COSTA RICA
A Natural Destination

COSTA RICA

A Natural Destination

SECOND EDITION

Ree Strange Sheck

John Muir Publications
Santa Fe, New Mexico

John Muir Publications, P.O. Box 613, Santa Fe, NM 87504

Second edition. First printing March 1992

Library of Congress Cataloging-in-Publication Data
Sheck, Ree.
  Costa Rica : a natural destination / Ree Strange Sheck. — 2nd ed.
    p. cm.
  Includes bibliographical references and index.
  ISBN 1-56261-014-7
  1. Costa Rica—Description and travel—1981   —Guide-books.
2. Natural parks and reserves—Costa Rica—Guide-books.   3. Outdoor
recreation—Costa Rica—Guide-books.   I. Title
F1543.5.S52   1992
917.28604'5—dc20   91-39998
                                                            CIP

Distributed to the book trade by
W. W. Norton & Company, Inc.
New York, New York

Typeface: Plantin
Typography: Copygraphics, Inc., Santa Fe, New Mexico
Cover Art and Book Design: Susan Surprise
Map Art: Michael Taylor
Printer: Banta Company

Contents

Río Celeste near Magil Forest Lodge (Photo by Ree Strange Sheck)

Acknowledgments

My deep appreciation to Yehudi Monestel, director of the daily newspaper *La República* and longtime friend and colleague, who first showed me around Costa Rica in 1968 and continues as an incomparable guide in a country he knows from top to bottom. Thanks to his parents, Don Bolívar and Doña Elena, who have opened their home and hearts to me.

Invaluable assistance on the book was provided through the Costa Rican National Tourist Bureau (ICT). Special thanks go to Mauricio Hernández in the San José office; drivers Jorge Chacón González, Victor Julio Araya, and Miguel Aguilar; and Grettel Aguero, Carolina Flores, and Mario Alfaro of the Plaza de la Cultura Information Office.

To the naturalist guides I was privileged to travel with, the tour operators in Costa Rica who arranged a few of my trips (especially John Aspinall of Costa Rica Sun Tours, who also offered telephone, typewriter, and fax machine when needed), and owners of private nature reserves and hotels I visited, thanks for gracious attention.

In October 1988, as a member of the press, I was invited to attend Expotur, an international meeting of tourism wholesalers and retailers in San José. Information gathered there got the book off the ground. I would like to thank Mario Quirós, then head of ICT; Yadyra Simón, executive director of Expotur; Marie Jeanne Oliger, editor of *Tecnitur*; and Mayela Pacheco of LACSA for making that trip a reality.

Travels in national parks, reserves, and refuges have given me profound respect for park rangers, who often live and work under difficult circumstances. Thanks to each one who took time to talk or walk with me. In the San José office of the National Parks Service, special thanks to Juan Carlos Romero, José María Rodríguez, and Fernando Cortés. Mario A. Boza, then director general of the National Parks Foundation and the Neotropical Foundation, spurred my interest in environmental education on the tropics in 1985 and was a valuable source for my research.

My appreciation to Mayra Bonilla and Álvaro González of Audiovise S.A., who so generously offered photographs for the book.

On the home front, help of many kinds during preparation of the manuscript came from Sally Venerable, Pat Patterson, and Pat Brandenburg of Santa Fe, New Mexico. Thanks to Gary and Margaret Elbow of Lubbock, Texas, who read the first manuscript and made suggestions. Thanks to my co-workers at the Monteverde Conservation League for their support during revisions for the second edition and to the Eston Rockwell family of Monteverde for seeing me through any number of seeming emergencies.

For unfailing support during research and writing of the book, my thanks go to my husband, Ronald Sheck (who also counseled me about map content and produced the preliminary maps), and my daughter, Claren (her marvelous sense of humor and perspective kept me on course). Continuing love and gratitude go to my son, Curt, whose death in 1984 was the beginning of a new journey for me, a journey that led me back to Costa Rica and to this book.

Finally, I express my appreciation to the people of Costa Rica for their generosity of spirit, those I know and those whose names I never knew—for smiles, for helping me get on the right bus, for walking with me to the corner to point to the street I needed, for reminding me that neighborliness transcends international boundaries.

1

Why Costa Rica?

Costa Rica touches the heart and mind, not through elegant boulevards, towering cathedrals, or an imposing place in history but through its incredible natural beauty and a gracious people disposed to peace, kindness, and a generosity of spirit. No one feels a stranger here for long.

It is one of the most biologically diverse countries in the world—a treasure house of flora and fauna unequaled in so small an area. Casual tourist and dedicated nature traveler alike come under the spell of a natural wonderland studded with tropical forests, rushing rivers, exotic animals, uncrowded beaches, high mountains, and awesome volcanoes.

Struggling to explain why increasing numbers of people are making their way to this small Central American country, one observer finally said simply, "The greatest tourist attraction in Costa Rica *is* Costa Rica."

With more than one hundred years of democracy under its belt in a region rampant with political strife, Costa Rica boasts "teachers, not soldiers." The country has had no army since 1948. It does lay claim to one of the highest literacy rates in the world and a national health care system that covers all its citizens. The people's inclination toward modesty, simplicity, and friendliness along with the country's commitment to peace create a climate of trust for travelers.

And what a place to travel. Visitors can walk among rain forest

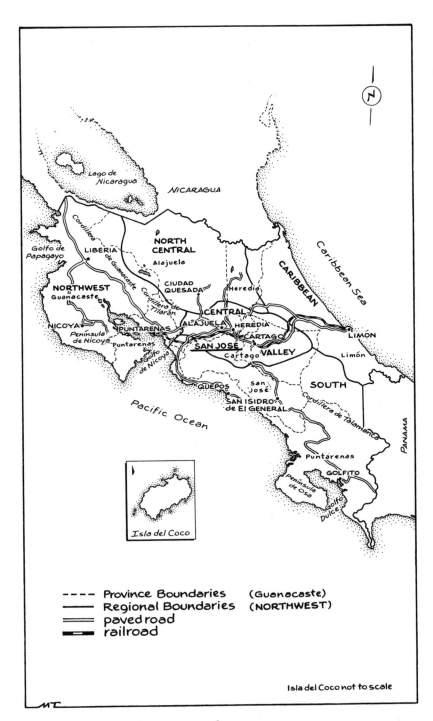

Province Boundaries   (Guanacaste)
Regional Boundaries   (NORTHWEST)
paved road
railroad

Isla del Coco not to scale

giants, see green turtles nesting, get a ringside view of one of the most active volcanoes in the world, ogle at the keel-billed toucan, and hear the howler monkey. Pristine beaches beckon on the Caribbean and Pacific. Trees alive with their own miniforests of bromeliads, lichens, and mosses assume mysterious forms in the high cloud forests; orchids grow wild amid lush vegetation that tumbles down along road cuts. Miles of coffee *fincas* (farms), sugarcane fields, and pineapple and banana plantations bear witness to a rural heritage and the influence of agriculture on the life of the country today.

Travelers can enjoy world-class white-water rafting, sunning on a deserted beach, bicycle touring, surfing, swimming, fishing, bird-watching, hiking, or shopping, or simply sit on the Plaza de la Cultura in the heart of San José and people-watch.

A small country, a little smaller than the state of West Virginia in the United States or Nova Scotia in Canada, Costa Rica abounds with plant species—North American, South American, and those native to the area. It would be possible to drive from Puntarenas on the Pacific to Port of Limón on the Atlantic in less than six hours, even allowing time to maneuver through traffic in the capital city of San José en route.

Elevations go from sea level to 12,529 feet (3,819 m). In general, temperatures are moderate, varying more with altitude than time of year. San José's average high is 77°F (24.9°C); its low, 61°F (16.3°C). Lowland zones range from the 70s to the 90s (21° to 37°C). Most people are surprised to learn that frost and ice can occur on some of the loftier peaks.

Costa Rica is known around the world for its national park system, now protecting about 12 percent of the land. With various other reserves and parks, almost 27 percent of its territory is protected, an enviable record for any country—remarkable for a developing one. That commitment to conservation makes it possible for resident and tourist alike to encounter the natural world in a special way. An agouti and I once surprised each other on a park trail; a paca (called in Costa Rica by the marvelous name of *tepezcuintle*) amazed me by rushing from bushes to plunge into a pool at the base of a waterfall where I had just been swimming. Giant blue morpho butterflies can turn any ordinary day into a mystical experience. There is always the chance that one will come face-to-face with a tapir or catch a glimpse of a scarlet macaw. Tropical trees towering to 150 feet and delicate, tiny flowers blooming in a high Andean-like climate open us not only to the magnificence of the universe but also to the interrelationship of all living things.

This guide is offered as a companion for your journey in Costa Rica, to help you touch and be touched by the land and people on paths most comfortable to you. It includes information about the national parks and privately owned nature reserves, beaches, volcanoes, and towns. It also tells what you will find at the end of the trail—a private room and bath with hot water or a bunk in a dormitory atmosphere with a shared bath and cold water. It lets you know whether you can fly in or drive in, or whether access is by foot, boat, or horseback.

There is a nutshell version of the country's history, focusing on what makes Costa Rica stand out from its neighbors, tips on what to bring along and how to call home, and a few highlighted odds and ends such as where and when you might see a quetzal, which beaches turtles lay their eggs on, water safety, and coffee from bean to harvest.

The book is intended to help you find your own adventure, to sense the heartbeat of this special place, from the quiet rhythm of its rural landscape to busy San José. Your experience will be your own. Just bring an open heart to contain it.

2
Marching to a Different Drummer

There's something different about Costa Rica. It is a country without an army in a world that counts tanks and missiles and nuclear warheads as the measure of a nation's strength. The national hero is not a general but a young, barefoot campesino (farmer). Schoolchildren, not soldiers, parade on Independence Day. While other countries debate the issue, Costa Rica abolished the death penalty one hundred years ago.

Located in a region where violence is too often the order of the day, Costa Rica lives in peace. It has one of the highest literacy rates in the Western Hemisphere and a Social Security system that offers health care to all of its people. Costa Ricans like to say they have gained through evolution what other countries try to attain through revolution.

This small nation has international standing in the conservation community for its commitment to preservation of forests and wildlife. National parks cover almost 12 percent of Costa Rica, while another 15 percent has protection of some kind as Indian reserves, wildlife refuges, and forest reserves.

Travelers often ask what has led this country on a path that sets it apart from its Central American neighbors. A brief look at Costa Rica's history sheds some light. Explanations about the current political and social systems and the economy are intended to answer some of the questions most visitors ask.

Historical Highlights

When Christopher Columbus dropped anchor off Costa Rica in 1502, near present-day Port of Limón, he still thought he had found a new route to the East and believed he was on the southeast coast of Asia, near Siam. Even today some people confuse Costa Rica with another country—Puerto Rico.

Stories about great wealth to be found here began at that time. The Indians offered Columbus gifts of gold, and Spanish explorers began to refer to the area as *costa rica*, or "rich coast." Later expeditions touched along the Caribbean and then the Pacific coasts, but it was not until the 1560s that the first permanent European settlement took root. Cartago in the Central Valley became the capital of what would become a province under the Captaincy General of Guatemala.

The first Spanish inhabitants of this new land found neither mineral wealth nor a large indigenous population that could be used as forced labor. The Indians they did find were not keen on servitude. Forms of resistance ranged from warfare to retreat into forested back-country. Colonizers were effectively reduced to small landholdings that they and their families could work. Communication was hampered by rugged terrain and lack of roads, made more difficult by seasonally heavy rains. Efforts went into survival rather than commerce, with the agrarian society based on subsistence farming and ranching.

Throughout the colonial period Costa Rica was a poor, neglected outpost of the Spanish empire. The poverty and isolation gave rise to a simple life, individualism, hospitality, and a spirit of equality that cut across social-class lines, creating the beginnings of rural democracy.

Even the name Costa Ricans call themselves, *ticos*, is said by some to come from a colonial saying: "We are all *hermaniticos* [little brothers]." Diminutive endings of -*ito* and -*ico* are characteristic of everyday speech. For example, you may hear *pequeñito* for "small" rather than *pequeño*.

The wars for independence from Spain were far removed from this peaceful enclave. When victory came in 1821, Costa Rica received word a month later. The story is that a messenger on a mule delivered the official letter. Costa Rica joined the Central American Federation for a time but declared itself an independent republic in 1848.

The war that did have an impact on the country came in 1856, when William Walker, a U.S. adventurer who had gained control of the armed forces of Nicaragua and dreamed of controlling all of Central America, invaded Costa Rica. The strong national identity forged during the colonial period of isolation brought volunteers from around the country to defend the nation. In a battle that lasted only minutes, the well-armed invading force was routed at Hacienda Santa Rosa in Guanacaste. (The site of the confrontation is now protected in Santa Rosa National Park. When you visit there, remember how remote this was at the time; the ragtag citizen army of 9,000 marched twelve days from San José to get there.) The army pursued Walker's forces into Nicaragua, where a second battle occurred. In the fighting at Rivas, a brave young campesino from Alajuela named Juan Santamaría volunteered to set fire to the Walker stronghold, losing his life in the act. He became the national hero for his part in this crucial battle. Walker's dream ended in 1860 before a firing squad in Honduras.

The first true popular elections came in 1889, which is why Costa Rica claims more than one hundred years of democracy. The president at the time tried to cancel the promised vote to name his own successor, but the elections were held when peasants invaded San José and demanded their say. By this time the exportation of coffee was ending Costa Rica's isolation. Soon bananas thrust it further into international commerce. Population grew, frontiers expanded, and transportation routes carried produce out and the world in.

Costa Rica's own brief "revolution" came in 1948, when Congress annulled the presidential election to keep the opposition candidate from taking over. It was a short but savage civil war in which more than two thousand people died. The leader of the revolt was José ("Pepe") Figueres, who took control of an interim government for eighteen months before the elected opposition candidate assumed office. Figueres abolished the army; military facilities were converted to schools, a prison, and the National Museum. The Constitution of 1949 set up a government full of checks and balances.

Monument in Alajuela honoring Costa Rica's national hero, Juan Santamaría (Photo by Ree Strange Sheck)

Succeeding governments have spent money on roads, schools, hospitals, electricity, and running water instead of arms. Compromise and negotiation are the key words in resolution of conflict. Citizens do, however, still take to the streets to pressure for governmental action or as a form of protest.

Today, large landholdings exist alongside small farms; wealth exists alongside poverty. But there is still a genuine faith in peace as a force, in democracy, in the fundamental dignity of man. Social, economic, and political mobility are possible. The national character is still tied to the land. Even in urban centers, Costa Ricans tell you their strength is in the hardworking, loyal campesino and the land. How this idealization of the past will hold up as more and more campesinos become *peónes* (day laborers) and the pressures on the land increase will be interesting. You can be sure of one thing: it will be a Costa Rican solution.

Political System

Governmental power is divided among executive, legislative, and judicial branches, with a Supreme Electoral Tribunal in charge of elections. The decentralized form of government reflects Costa Ricans' aversion to concentration of power.

A president is elected every four years by secret ballot and cannot be reelected. Two vice-presidents are elected at the same time. Numerous checks and balances were written into the 1949 constitution, under which the country is governed, to prevent abuse of power, especially by a strong president. The unicameral Legislative Assembly is considered to have more power than the president. Its fifty-seven deputies are also elected every four years and may not serve consecutive terms. Seats are allocated according to population in each of the country's seven provinces.

Magistrates of the Supreme Court of Justice are named by the legislature for staggered eight-year terms. These magistrates name justices at the provincial level.

To safeguard against electoral fraud, a kind of fourth branch of government is set up as an autonomous body. This Supreme Election Tribunal oversees everything from voter registration to the actual counting of votes. It also oversees registration of political parties and keeps an eye on political campaigns for misconduct. As a further check, six months before the election, command of the Civil and Rural Guard, essentially police forces, passes from the president to the tribunal.

Campaigning can get dirty, but election day itself is a party. Even children turn out to help get people to the polls, wave party flags, and shout slogans. Organized travel tours come just to observe the process and join in the civic fiesta.

Do not, however, mistake fanfare for frivolity. Ticos take their voting seriously; turnouts are high. Women have the vote, as do eighteen-year-olds. Even those who cannot read and write are entitled to cast a ballot. Women have been elected to high office—both in the legislature and as vice-president.

Municipal elections take place at the same time as the national elections. These are the two important levels of government.

Political parties come and go, the two principal ones today being the National Liberation party and the Social Christian Unity party. Factions split off and coalitions form. The Communist party is recognized but does not have much weight at the polls.

Costa Rica has a large bureaucracy. The government produces electricity, has the telephone service, runs the national banking system, feeds indigent pregnant women and small children, and distills liquor, along with all the things one expects a government to do. More than 20 percent of workers on fixed salaries are employed by either the central government or one of its numerous autonomous institutions such as Social Security.

Social Welfare

The Social Security system, referred to by ticos as the *Caja* and identified by the initials CCSS, was instituted in 1940 by the same president who helped enact a labor code that set minimum wages and guaranteed workers the right to organize. Though complaints about inefficiency and level of care are common today, no one denies the vital role Social Security has played in improving health care. Infant mortality rates are among the lowest in Latin America. Life expectancy at birth in the early part of the century was 40 years; today it is 77 years. When the system started, coverage was limited, but now practically every citizen in the country has access to care, whether they have paid into the system or not.

Rural health care programs geared to both prevention and treatment touch the lives of the poor in remote corners of the country. Scenarios may include a paramedic-staffed center supplemented with regular visits by doctors and nurses. I was once visiting a rural highland school when the doctor came for his scheduled community visit. One room of the two-room school was given over for consultations. In a coastal Caribbean village, a young mother told me the doctor came by boat once a month. Urban poor neighborhoods are also targeted.

The government has nutrition programs to carry out a constitutional mandate to feed indigent children. Most primary schools offer two meals a day not only to primary and preschool children but also to pregnant and nursing mothers. The community is a partner,

BOOKS AND THINGS

Travelers who receive so much from a country during their visit sometimes wonder what they can do to give something back. Several ways will be mentioned throughout the book. This is one possibility related to children and education.

The School Libraries Project is aimed at placing environmental education material in 3,000 primary schools, beginning with those in rural areas. The project is managed by the Neotropic Foundation, a private nonprofit organization dedicated to the conservation and sustainable development of Costa Rica's biological resources.

Packets of information include beauti-
fully illustrated laminated posters on tropical forests; a wall map and book about the national parks; nature storybooks for children; informative posters on geologic evolution, volcanoes, and sound pollution; and five resource books for the teacher and/or school library, when one exists.

Fifty dollars will put these materials in another school. You will receive the name of the school or schools that receive a packet thanks to your gift. Send checks to Fundación Neotrópica, Apartado 236-1002, San José, Costa Rica. Specify that the gift is for the School Libraries Project. Telephone number in San José is 33-0003 or 55-4254.

providing the cooks and transporting supplies. I have seen more than one rural school where growing a garden is part of the curriculum, and the fruits of the harvest go to the food program.

As you travel around the country, you will see clinics in small towns and a growing number of regional hospitals. The Red Cross, or Cruz Roja as it is called in Spanish, is a strong, highly respected organization in Costa Rica with dedicated staff members and volunteers in many communities. It works closely with health care agencies and provides ambulance service.

Costa Rica and schools are practically synonymous. The country was one of the first in the world to mandate free, compulsory, tax-supported education. This 1869 constitutional provision preceded passage of such laws in the United States.

In a rural place, the schoolhouse may be one room, with six grades divided between morning and afternoon classes. Continuing on to secondary school can mean real commitment for students, for while primary schools are abundant, secondary schools are centered in areas with larger populations. Two young people who stopped to rest near me on a mountain road explained that they were on the way to the nearest bus stop that would take them to school in Turrialba. The bus ride would be thirty minutes, while the daily walk to and from the stop was one and a half hours each way, with the return trip after dark.

Costa Rica has three state universities in the Central Valley, and there are branches in outlying areas. University education is not free, but tuition is generally low and scholarships are available. Technical and vocational schools are also located outside the San José metropolitan area to put higher education within reach of more students as well as promote other regions in hopes of stemming the flow of people into the heavily populated Central Valley.

Most visitors ask about the rationale behind school uniforms for primary and secondary students. This, too, harks back to egalitarian roots. The idea is to minimize differences between social classes. Private schools also have uniforms. Secondary schools may petition to have a uniform that differs from the traditional blue shirt and navy blue pants or skirt.

Debates on quality of education and even what constitutes an education rage here as elsewhere. Resources are stretched thin, and urban areas have an advantage because of backup facilities such as libraries and easier access to educational support. It is sometimes difficult to retain teachers in small, isolated areas. The overall picture, however, looks positive. Schools are frequently the nucleus around which a sense of community forms. Dedicated teachers do exist, often working with few of the materials teachers in the United States or Canada take for granted. Innovative projects include a shortwave radio learning program aimed at primary schoolchildren in rural areas, which brings whole communities to the school to listen. Bilingual materials in the six surviving Indian languages (Malecu, Cabecar, Térraba, Boruca, Guaymí, Bribrí) are incorporated into the curriculum on Indian reserves, including history and legends that had relied on oral tradition.

Housing is another focus of social programs, and it has been particularly emphasized in the last few years. Both urban and rural public housing projects have been implemented in an attempt to meet a serious housing shortage.

Economy

Starting from a base of subsistence agriculture in colonial times, Costa Rica moved into the world economy only in the latter half of the nineteenth century with the exportation of coffee to Europe. Exportation of bananas followed closely on the heels of coffee. A Costa Rican journalist, lamenting his country's dependence on agricultural exports, once said to me, "What makes it worse is that the country produces *postres* [desserts]—coffee, bananas, sugar, and chocolate. When importing countries are in an economic bind, demand for these things drops first."

If you hear Costa Ricans refer to the "crisis," they are talking about the years from 1979 to 1982, when the country went through probably the worst economic crunch in its history. World prices for these traditional crops collapsed at the same time that petroleum costs

13

Stalks of bananas covered with treated plastic for protection (Photo by Ree Strange Sheck)

soared. Since Costa Rica imports all the oil it uses, the dynamics were devastating. The country had borrowed heavily from banks eager to lend, the money used largely, as one Costa Rican put it, "to maintain our accustomed standard of living." It has been difficult to cut social programs citizens take as their due. National spending still outstrips income earned from exports and taxation, while juggling foreign debt payments demands enormous energy.

However, there is light on the horizon. Investment in nontraditional products to increase exports and cut dependence on the postres is starting to pay off. In 1988 for the first time, nontraditional exports edged past traditional exports in dollar value. Textiles, fresh flowers, ornamental plants, pineapple, frozen fish, and melons are among items filling out the menu. Check the label of the next shirt or pair of pants you buy. It could very well say, "Assembled in Costa Rica." The country has become one of the largest brassiere manufacturers in the world.

The country's stability, a large and educated middle class that provides a high-quality work force, lower labor costs, and national and international incentives are drawing foreign firms to establish joint venture operations with Costa Ricans. The U.S. Caribbean Basin Initiative, which provides preferential customs treatment to many products from the region, has been a stimulus; the United States is the country's biggest business partner, but multinational companies from Europe and the Far East are also setting up shop.

Someone once observed that Costa Rica has a way of turning fatal flaws into saving graces. Perhaps the national debt is a case in point. "Debt-for-nature" swaps are reducing that debt while providing money for in-country conservation projects. The plan works like this: conservationists raise funds to buy a piece of the debt on the secondary market—sometimes from a foreign bank willing to sell for as little as 20 percent of the face value. This debt is usually in dollars. It is usually the Central Bank of Costa Rica that buys the debt from the conservation group through interest-bearing government bonds, in local currency. The conservation group must use the money received to finance environmental projects. The foreign bank gets what it considers a bad debt off the books, Costa Rica lightens its burden, and money flows into the preservation of natural resources.

Natural Resources

Historically, Costa Rica's Indian population was low and dispersed, causing little human impact on the land. Spanish colonial settlement was also limited, both in size and location, being focused in the centers of San José, Cartago, Alajuela, and Heredia. As the limits of the frontier began to widen after independence from Spain, first around the Central Valley and then fanning out from transportation routes to the coasts and eventually to the north and south, occasional legislation began to appear to protect natural resources. Initial concerns seemed to be with wildlife and hunting or with prohibiting private ownership of certain tracts of land or a volcano crater. Precedents were set, though early enforcement was not terrific. Concerns evolved as more forests fell.

As time went on, foreign naturalists, who first began to arrive in the mid-nineteenth century, came in increasing numbers, drawn by the

SOME CONSERVATION ORGANIZATIONS

The National Parks Foundation and the Neotropic Foundation are leading private nonprofit organizations committed to conservation and sustainable development of biological resources.

Debt-for-nature swaps through the National Parks Foundation have acquired private land inside legally protected areas. The foundation's Conservation Data Center deals with the status of endangered, threatened, and endemic species of plants and animals and works with national institutions that have responsibility for planning and management of natural resources and those all-important environmental impact studies. Apartado 1108-1002, San José, telephone 20-1744, fax 20-0939.

The Neotropic Foundation supports sustainable development programs with communities near reserves, environmental education, and publication of technical literature relevant to environmental policy as well as materials for the public. Establishing interpretive trails and publication of brochures for several parks and reserves are under way. Nature Stores at Poás and Manuel Antonio national parks and at the National Museum, ICT information office at the Plaza de la Cultura, and Neotropica's office (Calle 20, Avenidas 3/5) sell handcrafts of natural materials made by neighbors of the parks and reserves. Apartado 236-1002, San José, telephone 33-0003 or 55-4254, fax 33-0617.

Books can be ordered through their Editorial Heliconia, along with slides, posters, T-shirts, and sets of gorgeous postcards of the parks and their tropical flora and fauna.

Write for a list of what they have for sale.

Friends of Lomas Barbudal was formed to help conserve and protect the Lomas Barbudal Biological Reserve in Guanacaste. Dr. Gordon Frankie, who helped organize the group, says even small donations make a difference.

Wildfires have been the greatest danger facing the reserve. Some are set by hunters to flush out game, some by carelessness, some by runaway flames from neighboring fields being cleared. Through efforts of the Friends, a fire plan is now in place.

Volunteers are needed to work on projects at Lomas Barbudal, Spanish-speakers preferred. Special needs are for people with skills in conservation education and in development and production of visual aids and publications. For general information, write to Friends of Lomas Barbudal, 691 Colusa Avenue, Berkeley, CA 94707, fax (415) 528-0346. Donations for the reserve can be sent there or to the National Parks Foundation.

Among other conservation groups are APROCA, which promotes conservation and rational and sustainable management of marine, river, and lake resources (Apartado 1863-1002, San José, telephone 55-3365); APREFLOFAS, a volunteer force that helps patrol protected zones to combat illegal hunting and lumbering and works to increase conservation awareness through environmental education activities (Apartado 1192-1007, San José, telephone 40-6087); and Tsuli Tsuli/Audubon de Costa Rica (Apartado 4910-1000, San José, telephone 40-8775).

biological richness of the area. By the middle of this century, natives and foreigners alike began pressing for preservation: unprotected, forests were obviously not going to last forever. Costa Rica began to build a national park system that today protects nearly as many bird species as found in all of North America and almost half its number of plant species. There are more butterflies in this tiny country than in the entire United States. Scientists now know that Costa Rica is one of the most biologically diverse areas in the world.

While preservation was the necessary initial step, the goal and challenge of protected areas today is not only conservation of biodiversity but putting people into the conservation equation. Population pressures are increasing at a time when public land available for new settlement is practically gone. Neighbors to those protected lands who receive some benefit from them will be more inclined to preserve them. New concepts are going beyond promotion of the areas as centers of scientific research, nature tourism, and environmental education, all of which when carefully carried out can benefit local people. In some of the parks, for example, local residents are being incorporated into park operations as rangers, teachers, caretakers, and even researchers. Their livelihoods will come from the parks.

Throughout the country, the challenge is to teach people that they can make a living from natural resources without destroying them. This is a crucial concept since practically all forest reserves are in private hands and 17 percent of the parks are still privately owned. Sustainable development is the watchword. Managed harvesting of trees or of plants or their seeds can bring more money than clearing the forest, and the resource survives.

Government and private reforestation efforts are a long way from replacing what is cut every year, but they are growing. Research and plantings with native trees are under way. A project that encourages natural regeneration of a tropical dry forest could have implications for projects around the world.

Costa Rica has come a long way from its beginning, poor and forgotten by the world. Its accomplishments in health and literacy put it in the ranks of highly developed nations. In conservation and commitment to peace, it seems a giant.

3

Lay of the Land

Rising up between the Atlantic and the Pacific as a land bridge between North and South America, Costa Rica lies in a region unique in the world: no other area is both between two oceans and between two continents.

What makes such a geographic location special? For Costa Rica, it means a rich biological and cultural mix. In a corridor between two continents, the land is home to plants and animals from both North and South America as well as to species native to Costa Rica. Indigenous peoples, though small in number compared with neighbors to the north and south, were influenced by the advanced civilizations of both Mesoamerica and South America.

The rugged terrain of this small Central American country, wedged between Nicaragua on the north and Panama on the south, springs surprises on those who come expecting tropical temperatures to be always balmy. Believe it or not, ice forms at certain times of the year at the highest elevations. Read on for some pertinent facts about the land, climate, population, and biological diversity.

Topography

From sea to shining sea in Costa Rica can be as short a distance as 74 miles (119 km). However, where the country is narrowest between two oceans, south toward Panama, it is also the most rugged and hardest to cross. The chain of mountains that forms a backbone down the length of the land becomes higher and wider as it curves from northwest to southeast.

In the north, near Nicaragua, the chain is known as the Guanacaste Cordillera (*cordillera* is the Spanish term for mountain range), giving way as it progresses southeast to the Tilarán Cordillera and Central Cordillera, all of which were formed as a result of volcanic activity. The Cordillera of Talamanca in the south is an uplifted mountain range. It contains the highest peak in the country: Chirripó, at an elevation of 12,529 feet (3,819 m).

You won't be long in Costa Rica before you hear people talking about the Meseta Central, or Central Valley. Since colonial times this region has been the center of population, and today it is home for more than half of Costa Rica's 3 million people. The Central Valley is not just the area around San José, as many visitors assume. Two

VOLCANOES

Volcanoes are a hot topic. Some 112 craters, including the 2 located on Coco Island, mark the landscape of Costa Rica. These craters range from extinct to dormant to active and from a mere remnant rising 328 feet (100 m) from the Tortuguero Plains to majestic peaks more than 11,000 feet high (3,350 m) which still fuss and fume along the country's spiny backbone.

If you have never heard a volcano breathe, consider a visit to Arenal (5,358 ft., 1,633 m), currently one of the most active in the world. Hearing the huff of its breath one unforgettable morning made me one with primitive peoples; the mountain became a living being. When it hurled fiery blocks high in the air, not a doubt remained: Arenal was angry. It has been angry enough to kill people since it began its current phase of

activity in 1968, including a tourist who climbed up its slopes. Be prudent when you visit. Keep a respectful distance.

Activity at Poás Volcano (8,884 ft., 2,708 m) has caused Poás National Park to close at times since 1989. The Vulcanological and Seismological Observatory of Costa Rica at the National University in Heredia (telephone 37-4570) monitors Poás and other active sites. They have published a map that pinpoints the craters and gives elevation and type of volcano.

Some of the other volcanoes you may come across in your travels which have some level of activity include Irazú (11,260 ft., 3,432 m), Rincón de la Vieja (5,925 ft., 1,806 m), Miravalles (6,653 ft., 2,028 m), and Turrialba (10,925 ft., 3,330 m).

small valleys comprise the meseta: the lower and larger is San José, where the capital is located, along with towns such as Heredia, Alajuela, Grecia, Naranjo, Atenas, and San Ramón; the higher, eastern valley of Cartago contains the colonial capital of Cartago as well as Paraíso and Turrialba.

Elevations in the Central Valley range from almost 2,000 to 5,000 feet (600 to 1,500 m). Separating the two depressions is the Continental Divide, which runs through the mountains known as La Carpintera at 5,085 feet above sea level (1,550 m). The San José Valley drains toward the Pacific via the Virilla and Grande rivers, tributaries of the Tárcoles River. The Cartago Valley is drained by the headwaters of the Reventazón River, which flows to the Caribbean.

The third major intermountain basin, the General-Coto Brus Valley, is between the high Talamanca Range and the coastal mountains in the southwestern part of the country. Elevations here are lower than in the Central Valley, ranging from about 330 to 3,200 feet (100 to 1,000 m). Significant population has really spilled over into this rich region only in the last half of this century, with San Isidro de El General serving as a center for shopping and transportation in a largely rural landscape of dispersed settlement. Two tributaries of the great Térraba River—the General and Coto Brus—drain the basin toward the Pacific.

The spine of mountains that winds its way down the country separates two coastal regions that have noticeable differences. A number of hilly peninsulas jut out from the Pacific coastline (Santa Elena, Nicoya, Herradura, Osa, and Burica); there are two large gulfs (Nicoya and Dulce) and many small coves and bays, creating natural ports. The two major commercial ports are Puntarenas and Puerto Caldera. For the most part, mountains come close to the sea on the Pacific side. The greatest expanse of flatlands in the Pacific lowlands is inland, centering around the Tempisque River drainage at the north end of the Gulf of Nicoya and narrowing northward to the Nicaraguan border. Total Pacific coastline is almost 780 miles (1,254 km).

The Caribbean coast, by contrast, is only 132 miles long (212 km) and has a natural harbor only in the Moín-Limón area. The largest area of lowland plains in the country stretches back from the eastern coast: the Plains of Guatuso, San Carlos, Tortuguero, and Santa Clara

Cattle pasture on the Nicoya Peninsula (Photo by Ree Strange Sheck)

form a wedge-shaped lowland reaching from the San Juan River, the border with Nicaragua, to near Limón. These *llanuras* (pronounced ya-NOO-rahs) make up about one-fifth of Costa Rica and generally have an elevation of less than 330 feet (100 m). There are small volcanoes even here, the tallest rising less than 1,000 feet (300 m) above surrounding lands. This region contains the only rivers navigable for any distance inland. You will not see large ships, but the San Carlos and Sarapiquí rivers allow smaller-boat travel for about 30 miles (50 km) from where they flow into the San Juan River.

In a shrinking world, Costa Rica grew a few years ago when sophisticated satellite mapping techniques turned up more territory. It is great when there is more of something nice than you thought.

Climate Patterns

Costa Rica lies in the tropics between eight and eleven degrees north of the equator, about the same latitude as the southern tip of India. Because it is a small country without much latitude variation, one might expect the climate to be relatively uniform. Wrong. Climate

21

can vary over short distances because of the rugged mountain chains that affect such factors as wind, rain, and temperature. The result is a series of microclimates where altitude is a key to change.

Microclimates make countrywide generalizations about rainfall and temperature misleading. What is helpful to the traveler are some rules of thumb for various regions, backed up with specifics for a few locations. We are going to hit the high spots; my apologies to climatologists for ignoring the intricacies.

Temperatures
Remember that temperature goes down as elevation goes up: it is cooler in the mountains than at sea level. Temperatures are generally higher on the Pacific side than on the Caribbean at the same elevation (there are more clouds on the Caribbean watershed year-round than on the Pacific). At sea level on either side, the annual average is always going to be above 75°F (24°C).

Some of the highest peaks in the Central Mountain Range and Talamanca Mountains average 54°F (12°C), though temperatures can fall below freezing. The lowest temperature yet recorded was in the Talamancas: 16°F (−9°C) at Chirripó, the highest mountain in the country.

Variation in temperatures is much greater from night to day than from season to season. Differences between the hottest month and the coldest month at a particular location average only 4° to 5°F (2° to 3°C), while the daily fluctuation averages 14° to 18°F (8° to 10°C). The greatest daily fluctuation occurs during the dry season, when cloudless skies permit lots of sunshine in daytime and lots of heat radiation at night back out into the clear sky. Add some wind, and it can be downright chilly.

Following are some average annual highs and lows at particular locations to illustrate the differences, along with median averages derived from the two (totals are rounded off). Elevations given are of the measurement sites.

Between November and January, cold air from the north can funnel down through the mountains of North America, and though much weakened by the time they get to Costa Rica, the breezes bring a bite to the air. This is one of the few places in the world where polar

Place/Elevation	Average High °F (C)	Average Low °F (C)	Average Median °F (C)
San José *3,845 ft. (1,172 m)*	77 (25)	61 (16)	70 (20)
Limón *10 ft. (3 m)*	87 (30)	71 (21)	78 (25)
Puntarenas *10 ft. (3 m)*	92 (33)	73 (23)	81 (27)
Liberia *279 ft. (85 m)*	92 (33)	72 (22)	81 (27)
San Isidro de El General *2,306 ft. (703 m)*	88 (31)	64 (18)	76 (25)
Golfito *49 ft. (15 m)*	91 (33)	72 (22)	82 (28)

air gets this close to the equator, so the coolest month anywhere in the country is probably going to be November, December, or January; the warmest, March, April, or May.

Rainfall and Seasons

While spring and fall have little meaning here, summer and winter are tied to rainfall. Ticos call the dry season summer, which can stretch from December through April in some parts of the country. The winter designation is reserved for rainy months, which generally fall somewhere between May through November. It reverses the standard Northern Hemisphere understanding of which months are summer and which are winter, but it makes sense to ticos.

There are some rainfall rules of thumb, always keeping in mind microclimatic differences. On the Pacific side, particularly from the central to the northern area, the rainy season usually begins at the end of May and ends in November. Wettest months are September and October. However, the length of the wet season increases the farther south you go. January to March are the only dry months in some places, and by the time you reach the Golfo Dulce area, there may be practically no dry season. Rainfall amounts vary from less than 59

Local fishermen net fishing on the Pacific side of the Nicoya Peninsula (Photo by Ree Strange Sheck)

inches (1,500 mm) in the northwest and central part of the country to 197 inches (5,000 mm) in the south.

On the Atlantic side, the rainy season can begin in late April and end in January. Wettest months are usually November, December, and January, while some areas also have higher amounts in July as well. Annual rainfall averages are higher on the Caribbean than on the Pacific side. Heaviest rainfall is inland, not along the coast; in some places on the eastern—windward—face of the mountains in the north, it exceeds 355 inches (9,000 mm) per year. In the rest of the Caribbean lowlands, annual rainfall usually averages from 118 to 200 inches (3,000 to 5,000 mm).

Throughout Costa Rica, less rain falls on valley bottoms, so places like San José and San Isidro de El General are drier than surrounding slopes. If you look at a map of precipitation for the country, you will notice that the most prevalent rainfall pattern is in the range of

79 to 158 inches (2,000 to 4,000 mm). Here are some specific locations and their average annual rainfall.

Place	Inches (mm)
San José	74 (1,881)
Limón	138 (3,499)
Puntarenas	63 (1,598)
Liberia	63 (1,600)
San Isidro de El General	117 (2,974)
Golfito	196 (4,976)
Tortuguero	214 (5,437)

Precipitation can come in the form of a tropical downpour—a gully-washer complete with impressive lightning and thunder—or a steady rain. The downpour is called an *aguacero*; a continuous rain for several days is a *temporal*.

Other weather terms you may hear are *veranillo* (little summer), which refers to a brief dry period in July or August in the Pacific zone; *papagayos*, strong winds blowing from the Pacific inland; and *nortes*, the winds coming down inland from the north and blowing toward the Pacific. Both of these winds are very strong in Guanacaste from January through March. *Alisios* are the northeast trade winds, felt during the dry season over the Pacific slope, except in the south.

Do not imagine that rain is constant throughout the wet season. Sunshine can dominate several days in a row. When the rains come, they usually begin in early afternoon in the Central Valley and other highland areas and later in the afternoon in the Pacific lowlands. Rain can drum steadily at night in the Atlantic lowlands and valley bottoms.

Each season has its beauty and its particular cares. In wetter times, plant life is profuse, with a vibrant greenness that seeps into the soul. In the dry season, a subtler background is a perfect canvas for deciduous trees that flower only at that time and for orchids and bougainvillea and *reina de la noche* (queen of the night, a datura).

Biological Diversity

Costa Rica is species rich. This small country that covers less than three ten-thousandths of the earth's surface is home to 5 percent of all the plant and animal species known to exist. As a matter of fact, species are still being discovered in the country's rich mix of tropical habitats. The National Biodiversity Institute has begun a multiyear project to discover and catalog all plant and animal species found here. The numbers bandied about for years have a good chance of becoming outdated even as you read this page, but here are a few to give you an idea of minimums that exist: birds, 850 species; insects, 350,000; vascular plants, 10,000; mammals, 208; reptiles, 220; amphibians, 160; freshwater fish, 130. Some scientists believe that as many as a half million species exist in Costa Rica.

As a land bridge between the continents, a bridge that dates back about three million years, Costa Rica became a corridor for the movement of plant and animal species north and south. This interchange was slowed by the gradual growth of humid tropical forests that became widespread sometime in the last two million years. Today Costa Rica has flora and fauna from both continents as well as some endemic species. They live in a variety of habitats: tropical dry and seasonally deciduous forests, rain forests, cloud forests, mangrove swamps, coral reefs, rivers, and *páramos* (high, cold, humid landscapes). Costa Rica is the northern limit for Andean páramo vegetation. You will find it above the tree line at Cerro de la Muerte and on Chirripó and other of the Talamanca's highest peaks.

Descriptions of Costa Rica often include mention of its twelve life zones. Defined by L. R. Holdridge, these zones classify vegetation. They are based on temperature and rainfall and their seasonal variation and distribution. Basically, the zones are tropical dry, moist, wet, and rain forests, with their premontane and lower montane versions, plus the tropical subalpine rain páramo.

The Tropical Science Center, a private nonprofit Costa Rican association that focuses on natural resources in the tropics, has a striking map of the country showing these zones in color. It is a vivid picture of variation over small distances—the microclimates mentioned

Gigantic *sombrilla del pobre* plants in Braulio Carrillo National Park (Photo by Ronald Sheck)

earlier. The map is for sale at their office in San Pedro, outside San José, along with other interesting publications for the serious nature traveler (telephone 53-3267). The Tropical Science Center also operates the Monteverde Cloud Forest Preserve.

Forest was the natural cover of this tropical land since about two million years ago, and until this century the forests continued to dominate. However, with commercial logging and the clearing of land for agriculture and settlement, less than one-third of the country remains forested, a substantial amount of which lies in protected lands. Though trees are still being cut, private and government efforts and national and international attention are focused on integrating conservation and sustainable development to preserve what remains. Private and public reforestion projects under way do not keep up with the estimated 98,800 acres (40,000 ha) cut every year.

Reforestation is tricky. Complex relationships between flora and fauna are not fully understood. What *is* understood points dramatically to the intricacies of nature. For instance, there are 65 species of fig trees in Costa Rica, adapted to a variety of habitats. Each one of these species is pollinated by a different species of wasp. After the female wasp pollinates the fig, she lays her eggs inside the fruit. The wasp depends on the fig and the fig depends on the wasp. Remove either and the cycle of survival is broken.

Animals are more important to seed dispersal of plants in tropical forests than in temperate ones, where wind is the primary factor. Maintaining the rich animal mix is crucial to maintaining the diverse plant species in a forest.

Around the world, species are being lost which have not even been identified, much less studied for their importance to mankind. Plants are gone whose medicinal values might have been important. Disappearance of a species of fauna can cut a link in a food chain that affects several species.

We are beginning to appreciate the necessity of maintaining natural forests. Replacing a primary forest of mixed species with one or two types of trees will not maintain the diversity: the fig wasp is not going to make it in a eucalyptus grove. While reforestation projects on already cleared lands are essential—erosion control and watershed protection alone merit the effort—they are not going to duplicate what has been lost.

A project to re-cover a part of Guanacaste with tropical dry forest largely through natural recovery has worldwide significance. It is a long-term project that could take from fifty to one hundred years; visitors can get a firsthand look when they travel to Guanacaste National Park. The object is to allow the forest to reclaim pasture and farmland, spreading out from the last remaining tropical dry forest in the area, protected by adjacent Santa Rosa National Park. Dr. Daniel Jantzen is the moving force behind this experiment.

Costa Rica's creation of national parks, reserves, and refuges is a step toward preserving a biological diversity important far beyond its national boundaries. Maintaining them in the face of increasing economic and population pressures may have to be a shared responsibility.

Population Patterns

The Central Valley, which today holds about 55 percent of the country's 3 million people, has been the center of population since colonial times. As was the pattern in other Central American countries, settlement centered in the highlands. Early Spanish colonists in Costa Rica shunned the hotter, rainier coastlands to settle in this mountain valley with rich volcanic soil. It was an enclave in the New World that continued in relative isolation until the nineteenth century. As late as 1700, Cartago, with a population of 2,535, was the only permanent urban center that existed. In 1821, when Costa Rica gained independence from Spain, 60,000 people lived in the country, with 90 percent in the Central Valley. About 5 percent had ventured out toward Esparza and Bagaces to raise cattle, and another 5 percent consisted of indigenous peoples living in dispersed settlements on their traditional lands north and south.

A small bean introduced into Costa Rica around the beginning of the nineteeth century ended up transforming the life of this agrarian society, pushing the frontier farther and farther away from the Central Valley. Coffee was its name. The export of coffee led to opening of a road to Puntarenas, for the first loads went to Panama, then Chile, and finally to Europe via the Strait of Magellan. Transport of the beans to the Port of Limón for more direct access to the European market instigated the building of a railroad to the Atlantic and indirectly the beginning of large banana plantations on the Caribbean. Blacks brought to work on the railroad and plantations, mainly from Jamaica, added another ethnic group and an English-speaking component. The Afro-American population today is about 2 percent. The estimated Indian population is about 29,000.

As land values went up in the Central Valley, small farmers sought new territory. Satellite towns took shape around colonial centers, but Costa Rica still had an abundance of unoccupied land at the beginning of the twentieth century.

In 1938, banana activity moved to the southern Pacific coastal region from the Atlantic; roads followed, and so did settlement. With the opening of the Pan American Highway south of the Central Valley to San Isidro de El General in 1946, the trickle of pioneers who had braved Cerro de la Muerte on foot or horseback became a flood of immigrants looking for new land, following the transportation route as it made its way to Panama in the sixties. (The Pan American Highway is called the Inter-American Highway in Costa Rica, as it is throughout Central America.)

POPULATION

Costa Rica	*3,029,746*
Provinces	
San José	*1,105,844*
Alajuela	*539,375*
Cartago	*340,298*
Heredia	*243,679*
Guanacaste	*242,681*
Puntarenas	*338,384*
Limón	*219,485*

Source: Oficina de Censos y Estadísticos, 1991 census figures.

Immigrants came from other lands: Italians, for example, developed San Vito, and North American Quakers settled Monteverde. The northern portion of the Inter-American Highway was important in the development of Guanacaste. Population pressure in the central region had grown: in 1956, Costa Rica had one million inhabitants; in 1976, two million. New transportion routes helped drain off some of this pressure as people left for available land elsewhere. Limits of settlement extended to the Plains of San Carlos and Sarapiquí, to Guanacaste and Tilarán, to the Nicoya Peninsula, and to the San Isidro de El General and Coto Brus regions.

Today, for the first time in its history, Costa Rica is facing the pressures of a growing population with little remaining public land. Most of what exists is in Indian reserves, forest reserves, national parks, and wildlife refuges. Since one of the frontier legacies is a belief that every campesino has a right to a piece of land to work, pressure on this protected land is going to be enormous.

As you travel on the road to San Isidro de El General, remember that most settlement along here dates from the middle of this century. As you drive over the new road to Limón through Guapiles, look at what has developed in this decade. If you sense a frontier spirit as you get to know outlying areas, you will understand why.

4

Ticket to Enjoyment: Planning the Journey

Entry Requirements

For citizens of the United States and Canada, entry requirements are simple: no visas are necessary. With a valid passport, you are on your way. In lieu of a passport, you can use a birth certificate or voter registration along with photo identification, such as a driver's license, to buy a $2 tourist card when you check in at the ticket counter of the airline flying you to Costa Rica. Citizens of other countries can check with the nearest Costa Rican consulate or the Costa Rican National Tourist Bureau for entry requirements.

From the date of entry, U.S. citizens with passports can stay for ninety days; however, those who enter with a tourist card (no passport) are limited to thirty days. Canadians also receive permission to stay ninety days. The law requires travelers to carry a passport or tourist card at all times while in the country.

Allow me a plug for passports. Routinely accepted at banks when you change money and at hotels when you register, a passport simply makes travel easier. If you don't have a passport, consider applying for one. Check with your airline. Some require passports for purchase of a ticket.

A note on traveling with children under eighteen years of age: there are no special requirements unless the stay exceeds thirty days. Then, if only one parent or someone other than the parent is traveling with the child, Costa Rican law requires written permission of both parents before the child can leave Costa Rica; this is the same law that pertains to residents of the country. You would want to arrange this permission before leaving home. Contact the nearest Costa Rican consulate for information. Costa Ricans love children; the law was written for their protection.

Immunizations

No immunizations are currently required. Traveling or staying at home, it is wise to have inoculations up-to-date. Is your tetanus booster current?

Incidence of malaria has increased in some parts of Costa Rica with the influx of refugees from neighboring countries. Mosquito eradication programs are used to control its spread. Most cases have been in the northern border area and around Limón. Check with your physician or contact your local health office for advisory information. The spread of cholera in the New World may also change immunization requirements.

Exit Requirements

All tourists must pay a departure tax; at this writing it is less than $5. You may pay it at the airport in either dollars or *colones*. That is all that is required if you leave before your original permission runs out. Whether you can legally extend your stay depends on entry documents. Tourist cards good for thirty days cannot be renewed. If you are traveling with a passport, you can apply for an exit visa good for thirty days from the date it is issued. This gives you an automatic extension of your stay. To keep legal, apply for it just before your original permit expires. The exit visa costs about $15; each month or part of a month that you stay beyond the original permission in your passport costs an additional $3.

The painless way to get the exit visa is to let a San José travel agency do it for you. The charge for the service is about $4 and you spare yourself the frustration of standing in lines at government offices.

The travel agency will need your passport for a couple of working days, so make a copy of the first pages with your name, photo, and passport number as well as the page showing date of entry. Copy machines abound downtown; just look for a sign advertising *Copias*.

Airlines

Time, distance, and political considerations lead most tourists from the United States and Canada to opt for air travel to Costa Rica, which means landing at Juan Santamaría International Airport, twenty minutes from San José. Don't be startled if you hear the pilot say the plane will touch down at Cocos International Airport; Cocos was the previous name. You are in the right country.

Work under way at the airport near Liberia will give Costa Rica its second international airport. Liberia is a gateway to Guanacaste Province and its beautiful Pacific beaches, folklore towns, and a number of the country's spectacular national parks. The expected completion date is late 1993.

Various airlines fly into Costa Rica from the north. Generally, only some flights from Miami and Dallas are direct; others involve stops en route, at such places as Mexico City, San Salvador, Tegucigalpa, or San Pedro Sula. A particular airline may have fewer intermediate stops on certain days of the week: be sure to inquire if you want to minimize ups and downs.

Commercial carriers include American and Continental (U.S. carriers), LACSA (the Costa Rican airline), Mexicana (Mexico), SAHSA (Honduras), and TACA (El Salvador). Phone numbers for these airlines are listed in Practical Extras at the back of the book. Following is a list of some departure points for these airlines.

Dallas: American, Mexicana
Houston: SAHSA, TACA, Continental
Los Angeles: LACSA, Mexicana, TACA
Miami: American, LACSA, Mexicana, SAHSA, TACA
New Orleans: LACSA, SAHSA, TACA
New York: LACSA, Mexicana, TACA
San Francisco: LACSA, Mexicana, TACA

A new Costa Rican airline, ACORISA, is scheduled to have flights to the United States.

If possible, have your ticket written up as if issued by the airline that has an office in San José. For example, if you fly from Atlanta to Miami on Delta and Miami to San José on American, be sure the ticket is written up on American stock. If you have to make a change for the return trip, American will help you if the ticket is on their stock; otherwise, you have to try to deal with Delta, which has no office in San José. I learned the hard way.

From Canada, several companies have scheduled direct charter flights: Fiesta Holidays (416-498-5566) out of Toronto, Mirabelle (514-632-0510, fax 514-632-5598) out of Quebec, and Fiesta West (604-688-1102) out of Vancouver. Their airfare/transportation packages are less expensive than airfare alone from most U.S. cities—a real bargain. KLM and Iberia come in from Europe.

Whichever airline you choose, you must reconfirm your return flight at least seventy-two hours before departure. Addresses and phone numbers of the airline offices in San José are listed in Practical Extras.

You will be told to be at the airport two hours early. It is good advice; check-in lines can be long, and you need time to pay the departure tax and change remaining colones into dollars. The airport bank is open 8:00 a.m. to 4:00 p.m. Monday through Friday. You can change up to $50 worth of colones (sometimes $100) and only into U.S. dollars, not Canadian dollars. Downtown banks will also change colones for up to $50 before you leave. There you must show your passport and have a copy of the airline ticket to leave with the bank. At the airport bank, the passport and ticket are enough.

Here's a tip to save possible embarrassment at the airport. Porters who carry your luggage from curbside will leave it as close as possible to the check-in counter. Many an unsuspecting tourist has followed his luggage, only to receive disapproving looks from fellow passengers because he did not take his place at the end of the line. Waiting your turn is a surviving piece of the "everyone is equal" mentality born in colonial times. No one is exempt. In fact, the more important a person is, the more essential it is that this tenet be respected. I observed this for myself one lunchtime when I noticed the Costa Rican president entering a downtown McDonald's. It was almost as if a ritual—understood by all the players—was being performed as he took his place in line and looked for an empty table. That president was Oscar Arias, winner of the Nobel Peace Prize.

The same decorum is expected when waiting for a bus or to be helped at a department store counter. (The sign that says Haga Fila means "get in line.")

What to Bring

Having read the weather section in chapter 3, you know that you can encounter everything from frost in the early morning on the high mountains to a hot midday sun on the coast. Even in San José the nights can be chilly, so bring a sweater or sweatshirt and jacket. Light clothes that can be layered will serve you well.

Costa Ricans dress on the conservative side. Women do wear pants or jeans even in downtown San José, but shorts for men or women are not acceptable except for sports—save them for the beach areas. In a nice restaurant in the evening, most men have on coats and ties or at least a dress shirt; the ladies, dresses.

Cotton and polyester long pants are good. It takes forever and a day for jeans to dry in the rainy season. I do, however, usually stick in a pair for horseback riding or hikes in chilly climes. A long-sleeved shirt or two is wise for protection from sun—remember, rays are direct at ten degrees from the equator—and from insects and scratches on forest trails. Shorts are not recommended for hiking in rain forests.

Many researchers and naturalist guides prefer tennis shoes to hiking boots for forays into the tropical world. Whichever you choose, just be sure footwear is comfortable and can get wet; even in the dry season, some trails lead through small streams. In rainy times, rubber boots are a joy, and they are available in Costa Rica for less than $8. (Some lodging places have a few pair available for guests.) You can buy the boots, which are standard footwear for campesinos, in central markets and many shoe stores throughout the country. If you don't want the extra weight going home, make a gift of the boots to the last nature reserve you visit. If you have a large foot, consider bringing a pair from home.

Rubber boots *(botas de hule)*, standard gear for tropical trails (Photo by Ree Strange Sheck)

There is also a lively debate on rain ponchos versus umbrellas for experiencing a tropical rain forest in the rain. Just remember, you can swelter under a poncho, ending up as wet from sweat as from the rain. I pack an umbrella and a lightweight, hooded poncho that opens up on both sides so I can drape it over my shoulders and allow more air circulation. The poncho gives better protection to backpacks or fanny packs, binoculars, and cameras, and it is handy for boat rides or trips on horseback. The umbrella is great for town time and for when you are not carrying thirteen other things on the trail. Bring an inexpensive umbrella so that if you would rather stick an extra poster or gift in your bag when you leave, you can present the umbrella to the maid or bellboy at your hotel, who will probably be your friend by now, or the street vendor on the corner. Reasonably priced umbrellas are also available in San José.

If you will be staying at hotels or on nature reserves that have shared baths, consider a lightweight sweatsuit for trips to the shower. It can double as sleeping attire if the night is chillier than expected or for something comfortable to change into after a day of sightseeing or travel.

Here is a checklist of other items:

Wide-brimmed hat—for rain or sun
Flashlight—for nighttime hikes, to get from your cabin to the dining room in the middle of the forest, and in case the power goes off in town or the generator is shut off before you are ready for bed at one of the remote reserves.
Sunscreen
Insect repellent
Pocket calculator—simplifies currency calculations.
Moist towelettes
Pocketknife
Small mirror—some rustic facilities lack a bedroom mirror.
Anti-itch ointment—an antihistamine cream for insect bites or even an antihistamine to take orally to reduce discomfort.
Antidiarrhea medicine—better to have the kind you are comfortable with, just in case.
Washcloth—most Costa Rican hotels do not supply them.
Reclosable plastic bags—small ones ideal for keeping a passport or other important papers dry; larger one handy for packing a wet bathing suit.
Plastic water bottle or canteen—gives you some independence in what and where you drink.
Binoculars—to see the expression on the face of the sloth high in the tree.
Antifogging agent for eyeglasses—especially during the rainy season, when putting binoculars or camera to your glasses can result in one big blur. (If you are in the forest with Amos Bien of Rara Avis, he can show you a plant leaf that will do the trick, but otherwise, you had better bring your own stuff.)

Tissues or toilet paper—public rest rooms may not have any.
Coin purse—to accommodate an ever-growing supply of change.
(Unfortunately, it is only the small denominations that seem to self-generate: coins of 25 and 50 cents or one colón.)

If you stay in the rustic facilities at some parks, you need to bring soap, towel, and sleeping bag or sheets.

Leave expensive jewelry at home. Much to Costa Ricans' dismay, thievery is on the upswing, especially in San José. I had a chain snatched from my neck on a downtown street at midday.

The electric current is 110 volts, same as in the United States and Canada. Plugs and outlets are standard. Be aware, however, when packing electric razors and hair dryers and such that travel in the boonies may put you in a room without an electric outlet.

When packing your bags, remember that travel to some remote spot by small plane, boat, or jeep may limit what you can take for those few days. Some domestic airlines limit luggage to 26 pounds per person. You will generally be able to store your larger bags at the hotel until you return, so include a small bag with enough room to carry a change of clothes, swimsuit, toilet articles, another pair of shoes, umbrella or poncho, camera, and so on. A day pack of some kind comes in handy, even for city sightseeing. You can stick in a jacket, camera, umbrella, guidebook. Be sure it closes securely. To further foil the light-fingered in heavy street traffic or on crowded buses, put your fanny pack in front or move your day pack to your shoulder where you can control access to it. A water-resistant pack helps.

As for film, bring what you think you will need. You can get Fuji, Agfa, and some brands that may be unfamiliar to you at reasonable prices, but you will pay a premium for Kodak, and you will not find the variety of ASA ratings and types of film you may be accustomed to. Don't forget spare camera batteries.

Imported goods are expensive, so if you run out of toilet items, consider local brands. Bring any medicines you require and keep them with you. Do not pack them in luggage to be checked.

Reservations

Reservations are highly recommended for visits from December to April and are increasingly advisable in the low season. They are essential for Christmastime and Easter week. Think about reservations not only for hotels but for lodging at the privately operated nature reserves, where the number of rooms is limited. Even hotels, with the exception of a few in San José and at some beach resorts, tend to be small. Most are still owner operated. By the way, many hotels offer substantial discounts during off-season months. Phone numbers and/or addresses for hotels, private reserves, and tour companies are included in this book. Call once you are in the country to reconfirm reservations you made from home.

Keep in mind that tourist attractions also feel the impact of Costa Ricans during school vacation from December through February and again during midyear break for two weeks in July. Beaches and parks are prime destinations.

Thoughts on Itineraries

The first-time visitor to Costa Rica can feel overwhelmed by the banquet before him—tropical forests to explore, steaming volcanoes to photograph, beaches to comb, mountains to climb, rivers to raft, flowers to smell along the way. Hire a guide? Take a tour? Travel independently?

Here are some suggestions to help you get started. If it is your first trip, do not slight San José. It is big city, crazy traffic, and crowded downtown sidewalks, but it also is worthwhile museums, peopled parks, and the center of culture and government. Go on a day trip with a professional naturalist guide to a park or reserve in the first day or two; see chapter 9 on tours for possibilities. With a good introduction to the tropical world, your travels alone will be richer.

On the guided day trip, you will generally get Costa Rica's history in a nutshell, learn something about current economic realities, and have a chance to ask questions about what you are seeing or want to see. A naturalist guide knows where the crocodiles hang out, what time the scarlet macaws fly over the trail, what tree the hummingbird nest is in, and which orchids are in bloom. You will get an early taste of what is out there waiting for you while you leave the driving to someone else. If you want to see a monkey, there is no reason for you to go home without having seen one.

Neither do you want to limit your stay to San José. Costa Rica's essence is tied to its rural roots. Its people and its natural resources are what it has to offer. Several smaller towns now have adequate hotels, restaurants, and transportation to serve as bases for travel to nearby areas of interest. Traditional destinations are Limón, Puntarenas, and coastal resorts, but think about staying in Turrialba, San Isidro, or Liberia (see chap. 6 for some possibilities). Chapter 8 is a rundown of several privately operated nature reserves that cater to ecotourists. Chapter 7 guides you to the national parks that offer the level of comfort or adventure just right for you. In chapter 5, there are suggestions on ways to move around the country.

All prices given are in U.S. dollars. Hotel rates were given to me as valid for the 1992 high tourist season, but prices go up in Costa Rica as everywhere else. I have included the taxes in hotel rates, which at this writing are 15.39 percent. Bus and plane schedules can change, so please check once you are in the country at one of the places listed under Tourist Information in chapter 5.

By definition, vacations have to do with moving beyond one's ordinary activities. Let some of your dreams come true in Costa Rica: sail in a yacht, raft down a river, sit on a beach, walk in a cloud forest, hike in a jungle miles from nowhere, visit a banana plantation, see birds and animals you know only from National Geographic specials, bathe under a waterfall. Meet a warm and gracious people.

5

Bienvenidos: Welcome to Costa Rica

Bienvenidos means "welcome." Information in this chapter is intended to help you feel more comfortable as you move about city and *campo* (countryside). Here are details about money, calling home, where to find out what is going on while you are in Costa Rica, and how to get where you want to go. You'll find health and safety tips, with a special focus on nature travel, a list of holidays to plan around, and typical foods and drinks to try.

Language

Spanish is the official language of Costa Rica. However, major hotels have bilingual receptionists, and some restaurants have menus in English and Spanish (the English translations can be delightful). English is taught in public schools as a foreign language, so you will come across ticos who want to speak English with you or will try to help out if you do not speak Spanish. Do not, though, expect to find people who speak English wherever you go. Your taxi driver may not speak English, and no one at the bus station may understand a word you say. However, Costa Ricans are genuinely nice people on the whole, and they will try hard to help as long as you are polite.

Ticos are delighted when you try out whatever Spanish you know, so learn a few words and phrases—at least *por favor* (pronounced por fah-VOR) and *gracias* (GRAH-see-ahs), "please" and "thank you." You will soon be saying *buenos días* (boo-EN-nos DEE-ahs), "good morning," with the best of them.

At the Airport

One of the first welcomes you will hear as you make your way to *migración* (immigration) is from Nelson Villalobos, chief of the airport Tourist Information Office, or one of his staff. In English and Spanish, the voice over the loudspeaker welcomes you on behalf of the Costa Rican National Tourist Bureau, known by its Spanish initials, ICT. When you get to *aduana* (customs), look for the ICT counter. It is open from 8:00 a.m. to 9:00 p.m. every day of the year except Thursday and Friday of Holy Week, December 25, and January 1. For fourteen years Nelson has been helping people at the airport, and he or his people will have answers to your questions. They can help you make hotel reservations and give you a road map of Costa Rica, a San José city map, and a free poster (if they have any in stock). You can pick up brochures put out by ICT as well as by hotels and tour

COUNTRY ODDS AND ENDS

Population: 3.03 million
Area: 19,730 square miles (51,100 km²)
Capital: San José
  population 296,625★
  elevation 3,809 feet (1,161 m)
Official language: Spanish
Official religion: Roman Catholic; 10 percent belong to other religions
Government: Constitutional, democratic republic; elections every four years
Currency: Colón
Time: Central standard, no daylight savings time

Electric current: 110 volts
Telephone country code: 506
Highest point: Mount Chirripó, 12,529 feet (3,819 m)

★This figure is misleading, because it only counts population within the municipal limits of San José, but the metropolitan area includes other municipalities. Total estimated population of the metropolitan area is about 1.65 million.

companies. Nelson says that you should not hesitate to ask for help. If there is no time to stop at the airport tourist booth, you can get information at the ICT San José office.

At the baggage area, grab the first luggage cart you see. They are sometimes in short supply.

The bank at the airport is open from 8:00 a.m. to 4:00 p.m. Monday through Friday. It is across from the ticket counters on the ground floor of the airport.

A taxi ride for the 11 miles (18 km) into San José is about $10. (All dollar prices in the book refer to U.S. dollars.) *Colectivos* charge less than $2 per person if all seats are taken. Fare on the frequent public buses is about $.30, but there are no luggage racks, so if you have big bags, forget that option. You would also still have to get to your hotel from the bus terminal at Avenida 2, Calles 12/14.

Outside the front door of the terminal are offices of several rental car agencies, but be sure to read the section on transportation in this chapter before you rush out and rent one.

On the way into town, if you arrive during coffee harvest, you may get a whiff of something pungent as you cross a bridge—not exactly the sweet tropical fragrance you had expected. It is not the person next to you but *broza*, pulp washed from coffee beans during processing, that ends up in the river. Welcome to Costa Rica.

Money Matters

The monetary unit is the *colón* (co-LONE). Its symbol is ¢. Take time to look at the coins—some are *colones* (co-LONE-ess) and some are *céntimos* (SEN-tea-mos). Each is clearly marked, but it pays to recognize that the coin marked "20" is 20 colones, not 20 cents. Bills come in denominations of 5, 10, 50, 100, 500, 1,000, and 5,000. Coins are 10, 25, and 50 céntimos and 1, 2, 5, 10, and 20 colones. (Coins of 10 and bills of 5 and 10 are not much in circulation now.) The 5-colon bill, however, is a beauty, and you may find people around the Plaza de la Cultura selling them as souvenirs. It has the *guaria morada* on one side and a copy of the mural in the National

Theater on the other. You can sometimes purchase these new for 5 colons at the National Bank (Calle 4, Avenida Central/2); Banco Nacional (Avenida 1, Calles 2/4) will give one per person as long as the supply lasts. No more are being printed.

The colón floats in relation to the U.S. dollar; as of January 1992, the exchange rate was 135.65 to the dollar. Continuing mini-devaluations will bring changes in this rate.

From my experience, you can expect to pay a premium for colones in a departure airport, so change a minimum or wait until you get to Costa Rica. In the country, you may change money legally only at banks that belong to the national banking system or at your hotel. It is certainly more convenient at the hotel, but sometimes the cash drawer is low, so do not wait until the last minute to ask. You will find accommodating people who offer to change dollars as you walk around San José, especially on Avenida Central near the Central Bank. This is definitely illegal; both buyer and seller can be prosecuted. The difference in the legal and black-market rate is only a few colones— not worth the risk of being arrested. Besides, you could be cheated.

Hotels and banks usually charge a small amount for changing traveler's checks. Ask. For example, there may be a $1 minimum service charge for changing up to $200 worth of checks. Do not assume that all hotels will accept traveler's checks or credit cards, especially outside San José. Be sure to inquire when you make your reservation.

Do not take off for the countryside with only 5,000 colón notes, because small restaurants or shops may not have change. It is advisable to keep some smaller bills with you wherever you are.

Banks

Hours vary, but except on holidays and weekends banks are open at least from 9:00 a.m. to 3:00 p.m.; some have longer hours. One is Banco Nacional de Costa Rica, which is just south of the Metropolitan Cathedral at Avenida 4, Calle Central/2. (This means it is on Avenida 4 in the block between Calle Central and Calle 2. See the San José section of chap. 6 for more on addresses.) It is open 7:00 a.m. to

6:30 p.m. weekdays. Another is the Morazán branch of Banco Nacional de Costa Rica, which is on the corner of Avenida 1, Calle 7. It is open from 8:00 a.m. to 6:00 p.m. weekdays. Just ask the guard at the door of any bank if they change dollars (that much English everybody understands), and he will point you in the right direction.

Before you take a place in any bank line, ask again to be sure you are in the right place. You sometimes must hand over your identification documents (passport, tourist card) at one window and complete the transaction at another. It can be a happy five-minute experience, or it can take half an hour or more, depending on lines. That is why it is easier to change money at your hotel if you have the option. Most hotels stick to the official rate, posted for all to see.

Remember that banks are closed on holidays (see the list in this section) and that the current limit on the amount of colones you can change back into dollars on departure at the airport is $50 (sometimes up to $100).

Credit Cards

The number of establishments accepting credit cards is increasing, but check before you spend if you are depending on plastic. Major credit card companies have offices in San José. With an American Express card, you can write a personal check to purchase traveler's checks in dollars. The office is at Calle 1, Avenidas Central/1, open 8:00 a.m. to 5:30 p.m. weekdays. Look for the sign and take an elevator to the fourth floor of Edificio Alde.

You can get cash advances in colones, not dollars, with your Visa and MasterCard. A handful of hotels provide this service for their guests. Ask at yours. Otherwise, for Visa I have used the Banco Crédito Agrícola de Cartago, Avenida 4, Calle 2, near the Metropolitan Cathedral, open 9:00 a.m. to 3:00 p.m. Credomatic at Avenida Central, Calles 29/33 (second floor) will accept both Visa and Master-Card. They are open from 8:00 a.m. to 8:00 p.m. weekdays and from 8:00 a.m. to noon Saturday. If that seems too far to walk, use this as an opportunity to try the city bus system. Take a bus marked San Pedro that starts east of the National Theater on Avenida 2 and watch the street signs. There is a bus stop (*parada*) near Kentucky Fried Chicken, and Credomatic is one-half block east of the colonel. By the way, there is a very good restaurant called Paprika in the same building.

You will need to show your passport or tourist card for any of these transactions.

Tourist Information

In addition to the office at the airport mentioned earlier, ICT has an office in the heart of downtown San José, underneath the Plaza de la Cultura. Go down the stairs facing Calle 5, between Avenida Central and Avenida 2, and you will find some very kind people who can answer questions in English as well as Spanish about attractions, services, and transportation. They do their best to help, whatever the problem, and they do it with a smile. You can get a free ICT road map with good information on the back—available so far in English and Spanish—or a San José city map and ask to see a list of guides who have a stamp of approval because they have completed a training program. Hours are 9:00 a.m. to 5:00 p.m. weekdays and 9:00 a.m. to 1:00 p.m. Saturday. You may call there for information: 22-1090.

If you need help when that office is closed, call the airport office at 42-1820. It is open from 8:00 a.m. to 9:00 p.m. every day except Thursday and Friday of Holy Week, December 25, and January 1. There also are ICT offices at northern and southern borders for those who enter by land.

INFOTUR is a new computerized service that offers the traveler information on lodging, restaurants, bus schedules, embassies, museums, souvenir shops, and travel and car rental agencies. The bus list is a marvel, with departure times, addresses, and telephone numbers. Offices are at the ICT Plaza de la Cultura and airport information offices and at Calle 3, Avenida 10 (INFOTUR'S main office). Regional offices exist in Liberia, Puntarenas, and Limón as well as ports of entry from Panama and Nicaragua. Hours are 8:00 a.m. to 6:00 p.m. Monday through Saturday at the main INFOTUR office. Personnel there speak English, Spanish, German, French, and Italian. Telephone 23-4481, fax 23-4476. INFOTUR will make reservations for you.

The information is also available via computer with a modem for just the cost of the telephone call. Here is how. Connect your computer through one of these telephone numbers: 57-2000 and 53-2000. If you are outside the country, add Costa Rica's country code: (506). Press H (capital) and "Enter," then enter NINFRAC-211201000 and press "Enter." You can talk to the system via menus, entering the two first letters of the option. Internal selections are made by number codes. If you are a net user, the code is 0712211201000.

Communications

Mail
Some hotels sell postage stamps and will mail cards and letters for guests. However, it is fairly painless to do it yourself at the local post office; Spanish usually is not necessary. Just hand the card to the person at the window, who will sell you beautifully colored stamps, which you stick on; insert the card or letter in the slot marked *Exterior* (foreign). There may be a slot specifically for the United States and Canada. The line moves quickly at the Central Post Office in San José, Calle 2, Avenidas 1/3. Hours of window service are 7:00 a.m. to midnight weekdays, 8:00 a.m. to noon on Saturday.

Telephones
International calls are too easy. From a private phone you can dial direct, using the appropriate country code (001 for the United States and Canada), followed by the area code and the number. You can call collect or charge a call to your credit card by dialing 116 for the international operator, who speaks English. At most hotels you must go through the switchboard.

Radiográfica Costarricense in downtown San José, Avenida 5, Calles 1/3, and Comunicaciones Internacionales on Avenida 2 just around the corner from the Gran Hotel Costa Rica and Plaza de la Cultura are open from 7:00 a.m. to 10:00 p.m. They have phones where you can call the United States and Canada and pay on the spot. You can also call collect or use a telephone credit card. Communicaciones Internacionales also has an office in Puntarenas.

From any phone in the country, you can contact an operator in Canada or the United States to place collect or credit card calls. For the United States, dial 114 for AT&T, 162 for MCI, and 163 for US Sprint. You can contact an operator in Canada by dialing 161.

To make a local call from a public telephone, have a supply of 5-colón and 10-colón coins. Place the coin in the slot; if the phone is working properly, it will drop only when your call goes through. Sometimes a series of beeps at the beginning makes conversation impossible, but persevere. If the phone starts beeping after you have talked a while, feed it another coin or you will be cut off. When calling a friend, give the person the number you are calling from (posted near the phone) so he or she can call you back and avoid the problem.

Some hotels, grocery stores, and department stores have public phones inside which are quieter than those on the street. Public phones do not have phone books. Calls from your hotel can be expensive.

Notice the many public telephone signs as you travel around the country. Often they are in the local grocery store or sometimes even in a private home. To call from one of these, give the person in charge of the phone the number to be dialed. Time is metered and you pay when you finish. To call within the country, just dial the number; there is no long-distance code. Even on in-town calls, charges are based on time used, and that is one reason most businesses do not allow the public to use their private phones. It costs them.

Telex and Fax

If your hotel does not offer this service, go to Radiográfica or Comunicaciones Internacionales in San José, where you can both send and receive by telex and fax. Most post offices have telegraph services.

Taxes and Tipping

Be aware that a 10 percent service charge is automatically added to restaurant bills (along with a 12 percent tax). Tipping beyond that for extra-good service is at your discretion. Tips for hotel bellboys and porters are about $.50 per bag. Taxi drivers appreciate but do not expect tips; let it depend on courteous service as well. Do not forget the housekeeping staff.

Tour guides expect tips, and do not overlook the naturalist guide at the private reserve; his or her tip is not included in the package. Consider a minimum of $1 per person per day. If your tour has been by bus, give something to the driver as well. Some people prefer to tip individually, but another option is to put tips from everyone in the group together and present the combination tip on the last day. Perhaps you also want to leave a monetary thank you for the cook at the private reserve who turned out those good meals or the young girl who shyly served you every day.

Taxes, however, have nothing to do with courtesy. Hotels are going to charge you a 12 percent sales tax and a 3 percent tourism tax, which is similar to a lodger's tax.

Note: The sales tax was increased from 10 to 13 percent as a temporary measure, with the plan to reduce it to 12 percent in 1992, 11 percent in 1993, and finally back to 10 percent in 1994. It was indeed reduced to 12 percent in 1992.

Business Hours

We have already covered banking hours, which are at least 9:00 a.m. to 3:00 p.m. Government and professional offices are open from 8:00 a.m. to 5:00 p.m. Shops are generally open from 9:00 a.m. to 7:00 p.m., though some still observe the long lunch hour—closing doors from noon to 2:00 p.m. Downtown San José used to close up at midday Saturday and reopen on Monday. These days more stores observe weekday hours on Saturday, and a few are open on Sunday. Some restaurants close on Sunday, some on Monday; check before you charge off in a cab.

A note on daylight hours. Since Costa Rica is near the equator, it does not have the seasonal variations in daylight hours we to the north have. If you get up with the sun, you will be getting up between 5:00 and 5:30 a.m. Darkness falls around 6:00 p.m. year-round.

Transportation

You have options for getting around that you may not have considered. In San José, taxis and buses abound. To get out into the countryside, taxis, buses, planes, boats, bicycles, and rental cars are available.

The miles of paved roads grow yearly; Costa Ricans tell you the increase is always greatest the year before a presidential election. But highway construction and maintenance are expensive in this mountainous, rainy nation, to say nothing of the havoc wreaked by hurricanes and earth tremors. I traveled over the newly paved road between San Isidro de El General and Dominical in southern Costa Rica just after it was finished, marveling at what an easy, quick trip it was

Crossing a river south of Golfito on the way to Tiskita Biological Reserve (Photo by Ree Strange Sheck)

51

through a spectacular landscape. Six months and Hurricane Joan later, the landscape was still spectacular, though some of it had shifted onto the roadbed, and potholes required full driver attention. You can encounter superb highways, potholes, unpaved gut-busters, and charming country roads, and even the most recent road map cannot keep up with all the changes.

Taxis

Taxis are supposed to use meters, called *marías*. Don't be embarrassed to ask the driver if his meter works. If it does not or he doesn't have one, agree on a fare before you get in. If you are taking a taxi from the hotel, ask the receptionist or doorman what the fare might be. Rates are reasonable by U.S. standards. Taxis are painted red, except for the orange airport fleet.

Taxis will slow beside you when you do not need one, but they are, of course, impossible to catch when you are running late at rush hour on a rainy afternoon. Drivers are generally courteous, though some will refuse to take you if they consider the distance too short or the traffic too fierce. Do not be surprised if this happens to you at the taxi stand on Avenida 2 in front of Gran Hotel Costa Rica. It gets my vote for greatest percentage of surly drivers.

Drivers can be incredibly kind as well. One picked me up as I ran down a dark suburban street, carrying a backpack, to meet a 5:00 a.m. downtown departure for Tortuguero. Though he could not take me all the way because he was going off duty, he dropped me at the nearest bus stop without charging me a single colón and admonished me for being out alone: "Es peligroso, señora" (It is dangerous).

You can hire a taxi to go practically anywhere there is some kind of road. In outlying areas, taxis are often four-wheel-drive jeep types. Drivers have remarkable skill. If you do not fancy going on an organized tour to a particular location or do not want to take a bus or drive, you could hire a taxi. The fare will be based on distance and time. If you do not want to arrange it yourself, ask your hotel to call and get the fare and reserve the taxi. The fare Coopetico quoted for a trip to Poás Volcano, for example, was less than $45, leaving at 7:00 a.m. and returning at 2:00 p.m., allowing an hour and a half at the volcano for sightseeing. The advantage is that the driver will stop wherever you want to take a picture or have an extra moment to soak up the scenery; the disadvantage is that he may not speak English (airport drivers usually speak some English, but their rates are higher). There are a number of taxi companies. Look in the phone book.

Buses

Bus service in Costa Rica is reliable and inexpensive. It offers a good opportunity to mix with the people, perhaps in closer quarters than we of automobile-prone societies are accustomed to. You may actually have to rub shoulders with someone, but you will sense the nature of those people by the time the trip is over. And they might have a glimpse of yours.

My bus travels have revealed a genuinely courteous people—helpful, friendly, good-humored, dignified. No pigs and chickens inside these buses. The vehicles are usually clean (unfortunately, some carry a sign advising passengers to throw trash out the window rather than litter the bus!), and so are the Costa Ricans who use them. I have encountered some foreign tourists in Costa Rica who must have thought that "back to nature" in the tropics meant going without a bath. Not so for Costa Ricans: for them, cleanliness is truly next to godliness.

Let's talk first about intercity bus travel, leaving San José and the greater metropolitan area for last. You can take a bus from the capital to any destination in the country that has bus service for less than $6 one way at this writing. For that reason, I do not include exact fares with bus information in later chapters. I know some of us have to count pennies when we travel, but just allow $6 per ride and you will come out below budget. Departure points in San José for various towns are listed in Practical Extras for easy reference.

Sometimes reserved seats are possible with advance ticket purchase. If not, go to the bus stop at least an hour early. If the bus line has an office there, buy your ticket then and get in line. Sometimes there is no office; you will buy your ticket from the driver or his assistant. Get in line, but be sure to ask if you are in the right line. Verify that you are on the right bus when you get on. Some buses carry only the number of passengers there are seats for; on others, if you can get on or hang on, you can go. Check to see if your ticket gives you an assigned seat.

Some buses have compartments underneath for luggage; some have overhead luggage racks that usually are too small for anything but a sack or tote bag. Some have nothing but a small space toward the front where bags can be piled. Do not take any more luggage than you would be prepared to hold on your lap or put under your feet during the trip, and you will be OK. Some of the newer long-distance buses have adequate legroom, while some of the old ones bring back memories of riding on a school bus: the seats are the same, but you are bigger.

I include length of trip with bus information for specific destinations, so you can judge whether it appeals to you. Remember that the country is small. By the Inter-American Highway, it takes only six hours to get to the Nicaraguan border from San José; eight to get to the Panamanian.

On longer trips there is a short rest stop. I usually carry juice or fruit just in case; this is a good time to have your plastic water bottle or canteen with you. Do not expect a rest room on board.

If your destination is somewhere along the route, advise the driver and he will generally let you off as close as possible. Taxis usually wait where buses stop in towns.

Watch your belongings and, if you end up standing in a crowded bus, your pockets. Even with those courteous, helpful, friendly, dignified people around you, a bad apple may be on board (probably a foreigner). Be especially careful with checked luggage. Get off the bus quickly to claim it at your destination. I usually try to watch at intermediate stops to see that no one else claims my bag.

I look forward to bus trips off the major highways. They are so human. The driver may stop to chat a minute with the driver in the bus you meet or be flagged down by a housewife asking him to pick up something in town and drop it off on the return trip. These buses are a lifeline in rural areas. Once while I was on a trip from Monteverde, the bus stopped so the driver's assistant could move a piece of milled lumber to the side of the road. A few bumps later, another piece and another stop. Then another. Soon everyone on the bus was craning to see the next piece, laughing about the truck ahead that would arrive without its cargo, telling the driver to keep the pieces and add a room to his house. Even non-Spanish-speakers were caught up in the fun of it.

Some ability in Spanish makes bus travel easier, but with politeness, persistence, and imagination, someone who does not speak the language can manage. Carry a map and point to destinations, or write the destination down and show it when asking for guidance. *Bus* is spelled the same in Spanish but is pronounced "boos."

Thousands of people ride buses in San José every day. You can, too. City fares and even fares to other towns in the greater metropolitan area are minimal. You can take a bus to the airport or Alajuela or to some of San Pedro's good restaurants for $.30, or the art museum at La Sabana Park for about $.10. You do not need correct change. Hotel staff or the ICT office can tell you where stops are. Wait your turn in line and pay as you enter; the fare may be posted on the front window.

If there is no vacant seat, hang on. Men and women passengers relinquish their seats to pregnant women, parents with a small child or two in tow, the handicapped, and frail, elderly persons. It is not uncommon for men to surrender seats to females in any form, but that is strictly by choice. I have sometimes felt I was given a seat because I was a foreigner—a nice feeling after traveling in some other parts of the world. Microbuses cost more but are quicker, and you are guaranteed a seat.

Again, watch your money and passports. I had a coin purse lifted so skillfully on a Sabana-Estadio bus that I have yet to figure out how it was done. I have ridden the bus hundreds of times in Costa Rica and have had that happen only once. Buses are great for people-watching, for eavesdropping, and to get glimpses of people's everyday lives.

When it is time to get off, push a button, pull a cord, or yell "*parada*," and the driver will halt at the next scheduled stop.

Planes

SANSA is the national domestic airline, with scheduled service from San José to several locations. No flight is more than an hour, and they are inexpensive—none as much as $25 one way. This is the current schedule (no Sunday flights):

Six days a week: Coto 47, Golfito, Quepos

Three days a week: Barra del Colorado, Nosara, Palmar Sur, Sámara, Tamarindo

Since planes are small and service is limited, it is advisable to reserve at least eight days in advance by phone (21-9414, 33-0397, 33-3258) or fax (55-2176). Baggage is limited to 26 pounds (12 kilos) per person. You must pay for your tickets three days in advance. The office is just north of the corner of Calle 24 and Paseo Colón. Flights leave from Juan Santamaría Airport, but SANSA offers van service to and from the airport from its office. When flights are cancelled because of bad weather, you are on your own. SANSA makes no arrangement to get you to your destination.

Travelair is a new domestic service with daily scheduled flights to Barra del Colorado, Golfito, Quepos, and Tamarindo. One-way fares range from $30 to $57. Telephone 32-7883 or 20-3054, fax 20-0413. San José departures are from Tobias Bolaños airport. Several charter companies provide alternative air service, with five-passenger planes, out of Juan Santamaría or Tobías Bolaños airport in Pavas.

Do not schedule yourself too tightly. Once on a return charter flight from Marenco, humidity and temperature led the pilot to ferry two passengers and luggage to Palmar Sur, returning for the other three of us. From Palmar Sur we flew on to San José together. Standing on the short grass runway at Marenco with ocean on one side and rain forest on the other, not one of us questioned the pilot's decision.

Trains

The famous Jungle Train from San José to Limón is no more. It came to an end in 1991 when passenger service between the Central Valley and the Caribbean shut down. The Puntarenas service was also discontinued in 1991.

Ferries

Two vehicle/passenger ferries operate on the Pacific side. The Salinero route leaves from Puntarenas to Playa Naranjo across the Gulf of Nicoya at 7:00 a.m. and 4:00 p.m. daily, with an additional crossing at 11:00 a.m. on Thursday and weekends. Allow an hour and a half for the trip. The returns are two hours later. A smaller, faster ferry, with departures throughout the day, may be in service by this time. Check with ICT or INFOTUR.

The Tempisque Ferry crosses farther up the Gulf of Nicoya near the mouth of the Tempisque River from 7:00 a.m. to 6:00 p.m., taking about twenty minutes.

A passenger launch runs from Puntarenas to Paquera on the southeastern corner of the Nicoya Peninsula at 6:00 a.m. and 3:00 p.m. daily, a trip of about one and a half hours. Returns are at 8:00 a.m. and 5:00 p.m.

Car Rental

To rent a car, you need a valid driver's license, passport, and credit card. Minimum age is 18 or 25 years depending on the company. All major car-rental agencies have offices in Costa Rica, and there are several local companies as well. Offices are at Juan Santamaría International Airport and in San José either at major hotels or concentrated in the Paseo Colón area. Several beach hotels now offer car rentals, and there are agencies in Limón, Liberia, and Golfito.

Sample costs range from $21 a day plus $.21 a kilometer or $38 a day unlimited mileage for a small standard car to $31 a day plus $.31 a kilometer or $54 a day unlimited mileage for a four-wheel-drive vehicle. You can rent a nine-passenger van for as low as $33 a day plus mileage. These rates do not include mandatory insurance ($500 deductible), which runs from $10 to $15 a day. Weekly rates are discounted, and travelers in the low season from May to November may pay as much as 20 percent less.

Some agencies also rent coolers, surfboards (Toyota), beach chairs, and tents. You can even rent a driver for your rental car if you like. Get an ICT road map from the ICT for free and look on the back of that map for traffic regulations and numbers to call in case of an accident.

Gasoline is sold by the liter. Regular and diesel fuels are available now, and lead-free fuel may be available by the time you arrive. All petroleum is imported and refined in Costa Rica by RECOPE, the national refinery. In rural areas, watch the gas gauge. You will not find a service station at every intersection. While round-the-clock service is available in San José, service stations in other areas may open at 6:00 a.m. and close at 6:00 p.m.

The maximum speed limit is 50 miles (80 km) per hour on toll roads and primary highways unless posted otherwise. You will see plenty of 40- and 60-kilometer per hour signs. Speeders are subject to heavy fines, as are those in the front seat who do not buckle up.

Be sure to check the car over for any dents, scratches, or other damage before you accept it and have those noted in writing by the agent. It could save you some problems. Also be sure to check the spare and jack.

Before you decide to rent a car, please read the section in this book on traffic hazards. Just know what you are in for. If you do rent, do not leave belongings visible even in a locked car and do not leave luggage in the trunk at night or even unattended during the day. In fact, do not leave anything of value in a parked car.

Bicycles
Bicycle tourism is just beginning here. If you are going to do it on your own, remember that bike lanes do not exist. If it is your first trip to Costa Rica, you might consult with one of the tour companies before you set off: there are roads you should avoid.

Hitchhiking
Hitchhiking on major roads is practically nil since bus fare is so cheap. However, local people wait by the road for a ride in rural areas where bus service is nonexistent or infrequent. Tourists do not generally hitchhike in Costa Rica except in an emergency. For example, when my return flight from Golfito fell through and I had to be in San José the next day for an appointment—all the buses were sold out—I hitchhiked for the first time in my life. At the end of the seven-hour trip, the charming young man who rescued me advised, ''Ree, you should not do this anymore. Not everyone is good.'' He delivered me right to my door.

Other Transportation Options

Small companies licensed by ICT have vans or microbuses for hire, with driver. This option allows you to custom design your trip, stop as often as you like, and have someone else drive and take care of luggage. Here are three I know about.

Flor de María Castro, a former nurse, operates her own transportation company. If you are lucky, you may get her as a driver. She charges $125 a day for a nine-passenger microbus, driver, and fuel in the Central Valley; for tours out of the Central Valley the price depends on the destination. She also has a larger bus. Husband Marco Tulio Sbravatti, the other half of the team, speaks some English. Having traveled with them and observed their interaction with non-Spanish-speakers, I would say communication transcends language barriers. The two of them exemplify Costa Rican hospitality—they love sharing their country. Daughters Marcela and Ericka, who speak English, take care of reservations at 35-1072, fax 33-7932.

Eric Rockwell has a van for up to eight persons as well as a twenty-passenger bus. He is bilingual, English and Spanish. Charges vary according to distance and number of passengers, but to give you an idea, he charges $100 for up to four persons from San José to Monteverde. Though based in Monteverde, he will work out an itinerary with you for the other parts of the country. Telephone 61-2556.

Evelio Fonseca Mata, who regularly provides transportation to and from Monteverde in a fifteen-passenger van, will transport elsewhere in the country for $80 a day. Call him at 61-0958. He speaks mainly Spanish but has an English-speaking assistant to answer the phone. Charges for getting the traveler to Monteverde or from Monteverde to the next destination vary according to distance.

Traffic Hazards

For a tourist, there are easier ways to get around San José than by rental car: parking space is limited and traffic is fierce. I would suggest you walk or take a taxi or bus.

In the countryside, roads are for cars, buses, trucks, cows, dogs, chickens, people, and landslides. Be careful out there.

Some specific driving habits to look out for are passing on curves, use of climbing lanes by cars going downhill, and driving on whichever side of the road has the best pavement or fewer rocks or ruts. Tailgating is a national pastime.

Watch out for two-lane roads that feed suddenly into one-lane bridges, for *huecos* (oo-AY-cos), or holes in pavement, that can knock passengers and vehicle for a loop, and for tree branches laid across the road that warn of trouble ahead. Geography and climate team up to create landslides big and small.

Fog is a permanent possibility on the highest section of the Inter-American Highway south of San José toward San Isidro de El General —the range known as Cerro de la Muerte. The earlier you get through that section the better. The scenery is magnificent, by the way. The same advice goes for the new road to Limón through Braulio Carrillo National Park, though at least the road is wider there.

On the miles of the San José-Puntarenas highway that have yet to be widened, you may find yourself in a string of cars and buses and trucks belching diesel fumes on a narrow, winding road. Adrenaline flows as vehicles jockey for position without a clue as to what may be approaching just around the curve. I would avoid that road on weekends and after dark. In fact, for safety's sake, I would avoid driving at night in general.

Even with road map in hand, you will need to ask for directions when traveling off main roads. Additional signs are going up along main tourism routes, but choices to be made outnumber signs, especially on dirt roads. Be sure to read driving information on the back of the ICT road map, available in English, if you choose to drive.

Safety

Theft is a worldwide phenomenon. Use common sense: do not wear expensive-looking jewelry, do not flash around lots of cash, watch your belongings. Do not leave cameras or binoculars lying unattended on the beach. Watch your pockets and purses on crowded buses and streets. Use a sensible purse, one that closes securely; choose a bag that can be carried with straps over the shoulder, held tightly between arm and body. Travel stores now carry all kinds of hidden pockets and pouches to wear on practically any part of the body; investigate which serves your purposes. Keep your passport separate from your money. Carry only the credit cards you need.

Be alert on the street if approached by an overly friendly person who may claim to have met you somewhere. There are expert pickpockets around. I lost a watch while trying to explain to a man that I did not believe I knew him. I would know him now.

One of the most dangerous things facing a traveler in Costa Rica is crossing a downtown San José street. Your job as a pedestrian is to keep out of a driver's way, whatever he or she may decide to do. The tico's gentle nature seems to give way to individualism once behind the wheel. Cars turning right do not yield to pedestrians. Expect no mercy if the light change finds you in the middle of the street. To meet the challenge, I get beside a Costa Rican woman who is hanging onto at least two small children. When she goes, I go. By watching the natives, I have also learned that if I do not see the light turn green at a wide street like Avenida 2, the safest thing to do is to wait a full cycle and be ready to sprint across when it next turns green. You do not want to be in front of four lanes, or more, of cars gunning their engines when they get the signal to go.

One other word of caution: back up on corners where buses make turns on narrow streets; you could actually be hit by the body of the bus while standing on the sidewalk.

The pedestrian walkway along Avenida Central between the Central Bank and the Plaza de la Cultura is a delight; there is limited vehicle access, but generally you can walk right down the middle of the street. Lots of people crowd the narrow sidewalks; a study revealed that at one corner of the Central Market, an average of sixty-five thousand persons a day pass by.

Staying Healthy

Costa Rica feels like a healthy place to travel, but some precautions make travel anywhere healthier. Give your body a break: keep to a diet it can recognize at first, adding a few new things each day. Get plenty of rest. If you would not choose to eat in a "greasy spoon" or buy food from a street vendor at home, why risk it elsewhere in the world?

Food and Drink

I used to say it was okay to drink the tap water in San José and most other cities in the Central Valley. Then in 1991, a study revealed that only 50 percent of municipal systems have water not contaminated by fecal material. Costa Ricans are demanding action by government officials to remedy the situation, so it should improve. In the meantime, I tend to exercise more caution in coastal areas and try to follow the saying, "When in doubt, don't." When you stay at a hotel or reserve in a rural area, you have every right to ask what the source of water is. Bottled water—*agua mineral*—is available most everywhere, as are bottled carbonated drinks, beer, and packaged fruit juices.

A good substitute for water on a hot day on the coast is the liquid from a *pipa*, a green coconut. And remember, if you don't trust that the water is safe to drink, do not brush your teeth with it either.

You can get *té de manzanilla* (chamomile tea) practically anywhere, with water that most likely has been boiled. Several companies offer a variety of delicious, packaged herbal teas. Buy a box to carry with you in case the restaurant does not offer herbal tea. Some of the private reserves at low and medium altitudes have lemongrass (*zacate de limón*) in the garden. If you ask, the kitchen staff is usually delighted to brew a tea from it. It is not only delicious but is also used as a remedy for gastrointestinal problems and colds. You can always get fine coffee.

The two largest dairy product companies are Dos Pinos and Borden; both are reliable and offer pasteurized products. Even laser-treated milk that does not have to be refrigerated until opened is available.

Raw fruits and vegetables that can be peeled are safer. (That is one reason you carry a pocketknife.) Be sure to try the *mamón chino* (an exotic-looking red, spiny fruit with a succulent white flesh inside that you suck off of a large seed), several varieties of mangoes, pineapple, bananas with the taste of the sun still in them, and *cas* (wonderful in juice or ice cream).

If you hike, raft, or engage in a lot of physical exertion, remember that the salt content of sweat goes up with rising temperatures. Drink plenty of fluids and add salt to your food if you are sweating heavily.

Nature Travel Tips

Insects and snakes come with the tropics. Try to observe them on your terms. Plants can offer some surprises, so look before you grab hold of a tree along a steep or slick trail. It could have a protective coat of spines. If you choose to experience the jungle at night, take along a good light and go with a guide.

Remember that rivers can rise substantially with rain upstream; the river you waded across in the sunshine can look quite forbidding under a leaden sky. When you plan to hike along the beach, inquire about tides. Some beaches disappear at high tide, and the impact of high tide on the mouth of a river can render it dangerous to cross.

Do remember that the sun's rays are more vertical than you may be used to, so you can sunburn more easily. Be especially careful of the midday sun. Wear a hat with a brim large enough to protect your face and lips and use sunscreen. If tanning is a goal, limit yourself to brief exposures in early morning or late afternoon, building gradually.

Long sleeves and long pants protect from sun, insects, and scratches whether you are in open pasture and grassland or forest. Leave the shorts for leisure time at the beach. Loose-fitting clothes are cooler, and baggy pant legs can get the first full dose of venom in the unlikely case of a snakebite.

Insects

I am well acquainted with two insects in particular: chiggers (*coloradillas*—co-lo-rah-DEE-lyahs) and ticks (*garrapatas*—gahr-rah-PAH-tahs). Chiggers are actually mite larvae and live in grassy, bushy

The spiny pochote tree (Photo by Ree Strange Sheck)

areas waiting to climb up the legs of passersby. Bites itch like crazy, and the red bumps get worse if you scratch them. To discourage chiggers, dust sulfur powder on socks, feet, ankles, and lower calves before you walk in the grass. Put some on your pant legs. Mosquito repellents are not effective. For bites, Caladryl or Eurax cream helps; some people take an antihistamine for severe itching. The bites can last for weeks.

Ticks hang out especially where horses and cattle are found. You may notice some itching, but you may feel nothing, discovering their reddish black bodies under your skin when you undress. Be careful not to leave the biting end embedded (a tick doesn't really have a head), because it can fester and cause infection. Apply alcohol, gasoline, or kerosene to the bite or hold a lighted match or cigarette close to get the tick to let go and come out. Squeeze gently to help him along. Ticks can carry disease, so if you get a fever after being bitten, see a doctor.

In an area where mosquitoes are bothersome, use repellent and wear protective clothing. Some places provide mosquito netting for beds; if not, inexpensive mosquito coils, or "spirals" as they are known in Costa Rica, keep the population down. Buy them in grocery stores. The smoke from the end of the lighted spiral does the trick, but you also breathe that smoke. I would not recommend putting it right next to your bed.

Ants in a wonderful assortment of sizes and colors will bite or sting if you are where they do not want you to be. Try not to stand still without first checking out the area. Sounds easy, but the advice is hard to remember when you have just spotted a great green macaw or a coati and you freeze so it won't go away. Be alert in innocent-looking grass. A group of us waiting for a plane on a grass airfield were bitten by ferocious little black ants, and when we landed back in San José, we had to do battle again with the swarms that had infiltrated the luggage. For hikes and trail rides, hats and long-sleeved shirts give some protection against ants that live in trees you may brush against.

If you are bitten by no-see-ums, the gnats known as *purrujas* in Costa Rica, use an antibiotic salve. You will not only be in more agony if you scratch the bites but also risk infection. They live near the coast, but you can visit the coast many times and never encounter them; they prefer areas near salt marshes. Repellents are not effective; protective clothing works best.

African (killer) bees arrived in Costa Rica in 1982, and you would do well to assume that all colonies are now Africanized. Keep your distance from hives or swarms. The stings of Africanized bees are no more venomous than those of your garden variety bee, but these insects are aggressive and attack with less provocation. The cumulative effect of many bee stings is dangerous. If attacked, move in a zigzag motion; you can probably outrun them. Head for water if any is nearby, and cover your head. If someone with you is attacked and cannot move, cover both of you with something light in color and get the person to safety. Remove stingers with a knife or fingernails, careful not to squeeze more of the stinger's venom into the bite. Apply ice or cold water and, if badly bitten, see a doctor.

I routinely shake out boots or shoes before I put them on and shake and inspect my clothes. Having been bitten once by a scorpion when I did not, I rarely forget.

Snakes

Running on a path to catch a bus, I once came face-to-face with a snake racing to catch a gigantic frog. I had turned my head to glance at the frog as it leaped by and looked forward again to see a spectacular black snake with a luminous bright green stripe the length of his long body about four feet in front of me. The top half of that body was reared in the air, his head about the level of my thighs. Startled, we stopped in our tracks and stared at each other for a timeless moment. Then in one graceful move he melted to the ground and slid off into the leaves at the side of the trail. The lesson: if a giant frog passes you with incredible leaps and bounds, consider the possibility that something is in hot pursuit, headed your way.

Although seeing a snake in the tropical forest can be thrilling, be respectful and keep your distance. Minimize unpleasant surprises. First, running is not a good idea. Take time to look around. Never sit on or step over a log or rock without checking out the other side. Some snakes live in trees, with protective coloration, so watch where you put your hands and your head. Most bites, however, occur below the knees, so consider high boots—another benefit of those rubber boots.

Two pairs of eyes are better than one, so walk with a friend. At night, carry a strong light. If you want to familiarize yourself with which snakes are poisonous and which are not, visit the Serpentarium in San José, Avenida 1, Calles 9/11, open daily from 10:00 a.m. to 7:00 p.m., or visit the Clodomiro Picado Institute in Dulce Nombre de Coronado, about thirty minutes from downtown San José, open weekdays 1:00 to 4:00 p.m. Ask for directions at the ICT information office. Fewer than five hundred snakebites are reported each year—mostly farmworkers are bitten—with fewer than fifteen fatalities. The fer-de-lance, or *terciopelo*, accounts for almost half of the bites.

Most naturalist guides carry antivenin kits. Ask. All Social Security hospitals, Red Cross stations, and national guard posts have antivenin available. Bite marks of venomous and nonvenomous snakes differ, so if someone is bitten, look to see whether there are fang marks. There also may be small marks made by teeth. The bite by a nonpoisonous snake shows two rows of teeth marks but no fang marks. Keep the victim still (especially the affected part), squeeze out as much venom as possible with your mouth or hands within the first ten minutes of the bite (tourniquets and incisions are not recommended for amateurs). Get medical attention as quickly as possible. A description of the snake is helpful. There is an anticoral serum and a polivalent serum for use against all other venomous Central American snakes.

Swimming

Fungus infections, especially in the ears, from swimming in pools or rivers is not uncommon. To prevent infection, clean out ears with rubbing alcohol and a cotton swab after swimming. Common sense will guide you to avoid swimming in a polluted river. Check the water for visible pollutants before you get in and bathe with soap and water after swimming in any river. Read the information on water safety in this chapter before you swim in the ocean.

Medical Care

Costa Rica has good doctors and modern medical facilities, both in its public health care system (tourists have access to treatment in the Social Security hospitals and clinics in case of accident or sudden illness) and private clinics. Hospitals and private clinics are listed with phone numbers on the back of the ICT road map. One of the largest private hospitals is Clínica Bíblica: telephone 23-6422. Most hotels

WATER SAFETY

The beaches in Costa Rica are no more dangerous than those in southern California, according to Donald Melton of Quepos, architect of the newly established Foundation for Lifesaving and Coastal Protection in Costa Rica. A lifesaving training center is being set up at Manuel Antonio as a pilot project to cover Manuel Antonio, Jacó, and Esterillos beaches, with an eye to setting up similar centers on other major beaches.

Basic rules apply whenever you swim in coastal waters: do not swim alone, on a full stomach, or while intoxicated. Do not swim at the mouth of a river, where currents can be treacherous. For the same reason, be careful around rocky points. Look before you leap. How deep is the water? Are people standing? Is the slope gradual or is there a steep drop-off?

According to Donald, about 80 percent of the two hundred people who drown each year in Costa Rica are victims of riptides. Some rips are called permanent because they are always in the same place. Ask local people how safe the water is. In other areas, rips can come and go. Some telltale signs are discoloration of the water—brown spots where turbulence is kicking up sand—and areas where breakers do not return directly to the surf but run parallel to the

beach for a bit. Take a few minutes to watch the action of the sea before you go in.

If you are caught in a rip, remember that it will only take you out, not drag you under. Panic is a factor in drownings. Do not fight the current. See if you can use the energy of a big wave to push you toward the beach. Do motion to shore for help, but while it is coming, swim parallel to the beach, and then as the current weakens, swim at a 45° angle toward shore. Never try to swim directly toward the beach. If you cannot swim, float; keep your legs and body close to the surface. If you can walk when you feel yourself being pulled out, also go parallel to the shore as fast as you can to try to get out of it.

Some dangerous beaches are Playa Bonita near Limón; near the entrance to Cahuita National Park; Dona Ana and Playa Barranca near Puntarenas; and south Espadilla Beach at Manuel Antonio.

Anyone interested in helping with Costa Rica's first lifesaving program can contact Donald Melton at Apartado 15, Puerto Quepos, Costa Rica. Training of lifeguards will be done by World Lifesaving, a U.S. association of lifeguard professionals, and the National Program of Medical Emergency.

will contact a doctor for you, or the ICT information office in San José can help. U.S. and Canadian embassy addresses and phone numbers are listed in Practical Extras. Pharmacists often diagnose and prescribe. In addition to patent medicines, some medicines requiring prescriptions at home may be sold over the counter here.

Typical Fare

Gallo pinto is the staple of the Costa Rican diet—black beans and rice. Try to eat it somewhere other than a first-class hotel. A *gallo* is something with a tortilla wrapped around it, such as beef, cheese, beans, chicken, or pork. When faced with an unfamiliar menu in the countryside, you usually cannot go wrong ordering one of the rice dishes such as *arroz con pollo* (chicken and rice) or a *casado*, which often comes with beef, chicken, or pork and vegetables such as *yuca* (cassava, a tuber similar to a potato), plantain, or squash with the ever-present rice and black beans. *Olla de carne* is a soup of beef and vegetables—chunks of yuca, squash, potato, corn on the cob, plantain, or whatever is the house recipe for olla de carne.

Tico tamales, traditional at Christmas, are wrapped in banana leaves rather than corn husks, with a filling of pork most common, though it can be chicken. Try a *tortilla de queso*, a substantial tortilla with cheese mixed in the cornmeal. *Pupusas* are, I believe, of Salvadoran origin, but they have found their way to menus of typical restaurants in Costa Rica. Basically they are two tortillas fried with cheese inside—tasty and greasy.

Sea bass (*corvina*), prawns (*langostinos*), and lobster (*langosto*) are among fresh seafood available. An appetizer of *ceviche*, certain types of raw seafood "cooked" in lime or lemon juice and mixed with onion and coriander leaves, can serve as a good light lunch. Ceviche is, however, being served less now due to the threat of cholera in the Western Hemisphere.

The big bunches of bright red or orange fruit you see for sale along roadsides are *pejibayes*, a palm fruit that has been harvested for food since Indian times. When boiled, it is often served as an hors d'oeuvre with a dollop of mayonnaise on the top. Try it. You may not like it. The flesh is quite dense and on the dry side. Most ticos love them. Another product of the pejibaye palm is *palmito*, or heart of palm, served cooked or fresh. Some palm species do not resprout when cut for the "heart." The pejibaye does, and commercial plantations now supply the market. So you do not have to worry that your heart of palm salad cost a forest tree its life. Natives also make a fermented drink from the sap when a tree is cut. Have a guide point out the tree, a stately palm with hairy spines on the trunk.

Refrescos, or natural fruit drinks, may come mixed with milk, in which case they will be listed as *en leche*, or water (*en agua*). Let your surroundings guide you as to which is safest, or stick to bottled drinks. I often order *agua dulce* in the campo, a hot drink made of boiling water and brown sugar. You can also have that mixed with milk, *con leche*. It is especially good in the mountains when there is a chill in the air. *Guaro*, a cane-based liquor, is the national liquor.

For sweets, try a dessert (*postre*, POS-tray) of flan, a sweet custard, or *tres leches*, a moist cake. *Cajeta* is a fudge.

Current Happenings

The *Tico Times* is a weekly English-language newspaper published every Friday. It is an excellent source of information on what is going on in Costa Rica. Several newsstands sell it on downtown streets in San José, or look for it in gift shops, hotels, or in the Candy Shop in the row of stores off the Plaza de la Cultura, Calle 3, Avenida Central/2.

Holidays

Gaily decorated trucks carrying costumed children brightened the dusty road. We discovered it was the day of San Isidro, patron saint of the farmer, celebrated in the area we were passing through with a local fair and blessing of animals and carts and other vehicles. Many such religious or civic festivals occur throughout the year. Ask at the ICT Information Office to find out where festivals will occur during your visit.

On official national holidays, most businesses, including banks, close. Holidays are listed here so you can plan around them.

January 1—New Year's Day

March 19—St. Joseph's Day, patron saint of the capital, San José

Holy Week—Maundy Thursday and Good Friday rival Easter in importance. Banks and businesses close, some all week.

April 11—Day of Juan Santamaría, national boy hero from the battle against William Walker and his filibusterers in 1856

May 1—Labor Day

June 29—Day of St. Peter and St. Paul

July 25—Annexation of the Province of Guanacaste, formerly part of Nicaragua

August 2—Day of the Virgin de Los Angeles (Our Lady of the Angels), patron saint of Costa Rica

August 15—Mother's Day

September 15—Independence Day (independence from Spain)

October 12—Discovery of America, Columbus Day, celebrated here as Día de la Raza

December 8—Immaculate Conception

December 25—Christmas (many businesses close between Christmas and New Year's Day)

6

What to See and Do

If you have not guessed by now, I should tell you straight out that I love Costa Rica. My only reason for writing this book is to help other travelers discover what it has to offer. This section presents an overview of what awaits you in different parts of the country: the towns, parks and wildlife refuges, privately owned nature reserves, hotels, beaches, rivers, and good places to try typical food. You also will find out about some of the agricultural crops important to the country.

Not so long ago, most visitors used San José as a base for one-day trips into the countryside. Other towns now offer adequate hotels and services, opening up the option of staying in an area to explore it rather than returning to the capital every night. Places such as Turrialba, Liberia, and San Isidro de El General are not crowded with tourists; to experience the day-to-day rhythm of life in these areas puts you more in touch with the rural roots of Costa Rica than dodging traffic on San José's Central Avenue. Consider spending a few nights on nature reserves, either public or privately operated, to hear the birds as they greet the day, to have time on a forest trail, and to sit quietly after supper and visit with the guide or the cook or the ranger. Locations of such places are mentioned in this chapter; details on accommodations at each are covered in chapters 7 and 8.

As for hotels, I include those I visited. I have tried to cover a range of price possibilities. Information on tour options from hotels is included.

There are some excellent nature-oriented package tours to places mentioned in each region. Some companies feature naturalist guides and offer day trips customized to fit the wishes of as few as two people. Details on which companies offer what and price information are in chapter 9. How to get to the national parks and reserves on your own is included in chapter 7 with a discussion of what each has to offer the tourist. The privately owned nature reserves described in detail in chapter 8 are mentioned here; some of them offer one-day as well as multiday visits. We have already talked about the options of travel by public transportation, renting a car, and hiring a taxi or van with a driver (see chap. 5).

Costa Rica is a country of the unexpected. You may spot a sloth in a tree as you pass along a busy highway, round a bend to discover a herd of cows resting on the road, watch monkeys swing from tree to tree on shore as you swim in warm ocean waters, or spot a flock of parrots in downtown San José. It is a place to try things you have never done before: go rafting or kayaking, be pampered on a cruise in the Gulf of Nicoya, tramp along trails in a tropical forest, ford rivers with water to the hood of the car, stay up all night trying to photograph a volcanic eruption, or take off on horseback to explore the countryside. The following pages guide you to find the level of adventure you choose.

San José

San José (founded in 1737), like most cities, has its good and bad sides. It is the center of government, theater, and art, as well as of air pollution and congestion. It has beautiful parks and museums, along with a few beggars on the streets. It is big and often noisy, but even from its crowded downtown streets, one can manage a view of surrounding mountains, green against the sky. I find it a friendly, interesting city.

With all the traffic, it is hard to realize that the era of the automobile began here only in the fifties. It is not uncommon to see carts scattered among the cars even now, though they are generally pulled by a person rather than oxen or a horse, as you may still encounter in the

San José's Plaza de la Cultura, with the National Theater on the left (Photo by Ree Strange Sheck)

countryside. Walk along Avenida 1 to the area around the Central Market, Calles 6/8, or Borbón Market, Avenida 3, Calles 8/10, in the early morning to see carts being loaded and unloaded.

Avenida? Calle? These are words to add to your vocabulary. *Avenida* (pronounced ah-vay-NEE-dah) means "avenue." Avenidas run east and west in the city. *Calle* (CAHL-lyay) means "street," and calles—you got it—run north and south. It helps if you can get your bearings early, because when you stop to ask for directions, the answer will be in terms of so many blocks to the north, east, south, or west. Another handy word is *metros* (MAY-tros), or meters. One hundred meters is about the equivalent of a city block, so a helpful citizen will tell you to go "200 *metros al norte*," two blocks north.

About the hardest thing you will do in San José, other than get safely across busy streets, is keep the street numbering systems straight. Calle numbers originate from Calle Central, with odd-numbered streets running parallel to the east of it; even-numbered streets west. Avenida numbers originate from Avenida Central; odd numbers are north of it and even numbers south. For example, if you go north from Avenida Central, you cross in succession Avenida 1, Avenida 3, Avenida 5. Walking west from Calle Central, you encounter Calle 2, Calle 4, Calle 6. Few buildings have numbers, so a typical address is Calle 1, Avenidas 2/4. This means the place is on Calle 1 in the block between Avenida 2 and Avenida 4. Look at the map of central San José to fix the system in your mind.

Street and avenue numbers are posted on buildings at the corners of some intersections. Keep looking as you walk, and you will eventually find one. The Costa Rican National Tourist Bureau (ICT) has a free city map or you can buy one in hotels or shops; get one and carry it with you.

The downtown ICT office is underneath the Plaza de la Cultura (Avenidas Central/2, Calles 3/5). The steps are near Calle 5. Staff members, bilingual in English and Spanish, are helpful and courteous. Hours are 9:00 a.m. to 5:00 p.m. weekdays and 9:00 a.m. to 1:00 p.m. on Saturday. The telephone number is 22-1090.

The plaza is a good place to people-watch. A mime, juggler, marimba band, magician, or storyteller may be performing for whatever is collected when the hat is passed. Civic functions, book fairs, or a visiting music group from the Andes draw clusters of onlookers. Arti-

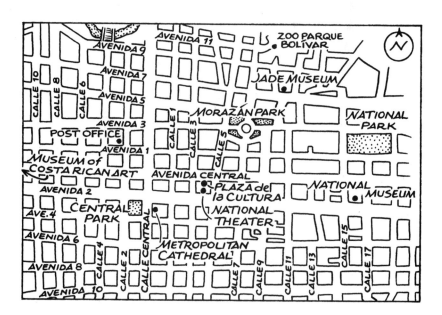

san booths have become common, creating a regular arts and crafts fair atmosphere. The adjacent open-air terrace of the Gran Hotel Costa Rica is a popular place to have refreshments or a meal while watching the activity or listening to the music.

On the Avenida 2 side of the plaza is a source of pride for ticos, the National Theater. Inaugurated in 1897, the building was paid for by coffee growers through a voluntary tax on every bag of coffee exported. The reason? A famous European opera star appearing in Guatemala had refused to perform in Costa Rica for lack of an adequate theater. National honor in this case resulted in a work of art. Because of severe damage in the December 1990 earthquake, performances have been cancelled here, but you can step inside for a tour. A fund-raising campaign for repairs is under way, and as work proceeds, certain areas may be closed off to visitors. The theater is open weekdays from 9:00 a.m. to 5:30 p.m., with an admission fee of $1.20.

Museums and Such

San José museums can be a good way to get a feel for the country before you take to the road. Most have reduced or free admission for students with an identification card.

National Museum (Avenidas Central/2, Calles 15/17). An exhibit on modern history joins pre-Columbian art, natural history, and religious art in this nineteenth-century building that was converted from a military fortress after the army was abolished. The Plaza de la Democracia next door, dedicated in 1989, commemorates one hundred years of democracy in Costa Rica. The museum is open from 9:00 a.m. to 5:00 p.m., closed on Mondays. Admission charge is about $.40. The museum has a good gift shop, with copies of Indian artifacts and ceramics.

Museum of Costa Rican Art (Calle 42, where Paseo Colón comes to La Sabana Park). La Sabana Park used to be the international airport (Charles Lindbergh landed here), and this museum is in the old terminal building. After looking over the art exhibits downstairs, climb to the second floor to see the Golden Room, whose embossed walls depict the country's history. Open 10:00 a.m. to 5:00 p.m., closed Mondays. Admission $.80. The Sabana-Cementerio bus will get you from Calle 7, Avenida Central to the museum.

Jade Museum (Avenida 7, Calle 9). The museum is on the eleventh floor of the Instituto Nacional de Seguros (National Insurance Institute) building. In addition to the marvelous collection of jade objects, there are pre-Columbian ceramic and stone works as well as displays with archaeological and ethnographic information. You also get some good views of the city from this height, and the rest rooms are clean. (Public rest rooms are in short supply; most museums do have them.) Open 9:00 a.m. to 3:00 p.m. weekdays except holidays. Free admission.

Gold Museum (Avenidas Central/2, Calle 5). Located underneath the Plaza de la Cultura, this spectacular collection of indigenous gold art belongs to the Central Bank of Costa Rica. Open Friday to Sunday, 10:00 a.m. to 5:00 p.m. Free admission.

Entertainment on the Plaza de la Cultura in San José (Photo by Ree Strange Sheck)

Museum of Natural Sciences La Salle (across from the southwest corner of La Sabana). Though some of the specimens appear a bit moth-eaten, exhibits show many of the mammals and birds to be found in Costa Rica. It may be your only chance to see the harpy eagle, an endangered species, even if it is stuffed. Some signs are in English and Spanish; some are only in Spanish, with Latin names. (See Practical Extras for a list of some of the more common animals in Costa Rica, with their English and Spanish names.) Do not overlook the butterfly collection above the shells. A few crocodiles and caimans live on a small island in the patio. Take the Sabana-Estadio bus from near the Cathedral on Avenida 2 and ask the driver to let you off at Colegio La Salle for the Museo de Ciencias Naturales. The museum is down a tree-lined drive, near the Ministry of Agriculture. Open 8:00 a.m. to 3:00 p.m. weekdays, 8:00 a.m. to noon Saturdays. Admission $.40.

Insect Museum (University of Costa Rica campus in San Pedro). This small museum in the basement of the Music Arts Building (Facultad de Artes Musicales) has a dazzling display of butterflies. There are bee specimens, exotic-looking beetles and walking sticks, poisonous spiders, the large *bala* ant found in the Atlantic zone, and a 162-pound wasp nest from near San Isidro de El General. Another display shows how animals protect themselves by mimicry and coloration.

The entrance, at the bottom of the stairs, will be locked. Ring the bell once for admission to the museum. Hours are 1:00 to 5:00 p.m. weekdays; admission $.80. The easiest way to find it is to go by taxi. Buses to San Pedro, leaving across from the National Theater on Avenida 2, will get you to within a ten- to fifteen-minute walk. Get off at the church in San Pedro and follow the street in front of it as it curves around to the north side of the campus. Watch for the Facultad de Artes Musicales and Museo de Insectos signs. It is a pretty campus, and students are extremely helpful when you ask directions.

Serpentarium (Avenida 1, Calles 9/11). You may not encounter a single snake during your forays into the natural world, so here is a good chance to see some of what lies hidden there: the boa constrictor, coral snake, brightly colored tree viper, and fer-de-lance. Forty species of live reptiles and amphibians (including the tiny poison dart frogs) are here, along with a nice photographic exhibit of Costa Rican wildlife. Most signage is in English and Spanish. Take time to look at the illustrations showing how to distinguish between venomous and nonvenomous snakes. You can also buy posters, T-shirts, postcards, nature books, and slides. A bilingual biologist is on hand. Open 10:00 a.m. to 7:00 p.m. year-round; admission $1.75. There is a sign at the entrance on the street, but the Serpentarium is upstairs.

Clodomiro Picado Institute (Dulce Nombre de Coronado). Snakes are "milked" at this snake "farm" for the production of serum to be used against Central American snakes, including most coral species. The low fatality rate from snakebites in Costa Rica is attributed to the widespread availability of antivenins; the lab also exports antivenins. The institute is about thirty minutes from San José. Take a taxi or the bus to Moravia (Avenida 3, Calle 3). Open weekdays from 8:00 a.m. to 4:00 p.m.; free admission.

Parque Bolivar—the zoo (Calle 9, Avenida 11). The zoo tends to be jammed on weekends with local folks. Most species of wildlife represented are found in Costa Rica, but an African lion, Bengal tiger, and assorted other foreign species round out the picture. Facilities themselves are on the shabby side, but the setting is beautiful. Plans have been announced to improve the zoo. Open 8:00 a.m. to 3:30 p.m. Monday to Friday, 9:00 a.m. to 4:30 p.m. weekends and holidays. Admission $.30. The information office of the national parks system is currently located here, with pamphlets, maps, and books for sale; however, a new information center may be opened at the National Parks office on Calle 25, Avenidas 8/10. Check with National Parks, 33-5284.

Zoológico de Aves (La Garita de Alajuela). More than 450 birds and a few species of mammals await the visitor on the spacious grounds of this former coffee plantation, a new location for the bird zoo. Here you can see the king vulture, toucans, parrots, scarlet macaws, and many other species that are so elusive in the rain forest. Signs give English and Spanish names. The animals are well cared for by owners Dennis and Susan Janik. Open daily 9:00 a.m. to 5:00 p.m. except

December 24 and 25. Admission $.80 adults, $.55 children. From Alajuela, you can take a La Garita or Atenas bus, which passes in front, or go by taxi for about $2.

Butterfly Farm (La Guácima de Alajuela). An enclosed tropical garden holds more than a thousand butterflies, representing more than 60 species. You can see all stages of the butterfly life cycle. Owners Joris and María Brinkerhoff have created a beautiful opportunity to observe and to learn and to photograph butterflies and tropical flowers. Open daily 9:00 a.m. to 4:30 p.m. Admission includes a one-hour guided tour when you arrive: adults $7, children $2. The last tour begins at 3:30 p.m. The La Guácima bus, which leaves from San José at 11:00 a.m. and 2:00 p.m., departs from Avenida 1, Calles 18/20 at the stop marked San Rafael de Ojo de Agua. From the last stop, the farm is about three blocks south; follow the signs. Call for other transportation information: 48-0115.

Souvenir Shops

Handcraft places are also mentioned in subsequent sections on the regions, but if you are shopping in San José, here are some with a wide variety of quality products: jewelry, wooden items, furniture, T-shirts, leather goods, artwork. Most also sell park posters, some natural history books in English, postcards, and slides; most accept credit cards.

La Casona (Calle Central, Avenidas Central/1). Two floors of shops; open Monday to Saturday 9:30 a.m. to 6:00 p.m.

CANAPI (Avenida 1, Calle 11). Open weekdays 9:00 a.m. to noon and 1:00 to 6:00 p.m., Saturdays 9:00 a.m. to 1:00 p.m.

Mercado Nacional de Artesanía (Calle 11, Avenidas 4/6). This is behind La Soledad Church, which offers a quiet place for reflection in this busy city and impressive stations of the cross. The artisan center is open weekdays from 9:00 a.m. to 12:30 p.m. and 1:30 to 6:00 p.m., Saturday from 9:00 a.m. to 12:30 p.m. and 1:30 to 5:00 p.m.

Travelers' Store, Costa Rica Expeditions (Calle Central, Avenida 3). Attention bird-watchers: you can get a locational checklist of birds of Costa Rica here. Open normal business hours including noon hours.

Pre-Columbian pottery in the National Museum (Photo courtesy of *La República*)

Annemarie's Boutique, Hotel Don Carlos (Calle 9, Avenidas 7/9). Lots of artwork along with one of the most complete selections of handcrafts around. Shopping here allows those not lucky enough to stay in this hotel an excuse to see it. Open 8:00 a.m. to 6:00 p.m. every day.

Suraska Gallery (Avenida 3, Calle 5) and La Galería (Calle 1, Avenidas Central/1) show off their handcrafts like the works of art that they are. Do not fail to go upstairs in each. Open weekdays 8:30 a.m. to 12:30 p.m. and 1:30 to 5:45 p.m., Saturdays 8:30 a.m. to noon.

Central Market (Avenidas Central/1, Calles 6/8). Handcrafts are sold here along with rubber boots, fish, flour, herbal remedies, shirts, and pots and pans. Watch your belongings and be ready for crowds.

Some city tours include a visit to nearby Moravia, well known for its leather goods. It is an easy bus trip to do on your own.

General Shopping

Head west from the Plaza de la Cultura on Avenida Central to find Librería Lehmann (Calles 1/3) for books and magazines, Librería Universal (Calles Central/1) for books, posters, maps, and department store items, and the La Gloria department store (Calles 4/6).

Next to the Avenida 1 "back door" of Librería Universal is a photo shop (look for the Fuji sign), where you can get film and same-day developing service for prints. Credit cards are accepted.

The Bookshop, one block east (Avenida 1, Calles 1/3), has English-language books, newspapers, and magazines.

The supermarket closest to the Plaza de la Cultura is La Gran Via, just west of the plaza; other large ones downtown are Mas x Menos and Automercado. Pharmacies (*farmacias*) abound, but there is a very complete drugstore/pharmacy about seven blocks from the Plaza de la Cultura at Calle Central, Avenidas 8/10. Look for the Botica Mario Jiménez sign. Another with courteous service is on the corner of Avenida Central, Calle 7. Remember, some stores require that you check packages when you enter and that you sometimes pay for a purchase at one counter or window (*caja*) and receive it at another (*empaque*).

Restaurants
San José and surrounding towns have many fine restaurants serving typical fare as well as French, Italian, Chinese, German, and Japanese cuisine. Look in the English-language weekly newspaper, *Tico Times*, and at tourist information in your hotel room. American restaurant chains are here: Pizza Hut, Mr. Pizza, Kentucky Fried Chicken, McDonald's, Burger King, Hardee's. A 12 percent tax is included in your restaurant bill, as well as a 10 percent tip.

If you want a light meal, look for a *soda*. San José also has good ice cream shops, such as Pops, two of which are near the plaza. Restaurant Internacional (Calle 9, Avenidas Central/1) and Sina (Avenida 1, Calle 7) have tasty, inexpensive *platos del día* (daily specials). Churrería Manolo (Avenida Central, Calles 9/11) has a typical Costa Rican breakfast for less than $2. *Churros* are those long, thin donutlike pastries for sale at the front.

Two hotels known for their good food are the Amstel (Avenida 1, Calle 7) and Bougainvillea (Barrio Tournon). Down from the Bougainvillea is El Pueblo Commercial Center, where you can have typical food at Cocina de Leña or seafood at Rías Bajas (more expensive). A personal favorite for a typical Costa Rican midday meal is the second-floor restaurant at the Hotel La Gran Via (Avenida Central,

Calles 1/3)—inexpensive, tasty, and filling. Others I return to are Casino Español (Calle 7, Avenidas Central/1), where the service makes you feel like royalty; La Nueva China, Tequila Willy's (for Mexican food), and Ambrosia (includes vegetarian dishes) in San Pedro; Tomy's Ribs (Avenida 6, Calles 11/13); and El Balcón de Europa (excellent), Avenida Central, Calle 9. La Hacienda has a nice atmosphere, good food, and friendly staff—Nils will do his best to make sure you enjoy your meal (Calle 7, Avenidas Central/2). The *flan de coco* is yummy. Las Orquídeas is a short drive north of San José on the road to Braulio Carrillo National Park, about 7 miles (12 km); nice atmosphere, good food, good service. Few people can resist the ambience of the outdoor terrace at the Gran Hotel Costa Rica next to the National Theater and Plaza de la Cultura. Food and prices are not bad either. At happy hour time, piano music from inside mingles with the sounds of a city getting ready to go home.

When I cannot stand the thought of one more meal in a restaurant, I drop by Spoon at Avenida Central, Calles 5/7, and choose among wonderful pastries, sandwiches, and desserts for a carryout lunch; they fix up natural fruit juice drinks to go, too. Morazán and España parks are a few blocks away on Avenida 3, a place to join ticos who are eating their sack lunches, watch schoolchildren play with the ducks, and watch the birds—lots of blue-gray tanagers, a few parrots, a woodpecker or two. The metallic school building you see nearby was built in the 1890s, the plates designed by Alexandre-Gustave Eiffel of Eiffel Tower fame and shipped from Belgium by boat to be assembled here. The National Park, farther down on Avenida 3 at Calle 15, is another good place to escape the crowds.

Hotels

This is not a comprehensive list of hotels, but it represents a range of prices. I do not list any that I would not be willing to stay in myself, depending on my pocketbook at the time. Most of these hotels are listed with the Costa Rican National Tourist Bureau, and the approved rates should be posted in the rooms. Some hotels have discounts in the off-season. Hotels that run their own nature tours are indicated.

Prices listed here include the 15 percent tax. If you arrive without a reservation, the ICT airport office will help you. Reservations are recommended. When calling from outside Costa Rica, use the country code: 506 before the number.

Costa Rica has a youth hostel association, with offices at Avenida Central, Calles 29/31; telephone 53-6588, fax 24-4085. The Costa Rican Network of Youth Hostels offers its members lodging at Toruma, its own facility in San José, and reduced rates at a growing number of other sites, including cabins or inns near Puntarenas, Rincón de la Vieja, and Tilarán as well as the private nature reserve, Rara Avis.

Aurola Holiday Inn. Singles from $119, doubles $131; seventeen floors, 201 rooms, including 12 suites; credit cards accepted. Air-conditioning, restaurant, swimming pool, cable TV, casino, parking, gym, spa. Avenida 5, Calle 5. Telephone 33-7233, (800) HOLIDAY (U.S.A.), or any Holiday Inn for reservations, fax 55-1036. Apartado 7802-1000, San José.

San José Palacio. Singles from $117, doubles $123; 254 rooms. Suites begin at $152. Restaurant, pool, tennis, squash and racketball, gym/spa (Jacuzzi, sauna, massage), air-conditioning, casino, satellite TV, beauty shop; credit cards accepted. Landscaped grounds on hill above highway in from airport, ten minutes from downtown. Telephone 20-2034 or 31-2202, fax 31-1990. Apartado 458-1150, San José.

Sheraton Herradura Hotel & Spa. Least-expensive single $108, double $118; 145 rooms (some suites). Five minutes from international airport, 20 minutes from San José. Restaurant, tennis, golf, pool. Air-conditioning, satellite TV, credit cards. Thirty species of orchids on grounds. Telephone 39-0033, (800) 325-3535 (U.S.A.), (800) 268-9393 (Western Canada), (800) 268-9330 (Eastern Canada), fax 39-2292. Ciudad Cariari, Apartado 7-1880-1000, San José.

Hotel Corobici. Single $105, double $117; 176 rooms. Air-conditioning, restaurant, cable TV, pool, spa, casino, credit cards. Near La Sabana Park. Telephone 32-8122, (800) 227-4274, fax 31-5834. Apartado 2443-1000, San José.

Tara Resort Hotel. Standard single $99, double $143; 30 rooms, including junior and master suites. Breakfast and pickup from airport included. Restaurant, satellite TV, gym, sauna, Jacuzzi, pool. Local naturalist guide for tour of Pico Blanco Mountain, rain forest. Arranges private tours anywhere. Southern-style plantation in country setting outside of San Antonio de Escazú. Veranda, balconies, and rooms with such names as Rhett Butler and Miss Melanie. Telephone 28-6992, fax 28-9651. Apartado 1459-1250, Escazú.

Albergue Campestre, Finca Rosa Blanca. Six rooms beginning at $88 single, $117 double, breakfast included. Three-bedroom colonial farmhouse next to main inn has daily, weekly, monthly rates. Credit cards accepted. Located at Santa Barbara de Heredia, 30 minutes from San José. Fantastic views of valley and coffee fields, 400 fruit trees on grounds, river with pools for swimming, walking trail, terraces, mural by Barva artist, two libraries, artwork, original decoration, much use of tropical hardwoods salvaged from a road-widening project. Unique. Horseback riding and nature tours arranged. Telephone 39-9392, fax 39-9555. In U.S.A. (800) 327-9854. Apartado 41-3009, Santa Barbara, Heredia.

Hotel L'Ambiance. Single $70, double $93. No credit cards or personal checks. No children under 15. Six rooms plus a suite (furnished in antiques) around an interior courtyard complete with fountain. Restaurant overlooks Parque Bolívar. Concierge can arrange private tours with driver. Cable TV, air-conditioning. Charming. Calle 13, Avenidas 9/11. Telephone 22-6702, 23-1598, fax 23-0481. Apartado 1040-2050, San Pedro.

Hotel Torremolinos. Single $64, double $72; 72 rooms are junior suites and full suites. Quiet neighborhood (Calle 40, Avenida 5) two blocks from Centro Colón. Shuttle service to downtown, pool, sauna, massage, cable TV, air-conditioning in full suites, parking. Telephone 22-9129, fax 55-3167. Apartado 2029-1000, San José.

Hotel Irazú. Least-expensive single $59, double $72 (you'll pay more if you want air-conditioning); 305 rooms, 16 suites. Restaurant, tennis, pool, casino, cable TV, spa, credit cards. Fifteen minutes from downtown; shuttle service. Daily bus service to sister hotel Jacó Beach on the Pacific. Telephone 32-4811, (800) 223-0888 (U.S.A.), (800) 268-7041 (Toronto), (800) 663-9582 (Vancouver, British Columbia), fax 32-3159. Apartado 962-1000, San José.

Hotel Grano de Oro. Singles begin at $58, doubles at $70; also deluxe rooms about $10 more and garden suite for $128. Each of the 21 rooms in this restored mansion is different, all with ceiling fans and private baths. Original art throughout, with rooms named for orchids, each having a watercolor of that orchid in the room. Small restaurant with breakfast and tearoom menu offering light meals for lunch or dinner. Atrium and courtyard with fountains. *Grano de oro* refers to the coffee bean, and the hotel serves its own blend and sells it in the gift shop that also features unusual items from self-help projects in Peru, Guatemala, and Costa Rica. Credit cards accepted, tours arranged. Short nightly program to bring guests together before dinner: for example, "Fruits of Costa Rica" one night gives people a chance to sample *guanábanas* or the *mamón chino*. Located near Paseo Colón, Calle 30, Avenidas 2/4. Telephone 33-4231, fax 21-2782. Apartado 1157-1007, Centro Colón, San José.

Hotel Bougainvillea. Singles from $58, doubles $64; 80 rooms. Restaurant, pool, Jacuzzi, parking, air-conditioning. Located near Barrio Tournon, 10-minute walk from city center. Telephone 33-6622, fax 22-5211. Bougainvillea Santo Domingo, under same ownership, is 15 minutes from San José on 10 acres: trees, orchards, coffee fields, flower gardens. Single $70, double $82; 44 junior suites with balconies. Restaurant, shuttle bus, cable TV, tennis, pool, jogging trail. Telephone 40-8822, fax 40-8484. Credit cards accepted at both. Apartado 69-2120, San José.

Gran Hotel Costa Rica. Single $56, double $76; 106 rooms. Restaurant, TV, casino, parking, credit cards. Located at Plaza de la Cultura, Avenida 2, Calle 3. Telephone 21-0796, 21-4000, fax 21-3501. Apartado 527-1000, San José.

Hotel Dunn Inn. Rooms from $53 to $64; 13 rooms. Continental breakfast included. Fans, cable TV, bar; credit cards accepted. Restored house in Barrio Amón, Avenida 11, Calle 5. Built around covered courtyard. Telephone 22-3232 or 22-3426, fax 21-4596. Apartado 1584-1000, San José.

Hotel Presidente. Single $53, double $67; 50 rooms, some suites with kitchens. Restaurant, air-conditioning, cable TV, credit cards. Adding 70 more rooms. Avenida Central, Calles 7/9. Telephone 22-3022, fax 21-1205. Apartado 2922-1000, San José.

Hotel Santo Tomás. Rooms from $50 to $76; 20 rooms. Restored mansion about 90 years old in the area north of Morazán Park. Continental breakfast included. Fans, high ceilings, bar, cable TV in parlorlike lobby; credit cards accepted. Each room different, some with bathtubs. French provincial furniture. Helps arrange individualized tours. Telephone 55-0448, fax 22-3950. Avenida 7, Calles 3/5, San José.

Hotel Royal Dutch. Single $50, double $63; 25 rooms, some suites with refrigerator. Restaurant, air-conditioning, TV; credit cards accepted. Calle 4, Avenidas Central/2. Telephone 22-1414, fax 33-3927. Apartado 4258-1000, San José.

Amstel Hotel. Single $46, double $54; 55 rooms. Air-conditioning, bar, fine restaurant. Calle 7, Avenidas 1/3. Telephone 22-4622, fax 33-3329. Apartado 4192-1000, San José.

Hotel La Gran Via. Single $43, double $56; 32 rooms. Located on Avenida Central, Calles 1/3; much quieter now that the avenida is closed to through traffic in this block. Restaurant, credit cards. Telephone 22-7737, fax 22-7853. Apartado 1433, San José.

Hotel Europa. Least-expensive single $42, double $55; 72 rooms. Restaurant, cable TV, outdoor pool, credit cards. Calle Central, Avenidas 3/5. Telephone 22-1222, (800) 223-6764 (U.S.A.), fax 21-3976. Apartado 72, San José.

Hotel Don Carlos. Single $41, double $47, including continental breakfast; 25 rooms, some suites. Accepts Visa. Calle 9, Avenidas 7/9. Small restaurant, cable TV, gym, marimba band three evenings a week, great gift shop, parking. Tours for guests to volcanoes, museums, city tour, and bird-watching and conservation trips. Provides maps for people with own transportation. Hotel was home of ex-president Tomás Guardia. Telephone 21-6707, fax 55-0828. Apartado 1593-1000, San José.

Hotel Petit Victoria. Single $41, double $47; 15 rooms. Breakfast included. Seventy-year-old Victorian house next to Sala Garbo theater near Paseo Colón at Calle 28, Avenida 2a. Elaborate tile floors, mini-bars in rooms, cable TV in lobby; credit cards accepted. Telephone 33-1812 or 33-1813, fax 33-1938. Apartado 357-1007, San José.

Tres Arcos Bed and Breakfast. Doubles with shared bath $40, private bath $47; 7 rooms. Breakfast included. Suites for up to five persons available. In lovely Los Yoses neighborhood only a fifteen-minute walk from downtown. Private, quiet, birds, orchids, bromeliads in garden. The Warringtons will help arrange tours, including a visit to Genesis II, a private nature reserve. Avenida 10, Calle 37. Telephone/fax 25-0271. Apartado 161-1000, San José.

Garden Court Hotel. Single $35, double $46; 70 rooms. Buffet breakfast included. Restaurant, pool in courtyard, TV, parking, air-conditioning; credit cards accepted. Avenida 7, Calles 6/8 (good hotel in a marginal neighborhood). Daily tours to Jacó Beach. Travel agency. Telephone 22-3674, fax 32-3159. From U.S.A., (800) CR-BOOK-H. Apartado 962-1000, San José.

Hotel Pico Blanco Inn. Singles from $35, doubles $41, two-bedroom cabins $70; 20 rooms. Restaurant/bar, private balconies, breathtaking views of Central Valley below. Located above San Antonio de Escazú twenty minutes from San José. Elevation 5,000 feet (1,524 m). Owners John and Flor are gracious hosts. Hiking trails nearby. A pair of free-flying macaws call this home. Telephone 28-3197, fax 28-5189. Apartado 900-2050, Escazú.

Hotel Plaza. Single $29, double $40; 40 rooms. Restaurant, TV, opens on to pedestrian mall. Avenida Central, Calles 2/4. Telephone 22-5533 or 22-5805, fax 22-2641. Apartado 2019-1000, San José.

Hotel Diplomat. Least-expensive single $25, double $34; 30 rooms. Optional TV, restaurant. Calle 6, Avenida Central/2. Telephone 21-8133, 21-8744. Apartado 6606-1000, San José.

D'Galah Hotel. Single $24, double $30; 25 rooms, some with kitchenettes; suites. Sauna, coffee shop, pool, parking, credit cards. Arranges tours to neighboring University of Costa Rica—Insect Museum, Botanical Gardens. Located on north side of campus in San Pedro. Telephone 34-1743, 53-7539. Apartado 85-2350, San José.

Petit Hotel. Single with private bath $24, double $30, rooms with shared bath begin at $16; 15 rooms. No credit cards. Free coffee, kitchen privileges—no restaurant. Television in lobby, pleasant interior courtyard. Calle 24, Paseo Colón/Avenida 2. Telephone 33-0766, fax 33-1938. Apartado 357-1007 Centro Colón, San José.

Hotel Galilea. Single $19, double $24; 23 rooms. TV in lobby, friendly staff; no credit cards. The Captain and staff befriend their guests. Nicer people would be hard to find. Telephone 33-6925, fax 23-1689. Avenida Central, Calles 11/13.

Hotel Bienvenido. Singles from $7, doubles $14; 44 rooms. Private baths, clean, hot water; no credit cards. Access to refrigerator and hot plate. Calle 10, Avenidas 1/3. Telephone 21-1872. Apartado 389-2200, Coronado.

Toruma Youth Hostel. Bed and breakfast $5; 95 beds in 9 rooms, men and women separate. Shared baths, bedding supplied. Small restaurant also open to public, with lunch less than $1.50. On Avenida Central, Calles 29/31, the building has been a home of ex-president José Figueres as well as the Italian Embassy. Use of washing machine and iron for minimal charge to guests. Telephone 53-6588, fax 24-4085. Apartado 1355-1002, San José.

One-Day Package Tours from San José
Because of the small size of the country and San José's central location, the traveler who wants to use the capital as a base can touch many parts of the country in one-day excursions. Tour companies that offer a limited number of one-day air trips expand the horizon even farther.

National parklands with easy access are Irazú and Poás volcanoes and Braulio Carrillo. Package tours by air bring Tortuguero and Barra del Colorado national parks into the picture. Guayabo National Monument, the only archaeological park, and Tapantí National Wildlife Refuge are also good road trips. A cruise in the Gulf of Nicoya or a tour to Carara Biological Reserve takes you to the Pacific. Exploring the historical and biological treasures of the Central Valley is possible with tours to the Orosi Valley, Lankester Gardens (for orchids), the colonial capital of Cartago with its religious shrine, and the handcraft city of Sarchí. One-day tours take you rafting or kayaking on the country's waterways and hiking on Barva Volcano. Find specifics on all of these in chapter 9.

If after all this physical activity, you return to San José and could use a massage, you might call Integree, where a relaxing massage is less than $15. Herbal wraps and a sauna are also available. Manager Nazira Naranjo and her staff are qualified professionals, and the facilities are pleasing. Telephone 33-3839. Located on Avenida 14, Calles 1/3.

Central Valley

The four colonial cities of Costa Rica were San José, Cartago, Alajuela, and Heredia. Each had its own character and strong sense of identity. That is still true today. When a person tells you he is from Alajuela, he has centuries of pride in his voice.

As you travel to or through these places, remember that this land was once covered with forest. Try to imagine what travel must have been like on foot or horseback up and down these mountains and across the rivers now gentled by bridges. Life here was hard; it forged the national character.

Beauty, not hardship, is the sensation one experiences when traveling through today. Patches of protected forest remain, but the landscape is largely one of coffee fields, sugarcane, small farms, picturesque villages, pastures for dairy cows. Each rural house has its flowers, a porch to sit on when the work is done, a few banana and coffee plants, some fruit trees, and perhaps some beans, squash, and corn—a link back to agrarian self-sufficiency.

Alajuela (pop. 44,358) was the home of Juan Santamaría, the country's national hero. He is honored here with a statue and the Juan Santamaría Historical Museum, open every day except Monday from 2:00 to 9:00 p.m. The Central Park is a veritable orchard of mango trees. Blue-gray tanagers are among birds that flock to eat the ripe fruit when it falls on the ground. In July, the Festival of Mangoes brings nine days of music, parades, farmers' markets, and an arts and crafts fair. Alajuela can be a stop on your way to Sarchí or Poás Volcano, or you can take a twenty-minute bus ride from San José (leaving from Avenida 2, Calles 12/14) to explore the town. This is the capital of the province of Alajuela.

Sarchí is an artisan center where even the trash cans and bus stops are decorated with colorful paintings. The most famous product is

Colorful ox carts in Sarchí (Photo by Ree Strange Sheck)

the painted ox cart. Ox carts played a vital transportation role in earlier times, carrying coffee from the highlands down to the Pacific for export. Carts, painted and unpainted, still transport produce. Farmers are usually pleased to stop to allow you a photograph of their carts and oxen when you encounter them on a rural road. At Sarchí, you find the genuine item as well as replicas turned into bars, napkin holders, and miniatures, complete with a few beans of coffee stuck on. There are salad bowls, wooden fruit, lamps, furniture, jewelry, and more. At the Joaquín Chaverri store and factory, watch artisans paint the delicate designs freehand. The ICT information office in San José can tell you the best way to get to Sarchí by bus. Some tours to Poás include a stop here.

The fields covered with black shade cloths on the way to Poás Volcano consist of ornamental plants and flowers, a growing nontraditional export. Strawberries grow through here as well, and you can often buy them at roadside stands.

Heredia (pop. 27,117) is the gateway to another volcano, Barva. It is also the home of the National University and a church that harks back to colonial times, built in 1796. The tower of an old fort remains in pretty gardens near the church. Buses for Heredia leave San José

from Calle 1, Avenidas 7/9, every ten minutes for the twenty-five-minute trip. Heredia is the capital of the province by that name.

Barva Volcano is in Braulio Carrillo National Park. It is possible to see the resplendent quetzal here, along with a variety of other birds. Even veteran hikers have gotten lost, so consider going with a guide. One nature tour company (Jungle Trails) offers a one-day hike here with a minimum of two people.

On the road between Heredia and the jumping-off place for the volcano at Sacramento is the historic town of Barva, with its large church and tiled-roof adobe houses. Farther along, in the area of San José de la Montaña, are three hotels that offer a chance to spend the night in this chilly clime, to hike, to bird-watch. Bring a coat: it is cold at night and brisk in the early morning, and I have wished for my long johns to sleep in. Cypresal has 24 rooms, a small swimming pool, sauna, horse rental, and a restaurant. Singles are $36, doubles $47. Telephone 37-4466, 23-1717; fax 21-6244. Across the road are Cabañas Las Ardillas, seven rustic cabins that hold up to four people each, complete with fireplace and kitchen area; $42 a night. A trail leads down through a forest behind to the river. Telephone 21-4294, 22-8134. Walking distance up the road is El Pórtico, which does have heat in the rooms, along with a Jacuzzi, sauna, pool, and restaurant; 14 rooms. El Pórtico also has a river trail. Rates: $36 for a single, $49 for a double. Telephone 37-6022, 38-2930; fax 38-0629.

Between Alajuela and Heredia is a small mountain inn called Finca Rosa Blanca, near Santa Barbara de Heredia. It looks like a castle rising above the fields of coffee. The Bougainvillea's Santo Domingo Hotel between San José and Heredia offers another rural setting in the area. Both are described under the hotel section for San José.

Northeast of Heredia about 2.5 miles (4 km) from the highway to Braulio Carrillo Park and Limón is La Posada de la Montaña. This mountain inn bed and breakfast has economy rooms with shared bath and deluxe rooms and one- or two-bedroom suites with kitchenette, sitting room, fireplace, and private bath. Doubles in the economy rooms are $35; deluxe doubles, $47, including full breakfast. Credit cards accepted. Only twenty minutes from San José, the inn has 5 acres (2 ha) of grounds in coffee, tropical fruits, flowers, and trees.

COFFEE

Coffee was the number one export for Costa Rica from the middle of the last century until this decade, when bananas edged it into second place. Its cultivation and export brought the country into the world market and initiated a cash economy in a land previously tied to subsistence agriculture. The instability of world market prices for coffee brings good years and bad years, and even though Costa Rica is working hard to diversify its economy through nontraditional exports, a drop in the price of coffee still sends a shudder through the country.

Coffee, which originated in Ethiopia and Arabia, was brought to the New World by the French, Spanish, and Portuguese. Seeds were first planted in Costa Rica around the beginning of the nineteenth century, but coffee did not become an export until 1840. Most of the crop today is sold to West Germany, the United States, and England.

According to a coffee specialist at CATIE, the agricultural center at Turrialba, coffee grown above 4,000 feet (1,200 m) gives the best flavor, on land where temperatures average between 59° and 82°F (15° and 28°C). A definite dry season helps because plants then flower evenly once the rains start. That means the fruit will mature over a few months, creating a short harvest period. Coffee is picked by hand; only mature fruit is taken. Since all the berries even on a single plant do not ripen at the same time, much labor is involved. Reducing the duration of that labor-intensive period is economically important to the grower.

Coffee plants are grown in nurseries until they are about one year old, and then they are transplanted to the field. After two years, they begin to bear commercially. Some growers harvest from coffee trees for fifteen or twenty years and then prune them way back for twenty more years of production before replacing the plant. (Coffee wood is highly prized for cooking because it burns slowly and produces little smoke.) Others replace more often.

Notice that some fields have trees planted to shade the coffee. Varieties that do not need shade first showed increases in production per acre, but over time production dropped and more nutrients had to be added to the soil. Some growers who switched are now returning to shaded coffee. Some trees used, such as the poró, are legumes with nitrogen-fixing properties, so they add to the soil as well as provide shade. Sometimes fields have banana or citrus trees for shade.

Coffee is planted in May and June once the rains are established. Harvest depends on elevation: October to January in the Central Valley, June to October or November in Turrialba and Coto Brus. Pickers are paid by the arroba (25 lbs.). A good picker can earn about $11 a day. All ages take to the fields for harvest. Each berry, which turns from green to red when ripe, contains two seeds. These seeds are the coffee beans. The pulp of the fruit must be removed and the beans dried before they can be roasted or exported.

Transportation from San José arranged. Telephone/fax 39-8096. In the U.S.A., (417) 637-2066. Apartado 1-3017, San Isidro de Heredía.

Cartago (pop. 29,564) lies 13 miles (21 km) southeast of San José, on the other side of the Continental Divide. Once the colonial capital, it now is capital of the province of Cartago.

If you like markets, stop by the one here—gorgeous vegetables. Ruins of a church surround a tranquil garden of trees, flowers, and fountains; the town gave up on trying to finish it after a severe earthquake in 1910. In front is an example of a cobblestone street from the colonial era. The most famous church in Cartago—in the entire country—is the Basílica de Nuestra Señora de los Angeles, built in honor of La Negrita, Costa Rica's patron saint. An image of the dark-skinned Virgin is inside. Go downstairs to see the site of the spring where the Virgin first appeared. Holy water from the spring flows out behind the basilica, where people can fill bottles or jars. Many miracles are attributed to the saint. On August 2, thousands of pilgrims gather at the shrine; the road from San José to Cartago is jammed with marchers beginning the preceding day. Some arrive from as far away as Nicoya, Guanacaste, Panama, and Nicaragua.

Cartago has felt the effects of activity from Irazú Volcano as well as from several severe earthquakes. The drive to the volcano offers spectacular views of the valley. Farmers tend fields of potatoes and onions and cabbages. Milk cows move along the road. We once stopped to photograph a young man forking hay into an ancient-looking barn along the way. He insisted on taking us into the barn to see his bull.

From Cartago it is a 15-minute drive to the Lankester Gardens, operated by the University of Costa Rica. Begun by Charles Lankester to preserve local flora—especially orchids, bromeliads, and arum plants—as well as to regenerate a natural forest, the Jardines Lankester stands as a gift from one nature lover to thousands who have walked these paths. Most come to see the more than 800 species of orchids. Some are blooming at any time of year, but peak months are February through April. Trails lead over brooks, under arbors, to greenhouses, through a breathtaking display of flowers and trees that attract at least 150 species of birds. The gardens are open daily from 8:30 a.m. to 3:30 p.m. Guided walks leave on the half hour. Admission $.80. Tours come from San José; a bus from Cartago for Paraíso (Paradise) brings you close to the entrance. Ask the driver to advise you where to get off.

From Paraíso, roads go east and south for magnificent views of the Orosi Valley, Reventazón River, and the lake formed by the Cachí Dam. The east road leads to ruins of the seventeenth-century church of Ujarrás. Archaeological digs indicate the colonial town that once surrounded it lies over pre-Columbian roads. There is a restaurant at the view point (*mirador* in Spanish) overlooking Ujarrás. Ten minutes away by car is the Charrarra Recreation Park on the lake, with swimming pool, restaurant, picnic areas, tour boat, and trails. The distinctive call of the oropendola, a large dark bird with yellow tail feathers, resounds through the trees. Crowded on weekends, the park is peaceful on other days. The road continues on to the dam.

The road south of Paraíso goes to the town of Orosi and its eighteenth-century church. Beside the church is a small historical museum, closed on Mondays. A mirador before you reach Orosi offers glorious views. Just beyond the town is Hotel Río Palomo, on the Palomo River, with its popular restaurant. Cabins with a small living room and private bath (hot water) are $19 for two persons; those with kitchenettes and beds for up to six persons are $28 for two. Tours are offered to Tapantí, Orosí, Ujarrás, and a coffee plantation. Horseback tours are also available, and there is a large swimming pool by the restaurant. Telephone 73-3128, 73-3057. Apartado 220-7050, Cartago.

The Tapantí National Wildlife Refuge is about 6 miles (10 km) from Orosi. Tours combine some of these sites out of Cartago in day trips from San José. Public buses from Cartago go to Orosi and Ujarrás (ask at ICT), with a taxi extension for Tapantí. If you are driving, you can make a loop from Ujarrás around the lake, but the unpaved section from the dam to Orosi is very bumpy (and dusty in the dry season).

The road from Cartago to Turrialba is spectacular as it winds up and over the mountains. This was the route to Limón before the shorter highway from San José to Guapiles opened. When you get to the town of Cervantes, watch on the left for the Posada de la Luna restaurant. I am unable to pass this place without stopping for a freshly made *tortilla de queso* (cheese tortilla) and glass of hot *agua dulce con leche*. The agua dulce is a typical hot drink made from raw sugar and water. Here they bring a pitcher of hot milk to add if you request con leche. Some people swear the best *gallo pinto* (beans and rice) in the

Coffee harvested by hand near Turrialba (Photo by Ree Strange Sheck)

country is served here; buy some *cajeta* (fudge) to take with you. Showcases hold bits of history from Indian artifacts to flatirons. La Luna is quite a place.

The agricultural lands around Juan Viñas are among the most beautiful in Costa Rica. Fields of sugarcane wave across this top-of-the-world setting. Then comes the winding descent into the Turrialba Valley.

Only 40 miles (64 km) from San José, Turrialba, with 29,488 people in the city proper, is the center of a rich agricultural region and is increasingly a destination for tourists. Kayakers and white-water rafters use the town as a base for forays on the mighty Reventazón and Pacuare rivers. Its location makes it ideal for travelers interested in archaeology, agriculture, and nature. From here you can visit Guayabo National Monument (11 mi., 18 km away), Turrialba Volcano, plantations of coffee, macadamia, cardamom, sugarcane, and bananas, and tour CATIE, a tropical agricultural research and education center. Located a few miles from Turrialba, CATIE prefers that visitors come with an organized group to receive the most from a visit. A tour can include a look at meat and dairy operations, forest management, orchids, coffee, cacao, macadamia, plantains, and plant genetics, with a stop at their seed laboratory and seed bank. Individual visitors can go on the nature trail but will not have access to the facilities. Telephone number of CATIE's tourist office is 56-6431, extension 210.

The 18-room Hotel Wagelia near the center of town is comfortable; international visitors to CATIE often stay here. Singles are $31, doubles $47. There is parking, a gift shop including items made locally by handicapped children, and a good restaurant. Credit cards accepted. An annex to the hotel has opened on a quiet street backed by coffee fields at the edge of town. Rates are the same for its 11 rooms. It has a restaurant, sports areas, and a pool for adults and one for children. Both hotels have private baths. Rafting tours can be arranged as well as visits to CATIE, Guayabo National Monument, and Turrialba Volcano (travel by car and horseback), all with bilingual guides. Telephone 56-1566, fax/telephone 56-1596. Apartado 99-7150, Turrialba.

SUGARCANE

Sugarcane was brought to the New World by Columbus and was introduced into Costa Rica in 1530. Though it is grown in most of the country, there are five major cane-producing regions: the area of the Central Valley around Atenas and Grecia; the Turrialba and Juan Viñas area of the Central Valley; Guanacaste; San Carlos; and Pérez Zeledón and Parrita to the south. Some 98,840 acres (40,000 ha) are in production.

At 3,280 feet (1,000 m) or less, cane takes twelve to eighteen months to reach harvest; above that elevation, it takes twenty-four months. Almost all is cut by hand except in Guanacaste, where machines are used because of insufficient labor. In Costa Rica, most cane is burned before it is cut to make the cutting easier: a worker can cut two to three tons of unburned cane per day compared to three to six tons of cane that has been burned. Harvest is from January to May, though in higher regions around Juan Viñas it can last until August. Large sugar mills are called ingenios, and companies often provide a school and housing for workers. Small trapiches, where juice is extracted by oxen power, can still be found.

More than 4,400 people have cane operations, ranging from a few acres to 7,400 acres (3,000 ha). Some 59,000 people depend on cane production, including workers and their families. Where cane harvest alternates with coffee harvest, especially in the Central Valley, field hands work in both.

The United States is the biggest buyer of Costa Rican sugar and has been since 1963 when it stopped buying sugar from Cuba. The Soviet Union buys tico sugar as well. Some cane is used to produce alcohol for fuel, which is also exported to the United States. You may notice the distilleries in Cañas and Liberia.

Price is fixed by the government, and the Sugarcane Agricultural and Industrial League (LAICA) regulates buying and selling in and out of the country and conducts research to improve production. Costa Rica is third in the world in production per hectare.

Do not plan to sleep late anywhere in town. The peaceful air of the place is broken by three strong blasts of the town's fire alarm announcing 6:00 a.m.

You can get from San José to Turrialba by express bus. If you have a car, there is a back door to Turrialba, which winds through San Isidro de Coronado and Rancho Redondo, dairy country and oak forest often shrouded in mist. The last time I was on this road was a Corpus Christi Sunday. Flowers strewn in the road marked the path of religious processions in village after village. In one, a milk cow stood in the middle of the road eating the flower petals while worshipers sang inside the church. Past Llano Grande is the turnoff for

Irazú Volcano. Continue on to Cot and Pacayas for Santa Cruz, watching for waterfalls on the skirts of Turrialba Volcano. At Santa Cruz, turn to Turrialba. This road is passable even in the rainy season with a regular car. From Santa Cruz there is a jolting road—which is supposed to be surfaced this year—on to Guayabo and the national monument.

There is a small mountain lodge called La Calzada on the road between the town of Guayabo and the national park. Currently there are four doubles with a shared bath, but construction is under way on three rooms with private baths. Cost is $14 per room for one or two persons; Visa accepted. An Indian road (*calzada*) passes through the property, hence its name, and a walk along the road through plantains, macadamia, and coffee to the forest and river may reveal potsherds. José Miguel and Grettel García are great hosts. Food at the thatched, open-air restaurant is typical fare—delicious. Stop by on your way to the park even if you do not spend the night.

La Calzada is a ten-minute walk from the park. José offers a number of optional tours to his guests: to see the juice extracted from sugarcane at an old-style *trapiche* using oxen (open one day a week) as well as at a newer steam-powered plant, to visit a coffee farm and processing plant, and to see a local cheese factory. Call for reservations: 56-6091, 56-0465. José offers a pickup service in Turrialba for $16. The bus from Turrialba to Guayabo passes in front. Check the schedule: it only runs once a day, none on Sunday.

Two other small mountain lodges are located outside of Turrialba on the road toward Limón. Turrialtico is about 4 miles (7 km). Twelve rooms with private baths (hot water) are above the locally popular restaurant. Owner Hector Lezama will pick you up in Turrialba, or you can come by bus. He arranges tours to Guayabo, macadamia and coffee plantations, rafting trips, and with enough notice, a trip to Turrialba Volcano—part by car, part on horseback. Rooms are $23, no credit cards. Telephone/fax 56-1111.

Pochotel is 7 miles (11 km) from Turrialba. From its mirador on a clear day you can see the Caribbean. Six two-room bungalows with private baths and hot water go from $23 for a double to $37. Bungalows are separate from the restaurant. Owner Oscar García will arrange pickup in Turrialba and tours to Guayabo and sites around Turrialba. Visa accepted. Telephone 56-0111, fax 56-6222.

On the banks of the Reventazón River off the road to La Suiza southeast of Turrialba is the new Casa Turire, built inside the Atirro Hacienda. Surrounded by sugarcane, coffee, and macadamia fields, the 12-room, 4-suite grand "plantation house," two stories, sits amid landscaped gardens, with a pool, Jacuzzi, and five-hole golf course on the grounds. Guests can visit a sugar mill and processing plants for coffee and macadamia nuts. Bike and horse rentals available. Kayaking and rafting on the river arranged. Stunning views of mountains from balconies. Private landing strip. Standard rooms for one or two persons, $99; suites begin at $128; credit cards accepted. The breakfast buffet is $6, lunch is à la carte, and a set menu for dinner is $13, plus tax. The hotel does not accept guests younger than 17 years of age, and it is not equipped for the handicapped. Telephone 73-1111, fax 73-1075. Apartado 303-7150, Turrialba.

The privately owned nature reserve Rancho Naturalista, a favorite with bird and butterfly enthusiasts, is near Turrialba, southeast through La Suiza (see chap. 8).

North Central

Mountains, plains, volcanoes, lakes, rivers, forests, fruit farms, and cattle ranches form a colorful and diverse mosaic in this region of Costa Rica. Three principal roads take the traveler into the north central area from San José: the Zarcero-Ciudad Quesada-Arenal route; the Varablanca-San Miguel-Puerto Viejo route; and the route through Braulio Carrillo park, turning north before Guapiles to Las Horquetas and Puerto Viejo. (There are several towns named Puerto Viejo in Costa Rica. This is Puerto Viejo de Sarapiquí.)

Zarcero is a mountain town famous for its animals; that is, animals sculpted from plants, topiary art. The fantastic gardens in front of the church hold an evergreen elephant, bull, and rabbit, plus dozens of other forms. Roadside stands offer fruits, *cajeta*, delicious cheeses, and other specialties of this rural center of some 3,200 people. The

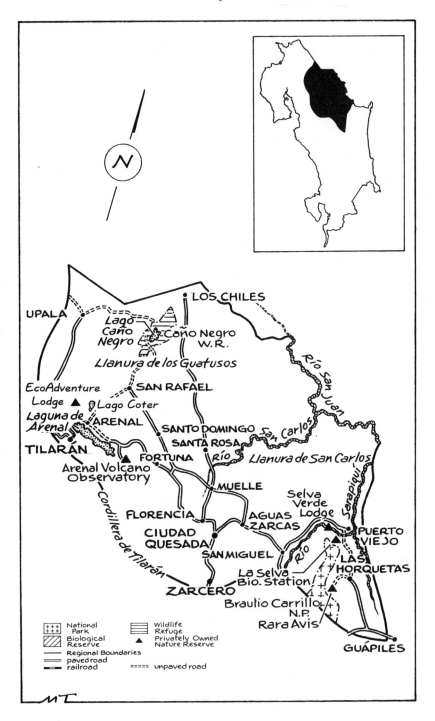

cheese known as *palmito* is not made from heart of palm, as some visitors deduce from its name. It is a layered ball of white cheese.

Ciudad Quesada (pop. 28,210) is a center of this rich agricultural area. Located on the edge of the San Carlos Plains about 60 miles (95 km) from the capital, it is often referred to as San Carlos. The first view of the extensive plains from the mountains is always a little surprising for those who think of Costa Rica as all rugged terrain. Both of these towns can be reached via the Ciudad Quesada bus from San José. Some one-day tours include a stop in Zarcero to see the church. Tours on the way to Arenal pass through Ciudad Quesada. There are daily buses from Ciudad Quesada through La Fortuna and around Lake Arenal to Tilarán.

Five miles (8 km) northeast of Ciudad Quesada is Hotel El Tucán, a country inn set among the trees, complete with tennis courts, swimming pools, sauna, restaurants, and 62 rooms. A thermal river that flows through the grounds supplies a Jacuzzi; the waters are said to be effective in treatment of arthritis, skin and kidney disorders, and rheumatism. Single $58, double $70, suites begin at $93. Walking trails, horseback riding, tennis, minigolf; arranges tours to Arenal Volcano, Caño Negro, Sarapiquí River. Telephone 46-1822, telephone/fax 21-9095. Apartado 114-1017, San José 2000.

Fourteen miles north of Ciudad Quesada at Muelle is the Tilajari Resort Hotel, located in a rural setting on the banks of the San Carlos River in sight of Arenal Volcano. Facilities include pools, three lighted tennis courts, a three-hole golf course and driving range, racquetball courts, sauna, restaurant, and bar. You can sometimes spot a crocodile in the river, and an orchard brings in birds looking for *guanábanas* and other tropical fruits. Guests may rent horses and tennis and golf equipment as well as canoes to use on the five rivers in the vicinity.

Tours operated from the hotel include visits to the Caño Negro National Wildlife Refuge (full day with drive to Los Chiles and boat trip on the Río Frío through the refuge to the town of Caño Negro), Venado Caves, waterfall in Fortuna, Arenal Volcano (a late afternoon/night tour that allows time at the Tabacón hot springs complex), fishing, and nature walks in a nearby 750-acre tropical forest

Exploring Corcovado National Park (Photo by Ree Strange Sheck)

(300 ha). Children can get up early and help milk the cows if they wish, according to one of the owners, Jaime Hamilton.

Rates for the 44 rooms: singles $70, doubles $82; suites also available. All have air-conditioning and fans, private baths with hot water; credit cards accepted. The rooms are quiet, located apart from the sports areas, restaurant, and pools and surrounded by manicured lawns. You may want to investigate packages that include transportation from San José and specific tours. For example, a five-day, four-night package for $586 per person, double occupancy, includes lodging, meals, airport or hotel pickup, taxes, bilingual guide, visits to Poás Volcano, Sarchí, and Zarcero en route plus tours to Arenal Volcano (forty minutes away), Tabacón, Fortuna waterfall, Venado Caves, Caño Negro, agricultural installations, horseback riding, and the nature walk. Tilajari is 73 miles (117 km) from San José. Telephone/fax 46-1083. Telephone 46-0979. Apartado 81, Ciudad Quesada, San Carlos.

Another opportunity to experience the variety of natural beauty in the north-central zone is to visit the more rustic Magil Forest Lodge, 12 miles (19 km) from San Rafael de Guatuso, between Caño Negro and Lake Arenal on the map. Located on the skirts of Tenorio Volcano, the mountain lodge has 11 rooms with private baths, $123 for two, including meals. Inquire about packages. The dining room has a table made from a single log that must be seen to be believed. The lodge itself is in a cleared area, but the 1,035-acre farm (420 ha) has 700 acres (283 ha) of rain forests to explore, some concealing unexcavated archaeological sites of the Guatuso Indians. More than 250 species of birds have been identified here, and there are monkeys, sloths, brightly colored frogs, and a wealth of orchids and giant ferns in the forest.

Guests can take a trip on the Río Frío to Caño Negro, go horseback riding, swim in the rivers, find the hot springs, and visit Venado Caves or Arenal Volcano. A new day tour for $20 per person includes a one-hour boat ride to a crocodile and caiman farm where you can see the whole process from egg to animal. It may be your only chance to see the unusual gar fish (*gaspar* in Spanish), sometimes called a living fossil because species of that genus lived 90 million years ago. Telephone 21-2825, 33-5991; fax 33-6837. Apartado 3404-1000, San José.

If you are going on to Lake Arenal from Ciudad Quesada, the road takes you to Fortuna (pop. 5,882). You can stop by the Tourist Information Center, open 6:00 a.m. to 6:00 p.m., and talk to Gabino about such area attractions as the waterfall (a 230-foot cascade, 70 meters), the hot springs at Tabacón, and nearby walking trails. He has a microbus and offers night tours to the volcano as well as other tours.

Hotel Las Colinas is just around the corner from the information center. Ten spacious, plain but clean rooms, each with private bath and hot water. Rates range from $10 to $30 per room, depending on number of persons. MasterCard and Visa accepted. Telephone 47-9107. Apartado 6, Fortuna de San Carlos.

West of Fortuna 2.5 miles (4 km) is Jungla y Senderos Los Lagos, which contains four forest trails and two lakes. Admission about $.80. Peddle boats, rowboats, and horses may be rented.

Just a piece farther down the road is Balneario Tabacón at the base of Arenal Volcano. Completely remodeled, the complex now offers five pools, four with thermal waters from the volcano and one cold-water pool; two are for children. The beautiful landscaped grounds center on paths along the river and a waterfall of hot water that steams against the greenery. The water from the hot springs is more than 122°F (50°C).

The pools and restaurant are open from 10:00 a.m. to 11:00 p.m., and admission is $5 per person. Reservations are recommended. A 20-room, first-class hotel will be completed in 1992. Call for reservations at the balneario or for information about the hotel. Telephone 22-1072, fax 21-3075.

Arenal is one of the world's most active volcanoes, thundering and blowing since 1968. There are a number of dirt roads that take you near the volcano. Watch from there. Climbing to the crater can be hazardous to your health; in fact, it can be fatal. For more details on this wonder of nature, refer to Arenal Volcano Observatory in chapter 8. This privately owned nature reserve offers a front row seat for nighttime viewing. Day tours are also offered.

Archaeological studies show that Indians had small settlements around Lake Arenal, near the volcano, as long ago as 2000 B.C. That lake was a mere shadow of the one that exists today, greatly enlarged as the result of a dam built for hydroelectric energy. Lake Arenal is

Arenal Volcano in north central Costa Rica (Photo by Ree Strange Sheck)

a favorite for fishing and water sports, such as kayaking. The road around the northeast side takes you over the dam and on to the new town of Arenal, the one built by the Costa Rican Electrical Institute to replace house by house the old Arenal, which was flooded because of the dam. Past the town of Arenal near Lake Coter is a private nature reserve called the EcoAdventure Lodge. It not only has a view of the volcano from its property but operates overnight camping trips near the volcano for its guests (see chap. 8). Its own nature trails are marvelous.

Located on the slopes above Lake Arenal on its northwestern end, Mirador Los Lagos has a clear view of lake and volcano from its seven rooms and open-air restaurant. Singles $20, doubles $27, private baths; no credit cards accepted. Telephone 69-5484. The owner/ managers arrange horseback rides and day trips to the EcoAdventure Lodge at Lake Coter. Continuing around the lake, you can go to Tilarán and connect with the Inter-American Highway at Cañas. Or from Tilarán you can take a dirt road through Quebrada Grande to Monteverde.

Tilarán (pop. 8,232), about 2 miles (3 km) from Lake Arenal, is a pleasant town laid out around the traditional square. One-half block from the church is a 16-room hotel called the Spot, which is associated with the EcoAdventure Lodge. It has a movie theater on the premises and rents bikes, horses, boats, and windsurfing boards. Landscaped gardens. Single $34, double $42, private baths; credit cards accepted. Telephone 69-5711, fax 69-5579. Apartado 60, Tilarán, Guanacaste.

Less expensive hotels in Tilarán include El Sueño (private baths, double about $18, telephone 69-5347) and Hotel Central (double with private bath from $6, telephone 69-5363).

The Caño Negro Wildlife Refuge north near the border with Nicaragua can be reached either from Upala or Los Chiles on roads that take off from this route. A paved road to Upala leaves the Inter-American Highway northwest of Cañas.

The second route from San José to the north-central region through Varablanca is spectacular, with Barva Volcano and Cacho Negro on one side and Poás Volcano and Cerro Congo on the other. Just before Varablanca is a turnoff to Poás Volcano. On a clear day from the heights, you can see the plains stretching to the coast. The winding descent passes gorgeous waterfalls—the most photographed being the Peace Waterfall. The river that feeds the waterfall rises in the forests of Poás.

At San Miguel, the road west takes you to Aguas Zarcas and Ciudad Quesada. To continue on to Puerto Viejo, keep to the north. Several privately owned nature reserves offer opportunities to learn about tropical flora and fauna in this region. Near Chilamate is Selva Verde Lodge, and the Organization of Tropical Studies' La Selva Biological Station is just outside Puerto Viejo (chap. 8). Selva Verde has an evolving butterfly garden open to the public from dawn to dusk just down the road from the Chilamate school, across from the lodge. Watch for the large floral butterfly on the hillside. Admission is $5 per person for the 2.5 miles (4 km) of trails. Peter Knudsen has added plantings to attract the butterflies (more than 700 species are found in the area) and provide host plants for larvae to feed on. There is also a section for medicinal plants. Before or after the butterfly walk, you may want to drop by the Selva Verde gift shop managed by Betty Ann Knudsen to see the variety of interesting locally made handcrafts. Two small lodges also offer rooms (no credit cards). EcoAlbergue next to La Selva has 4 rooms with fans and shared baths. Rates are $45 per person, including meals. The lodge offers a river trip and horseback riding. Guests may visit the farm's small dairy. Telephone 35-9280. Islas del Río near Chilamate has 20 rooms; a double with shared bath is $42 per person and $49 with private bath, meals included. A cable across the river connects the lodge with three small forested islands and a nature trail. An agroforestry tour on the farm allows guests to see a sustainable development project in action. Bilingual guide available for tours. Telephone 33-0366, fax 33-9671.

River adventure companies in San José offer trips on area rivers, and trips to view wildlife along the banks can be arranged with local entrepreneurs who have boats in Puerto Viejo. One of these is William Rojas, telephone 71-6901, extension 260 or 227. He has a twenty-passenger boat that makes the trip from Puerto Viejo to Barra del Colorado, traveling on the Sarapiquí and San Juan rivers. He has a set trip leaving Friday and returning Sunday for $75 per person round-trip for the transportation. He helps arrange lodging. Trips on other days are possible, cost depending on number of persons.

Local naturalist guides trained in a course offered by the Organization for Tropical Studies at La Selva will accompany individuals or groups not only in the Puerto Viejo area but to Braulio Carrillo Park and other areas in the Central Volcanic Range. The charge is less than $7 for a half day, $15 for a full day. English-speaking guides cost more, but all of these local guides have received some instruction in English. By hiring them you will have the interpretive skills of a naturalist to help you see the tropical forest and also support a community-based project that ties rural self-development to conservation. Call 71-6897 at La Selva, and talk to Héctor González for information or reservations.

The San Juan River is the boundary between Nicaragua and Costa Rica, and the river is actually Nicaraguan territory. Costa Rica has the perpetual right by treaty to use it.

The third main route into the north-central region goes through

Braulio Carrillo National Park. Where the highway crosses the Sucio River as you drop down toward the lowlands, still inside the park, pull off if you can to take a look at the joining of the Hondura River with the Sucio, which is dirty-looking because of mineral content carried from its origins on Irazú. The interplay of the blue and brown waters as they flow together is fascinating. There is a wide place to park after you cross the bridge. Be careful of traffic if you walk on the bridge for a closer look.

A turnoff to the north before Guapiles leads to Puerto Viejo via Las Horquetas. This is the jumping-off place for a visit to Rara Avis, a private nature reserve you may have heard about in connection with Donald Perry's tramway built there to explore the forest canopy (chap. 8).

Past Las Horquetas, the road continues along the Puerto Viejo River to the town of Puerto Viejo. You will see commercial plantings of pejibaye palm. This species of palm has commercial value from its fruit, which Costa Ricans love, and the heart (*palmito*), eaten raw or boiled. Try a palmito salad during your stay in Costa Rica.

There is a day trip through spectacular scenery between the first and second routes described above to the magnificent waterfalls in the Bajos del Toro area. We started out on route one, via Alajuela and Grecia to Sarchí Norte, turning north near the Chaverri factory. (There also is a road from Zarcero to Bajos del Toro.) Pavement ends, ferns cascade down roadsides, the leaves of the *sombrilla del pobre* (poor man's umbrella) seem giants among the other leaves. Waterfalls appear across the canyon through the mist. The welcome sign at the town of Toro Amarillo—500 people, 4,593 feet high (1,400 m)—is in French, English, and Spanish. As you continue on, watch for a sign on the left: La Catarata (the waterfall). A short walk away, you get a top-to-bottom view of water cascading into the deep canyon. Past La Colonia, the plains spread out before you. You can either continue toward Río Cuarto to the highway or go to Cariblanco, in either case reaching route two for the return to San José. You can rent a car or taxi to do the trip.

Northwest

Cloud forests, cattle ranches, miles of long beaches, deciduous dry forests—the area defined here as the northwest region contains fifteen national parks, reserves, and refuges, numerous privately owned reserves catering to the ecotourist, and more resort-type beach properties than any other section. Essentially, these areas with access off the Inter-American Highway north of Puntarenas plus the region known as the Nicoya Peninsula are our focus here.

There is bus transportation to Puntarenas, two boat services across the Gulf of Nicoya, bus service all the way to the border with Nicaragua and down into the peninsula, flights to Tamarindo, Sámara, and Nosara, along with taxis in many small towns to fill in the blanks (see Practical Extras). Though the Inter-American Highway opens the biggest door, some travelers slip in the back way through the north-central region.

From San José, the highway passes through pretty highland mountains and valleys of coffee, cows, and cane on the way to the warmer lowlands. It is fun to stop at roadside stands in Esparza to stretch legs and give thanks for safely getting over the hair-raising stretch of winding road south of San Ramón that has yet to be widened. You will probably see some fruits you do not recognize, along with watermelons, pineapples, and avocados.

Puntarenas (pop. 37,390) is built on a narrow piece of land with an estuary on one side and the Gulf of Nicoya on the other. You can get the ferry across to Playa Naranjo here as well as a passenger boat to Paquera, farther down the peninsula's coast.

Travelers who have never been to Costa Rica sometimes choose Puntarenas for their beach experience. While this is the closest beach area from San José, it is neither the prettiest nor the cleanest. Go to Puntarenas to experience the laid-back coastal life-style, walk along the oceanfront promenade, swim in a pretty hotel pool under a warm, blue sky, or watch people and sunsets, but do not go for the beaches.

Among the most popular tours in the country are those offering a day on a yacht out of Puntarenas, cruising around islands in the Gulf

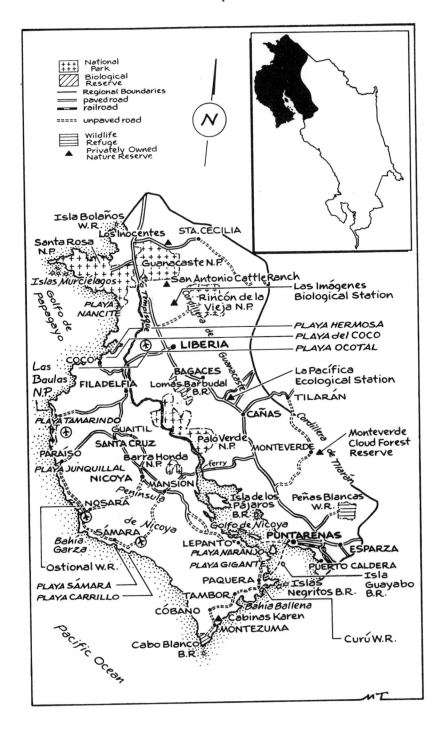

Ferry across the Tempisque River (Photo by Ree Strange Sheck)

of Nicoya (including Guayabo, Pajaritos, and Negritos biological reserves), eating well, and swimming and snorkeling in the clear waters off the island selected for a lunch stop. Packages can include transportation from San José.

There are hotels for every budget. Remember that rates are cheaper in the low season, and it seems discounts are even better in beach areas. Puntarenas is popular with San Josefinos on weekends, so mid-week visits are less crowded. The following are some hotels you might consider.

Hotel Fiesta. Ocean-view rooms with terrace $118, others $98; 174 rooms. Air-conditioning, pools, restaurants, casino, car rental, USA Direct phones; credit cards accepted. Tour agency offers trips to Monteverde, Manuel Antonio, Poás Volcano, and Carara Biological Reserve as well as an island cruise and rafting on the Corobicí. Located outside Puntarenas. Telephone 63-0185, fax 63-1516. Apartado 171-5400, Puntarenas.

Hotel Porto Bello. Single $58, double $70; 35 rooms. Air-conditioning, pools, mini gym, restaurant; credit cards accepted. On the road coming in from San José, not downtown. Arranges yacht excursions in Gulf of Nicoya. Telephone 61-1322, 61-2122, fax 61-0036. Apartado 108-5400, Puntarenas.

Hotel Yadrán. Balcony rooms $76, no balcony $64; 40 rooms. Air-conditioning, pool, restaurants, car rental; credit cards accepted. In town on the tip of the peninsula at the end of Paseo de los Turistas. Across road from beach. Spanish, English, and Japanese spoken. Telephone 61-2662, fax 61-1944. Apartado 14-5000, Puntarenas.

Hotel Tioga. Single $40, double $49, including full breakfast; 46 rooms. Air-conditioning, restaurant, beach umbrellas, pool, credit cards. Downtown across from beach. Arranges tours. Telephone 61-0271, fax 61-0127. Apartado 96-5400, Puntarenas.

Cabinas San Isidro. Fifty cabins with equipped kitchenettes from $32, five rooms at $18 each. Pools for children and adults, restaurant, no hot water; credit cards accepted. Day visits at $5 per person include lunch. Arranges cruises. Telephone 21-1225, fax 21-6822. Apartado 4674, San José. For special rates for youth hostel members, reserve through Costa Rican Network of Youth Hostels in San José, 24-4085.

Hotel Las Brisas. Smaller rooms from $28 for two, larger from $44; 19 rooms. Restaurant, pool, air-conditioning, car rental, no hot water; no credit cards accepted. Spanish, English, and Italian spoken. In town across from beach. Telephone 61-2120. Apartado 132, Puntarenas.

Shortly after the turnoff to Puntarenas from the Inter-American Highway is a road northeast to the Peñas Blancas National Wildlife Refuge, an important watershed protection area. Water takes on some different meanings as you continue into the drier Guanacaste Province. The concern can change from ''When will the rains stop?'' to ''When will they start?'' In the dry season, flowering red, white, pink, and yellow trees decorate a browner landscape. In any season, the national tree, the *guanacaste*, spreads its branches out like a great fan. Horses and cattle seek shade under its mimosa-type leaves in pasturelands.

The road to the town of Monteverde and the Monteverde Cloud Forest Preserve, a private biological preserve (see chap. 8 for information), turns right at the bridge over Río Lagarto. The bumpy 22-mile (35-km) route gives occasional breathtaking views of the lowlands below as you climb up on roads that seem to hang by grace along the edge of the mountains. As you wind through thin clouds, cows across deep valleys look like brown and white dots scattered on the steep pastures. You have plenty of time to enjoy as it is slow going. An alternative route, also unpaved, leaves the Inter-American before Lagarto, going through Sardinal and joining the Lagarto road past Guacimal.

The progressive community of Monteverde is itself worth a visit. Many tourists have heard of the North American Quakers, who founded the community in 1951. Drawn by Costa Rica's disarmed environment, they set up a cheese-making business that produces some of the finest cheeses in the country. The company also bought milk from neighboring farmers, and today there are 350 shareholders, including milk producers, employees, and neighbors. You can visit the modern dairy plant, La Lechería, Monday through Saturday from 7:30 a.m. to 4:30 p.m.; on Sunday it closes at 12:30 p.m. Cheese makers work from 9:00 a.m. to 4:00 p.m.: visitors may watch through a glass partition beside the sales room.

The CASEM gift shop sells locally handcrafted items, many with intricate embroidery or weaving. Save some of your souvenir shopping for here; the hand-painted cards and stationery make beautiful, easy-to-carry gifts. Designs used on the textiles and paper goods are drawn from the rich biological diversity of this place—quetzals, bellbirds, golden toads. This is a craft cooperative, so buying here directly benefits local residents. Open 8:00 a.m. to noon and 1:00 to 5:00 p.m. Monday through Saturday. Open on Sunday December through April.

The Monteverde Conservation League is a nonprofit conservation organization founded by residents and visiting biologists in 1986. The league works in land acquisition, forest protection, reforestation, research (some on native tree species), conservation of flora and fauna, and environmental education. It operates tree nurseries and works with local schools and community groups. One of its most exciting projects is Bosque Eterno de los Niños, the first international children's rain forest. The league office is open from 8:00 a.m. to noon and 1:00 to 5:00 p.m. weekdays, Saturdays 8:00 a.m. to noon.

For $2, visitors can wander along a privately owned nature trail managed by the league, the Sendero Bajo del Tigre, open 8:00 a.m.

INTERNATIONAL CHILDREN'S RAIN FOREST

Once upon a time there was a teacher from the United States who came to Monteverde, Costa Rica, to do biological research. Her enthusisam for the rain forest and her concern about its destruction found its way into a small primary school far, far away in rural Sweden. There a class of nine-year-olds wondered if there was something they could do to save the tall trees, the pretty waterfalls, the many animals who made their homes in the tropical forest. With their teacher, they decided there was. They sent enough money to the Monteverde Conservation League to buy 15 acres (6 ha) of threatened rain forest.

This idea of a rain forest saved by children for children spread to other schools in Sweden, to England, to schools in Maine in the United States where the biology teacher lived, and to Canada. Now children in other European countries, in Japan, and in Indonesia are selling homemade wildlife cards, having bake sales, and collecting materials for recycling to lend a hand. The result is Bosque Eterno de los Niños (Children's Eternal Forest), the first international children's rain forest in the world.

Since it was established in 1988, the children's rain forest has grown to cover thousands of acres of virgin forest. The Peñas Blancas River flows through this rugged land, whose steep slopes are not appropriate for farms and cattle. Living in the lush vegetation are quetzals, monkeys, bare-necked umbrellabirds, ocelots, jaguars, and tapirs. Long vines trail to the forest floor. There are species of plants that have yet even to be identified.

As children learn about this piece of forest in Costa Rica and why it is important, they begin to think in a new way about their own environment. Often their parents join in the campaign. One day, an educational center in Bosque Eterno de los Niños will bring together local children and children from around the world to learn more about natural history and each other.

One hundred dollars saves another acre. You will receive a certificate stating how many acres you have saved. Donations of any size can support crucial ongoing programs in environmental education, forest protection, reforestation, and information. Send donations to:

Monteverde Conservation League
Apartado 10165-1000
San José, Costa Rica
Telephone 61-0953, fax 61-1104

to 4:00 p.m. daily. The trail goes through forest and around pasture with plots for an arboretum and research; the haunting notes of the bellbird accompanied me on my walk. Near the view point, the trail is steep, but sections on either end are pleasant. The information booth at the entrance has material on league programs and gift items for sale.

The dairy, gift shops, league office, and hotels are strung along the road between Santa Elena and the cloud forest preserve. Stop in at El

Bosque restaurant near CASEM for a meal or refreshments. Verdant foliage cascades down the ravine beside the back dining terrace. The service is slow enough to allow ample time for birding; I got my best view of a blue-crowned motmot there. There are a number of small sodas along the road that serve good, inexpensive food. Several shops and galleries are scattered between Santa Elena and the preserve, a distance of a little more than 3 miles (5.5 km). Among the galleries are the Barn (near CASEM), Sarah Dowell's studio (up the hill from the cheese plant), and the Hummingbird Gallery (photographs by Michael and Patricia Fogden).

Drive out to the nearby rural community of Cañitas (a taxi will take you) for a meal at El Trapiche, typical food at its best in a picturesque setting beside a sugar mill. You can watch the process and buy fresh cane sugar. Open 10:00 a.m. to 5:30 p.m. Monday through Saturday. Visit the small gift shop next door for locally made handcrafts.

For a glorious experience with butterflies, visit the Monteverde Butterfly Garden. The $5 entrance fee for adults, $2.50 for children, entitles you to a guided walk through a botanical garden that includes a host of plants from the area. Afterward, you can have as much time as you want to walk along the paths or sit alone to watch or photograph the free-flying butterflies. It is a magical place. The information center includes displays of butterflies and other insects. You may get to see a butterfly emerge from its pupal case. There is a small snack bar. Open 9:30 a.m. to 4:00 p.m. daily.

Hotels are small and scattered along the road, so make advance reservations. Otherwise, if you arrive by bus, you may find yourself walking in the dark for several miles looking for a place to stay. You may note that most have the same address: mail comes up from San José twice a week on the cheese truck. Most hotels will help you find transportation to the preserve, rent a horse, and tell you about area attractions. All have hot water.

Monteverde Lodge. Single $59, double $68; 27 rooms. Located near Santa Elena, the hotel has a Jaccuzi, chandeliers, a huge wood-burning fireplace in the lobby, bathtubs, and views of the forest through large glass windows. Fixed prices for meals in the restaurant: breakfast $6.50, lunch and dinner $11, plus tax. Natural history slide shows arranged. Credit cards accepted. The hotel is owned by Costa

Rican Expeditions. Telephone 61-1157, fax 61-2651. Apartado 6941-1000, San José.

Hotel El Sapo Dorado. Single $53, double $64. Ten charming rooms in five bungalows, tucked among fruit trees and gardens in a clearing surrounded by forest. Each has a fireplace, sitting room area, and two full-sized beds. The restaurant, open to the public, offers gourmet dining. Daily specials may include dishes such as sailfish Niçoise, lomito in peppercorn sauce, or vegetarian pizza. Desserts are scrumptious. Marked trails through the forest take about two hours. Horse rental available. No credit cards. Telephone/fax 61-2952. Apartado 10165-1000, San José.

Hotel Belmar. Single $47, double $58; 18 rooms. Restaurant. Beautiful view of ocean on clear day. A Swiss chalet-type building with lots of stairs, balconies, wood paneling. Guests report seeing monkeys and even a quetzal from the balconies. Transportation to the reserve is $10 round-trip. Telephone/fax 61-1001. Apartado 10165-1000, San José.

The public bus passes on the main road in front of most of the hotels, but passengers may have to walk a few meters to get to the hotel. Both the Sapo Dorado and Belmar require short but uphill climbs from the main road.

Hotel de Montaña Monteverde. Single $43, double $58, 27 rooms including suites, one with its own Jacuzzi, $111. Gift shop, Jacuzzi with view of Gulf of Nicoya, restaurant has $5 fixed price for breakfast, $9 for lunch and dinner, plus tax. Credit cards accepted. Hotel has a small forest reserve with trails. Transportation from San José to Monteverde is $200; from Monteverde to Puntarenas, $130. Telephone/fax 61-1846. Apartado 976-1000, San José.

Hotel Fonda Vela. Single $42, double $49; 25 rooms including 6 suites. Each room is different in separated buildings situated to give privacy. One of the buildings was once a barn, with living quarters above, now tastefully decorated. Lots of windows, balconies, tropical wood, some spacious sleeping lofts, original watercolors throughout. Walking trails go through surrounding forest, and horses can be rented. In high season, daily slide show, with some of proceeds going to a reforestation project on the farm using native species. Gift shop and restaurant with fixed prices: $4 for breakfast, $6 for lunch, and

$8 for dinner, plus taxes. No credit cards. The hotel is on the road to the preserve, past the cheese plant and the last stop on the bus line. Telephone/fax 61-2551. Apartado 10165-1000, San José.

Hotel Heliconia. Single $40, double $45; 23 rooms. This two-story hotel started out as a pensión, but its growth has not diminished its friendly atmosphere. Curtains hand-painted with designs of local flora and fauna grace each room. Balconies, small library, bar/restaurant open to the public with meals à la carte. Boot rental, horseback riding, guide service. Offers horseback tour to mirador with view of Lake Arenal and Arenal Volcano (if weather cooperates). Transportation from San José and to Puntarenas, Manuel Antonio, and Guanacaste beaches. Telephone/fax 61-1009. Apartado 10165-1000, San José.

Pensión Quetzal. Meals included. Single $34, double $25 per person with shared bath; with private bath single is $40, double $28 per person. A two-room suite with private bath is $34 per person for a double. Vegetarian meals on request. No credit cards. Located next to Bajo Tigre Trail. This pensión has a resident ornithologist, the owner, who admits he spends a good amount of time advising people where to go to see particular birds as well as helping them try to decide what they actually did see. While they last, boots and ponchos are loaned to guests. Telephone/fax 61-0955. Apartado 10165-1000.

Cabañas Los Pinos. Six bungalows with equipped kitchenettes (refrigerator, hot plate, and dishes, all spotlessly clean): one bedroom, $32; two bedrooms, $58; three bedrooms, $85. Each room has a private tiled bath. Bungalows are among the trees, each with a porch to look out over the peaceful setting. Guests are free to explore the forest and farm. Owner rents horses, transports to reserve, and offers horseback tour to view point overlooking Arenal. No credit cards. Telephone 61-0905.

Pensión Flor Mar. Meals included. With shared bath $22 per person; with private bath $25. Twelve rooms, just across the river and up the hill from the cheese plant. Will pick up at the last bus stop with advance notice. Friendly, family-run operation. Boot rental, local transportation. Offers one- to two-day excursion to Arenal Volcano. Telephone/fax 61-0909. Apartado 10165-1000.

Villa Verde. Located between Monteverde and the preserve. Four rooms and restaurant in main building, $20 per person including meals, shared bath. Five cabins for up to four persons, with hand-made furniture and the walls a mosaic of tropical woods. Private baths, sitting areas, equipped kitchenettes, $25 per person without meals. In forested setting. Transportation from Santa Elena or Tila-rán. Arranges transport from San José. Horse rental and tours to mirador to see Arenal Volcano and to the San Luis waterfall. Telephone 61-1255.

Pensión El Tucán. In Santa Elena. Seven rooms, $5 per person, shared bath. Small basic rooms are above the restaurant, which serves tasty typical meals. The restaurant is open to the public, so you might stop by for a casado if you are in Santa Elena. It is a popular place for lunch. Horses can be rented. Telephone 61-1007.

The schedule of the direct public bus from San José changes, so check with ICT or call the company at 61-1152 or 22-3854 for information. When the bus leaves in the afternoon from San José, it arrives after dark, so bring a flashlight to make your way to your hotel from the main road. Listen for the driver to call out the name of your hotel so you will know where to get off. The bus stops first in Santa Elena before it continues to the final stop at the Monteverde cheese plant. The public bus from Puntarenas ends in Santa Elena, a few miles away. Most hotels arrange transportation from San José by private van. You can contact the van owner yourself: Evelio Fonseca Mata, 61-0958.

Another route to Monteverde is through the north-central section, traveling from Arenal to Tilarán and Santa Elena. The road from Tilarán to Monteverde is unpaved. The last 5 miles (8 km) before Santa Elena are the worst. There is a gas station in Monteverde. There is daily bus service between Tilarán and Santa Elena.

Back on the Inter-American Highway, continuing northward 11 miles (18 km) past the Monteverde cutoff at Río Lagarto, is a sign pointing to the Tempisque ferry, which carries cars and passengers to the Nicoya Peninsula.

The next major town on the Inter-American is Cañas; a few miles farther is the La Pacífica Ecological Center, which has a restaurant open to the public and offers day tours of its ranch and natural history areas. See chapter 8 for specifics. A little farther is the Rincón

Restaurant Coribicí on the banks of the Coribicí River, a river-rafting option; perhaps you will see a tour take off. While you have your meal on the open terrace facing the water and with a grand view of Tenorio Volcano, you can appreciate why birders like this area.

Bagaces is the turnoff for a visit to the Lomas Barbudal Biological Reserve and Palo Verde National Park, wonderful natural history destinations.

Liberia, 154 miles from San José (248 km), is the capital of Guanacaste Province. Less than 475 feet above sea level (144 m), the city lies within view of two of the volcanoes in the Guanacaste Range, Rincón de la Vieja and Miravalles. With a population of 29,362, it is a commercial center and a transportation hub. The highway to the Nicoya Peninsula and beach resort areas intersects here. Excitement grows in Liberia and this entire region at the prospects of what an international airport here can mean for increased tourism. The enlarged airport is expected to be ready by 1993. Direct San José-Liberia buses run daily.

Signs direct visitors to the El Sabanero Museum in the Casa de la Cultura, three blocks from the park, where an enthusiastic lady

El Sabanero Museum in Liberia (Photo by Ree Strange Sheck)

121

named Patricia Cardenas can help you with tourist information and reservations. If she does not know the answer to your questions, she will call until she finds out. The small museum, housed in a 150-year-old building, contains memorabilia related to the cowboy and early life in this "Wild West" region. Open Tuesday through Saturday from 9:00 a.m. to noon and 1:00 to 6:00 p.m., Sunday 9:00 a.m. to noon.

Several hotels open the possibility of using Liberia as a base for day trips to Rincón de la Vieja, Palo Verde, Las Baulas, Santa Rosa, and Guanacaste national parks as well as nearby beaches. Following are three that are located near the highway. All accept credit cards, arrange car rental, and have some English-speaking staff.

Hotel Las Espuelas. Single $53, double $67; 35 rooms plus 3 suites. Air-conditioning, pool, restaurant, gift shop, TV on request. On Thursdays and Saturdays, you will see typical dances of Guanacaste and hear marimba music. The hotel runs tours to Las Imágenes Biological Station and San Antonio Cattle Ranch (see chap. 8), one a day trip and the other with overnight possibilities, and to Santa Rosa National Park and Playa Hermosa. The hotel has a tourist information office. Telephone 66-0144, fax 25-3987. Apartado 88, Liberia.

Hotel El Sitio. Single $39, double $47; 52 rooms. Restaurant, pool, air-conditioning and fans, landscaped grounds. Telephone 66-1211, fax 66-2059 or 33-6883. Apartado 471-1000, San José.

El Bramadero. Rooms with fans: single $15, double $21; with air-conditioning: single $20, double $30. Pool, restaurant, bike rental. Call about possibility of transportation from San José. Telephone 66-0203, 66-0371, fax 66-1414. Apartado 70, Liberia.

The Office of Guanacaste Tours is in the Hotel Bramadero. The company offers natural history tours throughout the province. See chapter 9.

The road to the headquarters of Rincón de la Vieja National Park is from Liberia; the road to another part of the park leaves the Inter-American Highway at Guadalupe, 5 miles (8 km) north of Liberia, passing through Curubandé. A four-wheel-drive vehicle is recommended for the last few miles of the Curubandé route, which is through private property, the Guachipelín Hacienda. (Driving along a one-lane road through here at dusk, we once got behind a slow-moving skunk. We definitely felt he had the right-of-way.)

On the hacienda is Rincón de la Vieja Mountain Lodge, which offers a rustic setting for exploration of the park. Las Pailas, the "mud pots," are only thirty minutes from the lodge by horseback. Lodging is $16 with shared bath, $18 with private bath. Breakfast is $6 and lunch and dinner are $8 each. Packages including lodging, food, horse rental, and bilingual guide run from one day and two nights for $137 (tour to Las Pailas and Rincón de la Vieja Volcano) to four days and three nights for $252 (tours to Las Pailas, the volcano, waterfalls, and sulfur springs). Day trips for nonguests are to Las Pailas or the sulfur springs ($70), the volcano ($86), or to Las Pailas and the sulfur springs ($86). Prices include bilingual guide, horse, box lunch, and tax. Taxi transportation from Liberia can be arranged by the lodge—about $30. For youth hostel members, room and board is $27 a day, with a charge for horse rental and guide service. (Make reservations through the Costa Rican Network of Youth Hostels in San José, 24-4085.)

The lodge is the former main house of the hacienda: six bedrooms and three baths, no hot water. There are also three cabins with hot-water baths. Visitors have a chance to visit the dairy farm, with cheese-making facilities, a cattle operation, and a reforestation project. A 150-room hotel now under construction should be completed by August 1992. Telephone 66-2369, telephone/fax 66-0473. Apartado 114, Liberia.

Santa Rosa and Guanacaste national parks are farther north. A paved road goes all the way into Santa Rosa headquarters and the historical La Casona. Guanacaste National Park does offer overnight facilities (see chap. 7). Visits to both are offered by nature tour companies and through hotels and private nature reserves in the area.

Near Cuajiniquil, which is off the Inter-American at the northern end of Santa Rosa, is Junquillal Recreation Area, an example of the integration of local communities into the management and use of natural resources. A restaurant operated by the people of Cuajiniquil puts money into the community, as do horse and boat rental. Trails take visitors into the 1,248 acres (505 ha) of tropical dry forest. Junquillal Beach is down a dirt road passable without four-wheel drive; it is isolated, with tranquil waters, and forest. You can call the Guanacaste Conservation Area (tel. 69-5598) for information about Santa Rosa, Guanacaste, and Junquillal.

A delightful private nature reserve called Los Inocentes (see chap. 8) is east of the Inter-American, turning at La Cruz (paved road). It is possible to continue past Los Inocentes to Santa Cecilia and on to Upala.

Meanwhile, back in Liberia, some travelers choose the road southwest, Highway 21, for a visit to the beaches, historical towns, and nature reserves on the Nicoya Peninsula. Playa del Coco is the first beach area on that road. It is a popular destination for ticos. A bus runs daily from San José to Playa del Coco; several buses a day arrive from Liberia. There are a number of lodging places, on the more rustic side, right on the beach. Hotel Luna Tica has 37 rooms and 3 cabins. Single $7, double $14; credit cards accepted. Restaurant, fans or air-conditioning, no hot water, car and bicycle rental. Telephone/fax 67-0127. Apartado 67, Playa del Coco, Guanacaste.

Hotel La Flor de Itabo is not right on the water, but it offers comfortable accommodations. It has 8 rooms plus 5 bungalows containing 2 bedrooms and a kitchen, all with hot water. Singles are $55, doubles $60, bungalows $120; credit cards are accepted. Owners speak English, Spanish, French, German, and Italian. Facilities include restaurant, pool, air-conditioned rooms. They arrange scuba diving, fishing, and horseback riding trips and one-day excursions to nearby beaches, Nicoya and the Indian town of Guaitil, Santa Rosa, the geothermal project at Miravalles Volcano, and Rincón de la Vieja. The hotel also runs a fishing tour to Arenal Lake. Telephone 67-0292, 67-0011, fax 67-0003. Apartado 32, Playa del Coco, Guanacaste.

Just north of Playa del Coco is Playa Hermosa, where it is not uncommon to see dolphins in the bay or howler monkeys moving through the trees, especially in the dry season. If you do not have a car, you can take a Liberia-Sardinal bus and hire a taxi for the remaining 5 miles (8 km) or take a taxi from Liberia for about $10. Here are two lodging possibilities; English is spoken at both, and car rental is available.

Hotel Condovac La Costa. Single $88, double $100, 54 rooms; 101

villas with bedroom, living room, bath, kitchenette, and terrace over-looking bay are $94 on weekends, less on weekdays. Credit cards accepted. Air-conditioning and fans, pools, tennis, restaurant, disco, poolside bars, beachfront. Motorized carts transport guests around hillside resort complex. Arranges transportation to parks and from San José, offers scuba diving, snorkeling, sportfishing, jet-skiing, waterskiing, sailboating, and boat tours, plus kayaking, windsurf-ing, and hiking. Telephone 21-8949, 33-1862, fax 22-5637. Apartado 55-1001, Plaza González Víquez, San José.

Cabinas Playa Hermosa. Single $16, double $28; 20 rooms. On beach. Fans, restaurant, hot water, credit cards. Telephone/fax 67-0136. Apartado 117, Liberia.

About 1.5 miles (2.5 km) southwest of Playa del Coco is beautiful Ocotal Beach and Hotel El Ocotal, atop a cliff overlooking the Pacific. A big Guanacaste iguana is almost always somewhere along the steps going down to the beach. Tide pools are fascinating here; caves shoot the water of the incoming tide back out with tremendous force at the north end of the beach.

Diving safaris operate out of Hotel El Ocotal. You can rent tanks, regulators, snorkels, masks, and fins as well as cameras for under-water photography. To give you an idea of prices, there is a diving tour of five days and four nights for $437 each, double occupancy, includ-ing two days of dives, lodging, breakfasts, taxes, tanks, weights, boat, and guide.

Hotel El Ocotal. Single $84, double $100; 30 rooms, plus 6 two-room bungalows and 3 suites. Air-conditioning, TV, refrigerator in room, restaurant, gift shop, car rental; credit cards accepted. Offers sportfishing, scuba diving classes, equipment rentals, island cruises. Telephone 67-0230, fax 67-0083. Apartado 1, Playa del Coco, Guanacaste.

For the next cluster of accommodations along the beach, continue south on Highway 21 to an intersection on the other side of Filadelfia. Take the road that heads southwest. Turning north at Huacas, watch for signs to hotels at Sugar Beach (Pan de Azúcar), Playa Flamingo, and Playa Conchal. Here is what awaits you along those slow-going, gravel roads. Spanish and English spoken at each.

Hotel Sugar Beach. Room with fan $53, with air-conditioning $64;

Poolside at Hotel Condor Club above Playa Conchal (Photo by Ree Strange Sheck)

10 rooms. Open-air restaurant; credit cards not accepted. Lots of birds and monkeys, snorkeling in Potrero Bay. Owner/managers will arrange pickup from Tamarindo airport. Taxi fare from Liberia is about $30. Telephone 68-0959. Apartado 90, Santa Cruz.

Flamingo Beach Hotel. Rooms from $102; 112 rooms, 8 suites. The 23 presidential suites are $187. Restaurants, pool, tennis, volleyball, bike and horse rental; credit cards accepted. Yes, flamingos do appear along the estuary. Amigo Flamingo Tours on premises arranges trips to Los Inocentes, Tamarindo mangroves, Tempisque waterfall, Santa Rosa National Park, Guaitil and Santa Cruz, and San Antonio Cattle Ranch. Telephone 39-2921 or 39-1584, fax 39-0257. Apartado 692, Alajuela.

Hotel Condor Club (Playa Conchal). Rooms from $82; 40 rooms. Restaurant, pool, both fans and air-conditioning, TV, gift shop, tennis, horse rental. Another pool and restaurant next to beach below the hillside hotel. Ridley turtles nest here February to April. Both white sand and crushed-shell beaches. Tours handled through Guanacaste Tours. Transportation arranged from Tamarindo or Matapalo. Monkeys and parrots usually seen here, and no, those are not condors, as some tourists believed. They are buzzards, but it is nice to be in a place where even buzzards seem regal. Spanish, English, and German spoken. Telephone 68-0920, fax 68-0944. Apartado 102-2300, Curridabat, San José.

West from Huacas is Playa Grande and the new Las Baulas de Guanacaste National Park that protects an important nesting site of the leatherback turtle. Hotel Las Tortugas is steps away from the beach where the leatherbacks nest (November to March). Eight rooms from $81, three 2-bedroom suites $111. Restaurant, pool, airconditioning, outdoor Jacuzzi. Naturalist guides for walking, horseback, or canoe trips. No telephone. Apartado 164, Santa Cruz, Guanacaste. Can book through Tikal Tour Operators, telephone 23-2811, fax 23-1916.

Cabinas Playa Grande. Rooms $18, with kitchenette $22; 6 rooms. Not on beach. Restaurant, fans, Spanish only spoken. Will pick up from San José-Matapalo bus. Telephone 37-2552, fax 37-1790.

The road to Tamarindo is south out of Matapalo. The town of Tamarindo is bordered by Las Baulas park (chap. 7), important for turtles, birds, crocodiles, and mangroves.

Visitors to Tamarindo receive a warm welcome at the Tamarindo Information Welcome Center. The road into town leads right to it. You can get information on lodging, tours, and restaurants. Talk to Rosie or Roy.

Papagayo Excursions has jungle boat safaris on the saltwater estuary, where you will see a variety of birds and could possibly spot a caiman; nighttime turtle-nesting tours are also available, about $25 per person for either tour. Other possibilities are coastal cruises, guided diving trips (start at $60), and fishing and surfing. Telephone/fax 25-3648, 68-0859. Apartado 35, Santa Cruz, Guanacaste.

SANSA flies to Tamarindo three days a week (40-minute flight). Travelair flies daily. There is also a daily express bus from San José, a five-hour trip. Here are some lodging possibilities.

Hotel Tamarindo Diriá. Standard singles $78, doubles $84; 59 standard rooms, 9 deluxe, 2 suites. Air-conditioning, pools, tennis, gift shop, restaurant, satellite TV, on the beach. Credit cards accepted. Rents equipment for fishing, kayaking, windsurfing, scuba diving, snorkeling. Guided tours to Santa Cruz, Guaitil, Santa Rosa, Conchal and Flamingo beaches, and Arenal. Telephone 33-0530, fax 55-3355. Apartado 4211-1000, San José.

Pueblo Dorado. Single $37, double $47; 23 rooms. Air-conditioning, pool, restaurant, hot water; credit cards accepted. Across road from beach. Tours to Manuel Antonio, Santa Rosa, Guaitil, Playa Grande. Snorkeling equipment. Arranges microbus transport from San José and Puntarenas. Telephone/fax 22-5741. Apartado 1711-1002, San José.

Cabinas Pozo Azul. Room with fan $14, with air-conditioning $25; 27 rooms. Pool, hot plate and refrigerator, across road from beach, no hot water, accepts Visa. Telephone 68-0147.

Cabinas Zullymar. Single with fan $15 or $23 with air, double with fan $21 or $36 with air; 27 rooms. Some hot water, parking, no credit cards. English spoken. Arranges fishing and beach trips, horseback riding, boat rentals. Telephone 26-4732. Manager Edwin Martinez is a happy, helpful man.

Cabinas Marielos. Single $12, double $14; 6 rooms. Fans, no hot water, across from beach. Telephone 41-4843.

Sharing the road in the Nicoya Peninsula (Photo by Ree Strange Sheck)

As you travel by car over some of the back roads through the Nicoya Peninsula, you will see local residents along the road looking for a ride; bus service is thin to nonexistent in some parts. You can meet some interesting people who just need a lift to the next town or crossroads. We once picked up a one-armed man waving a big saw; he turned out to be a deaf-mute, but he let us know where he wanted out. A few area hotels offer car rentals, which allows you to get to the area initially by bus or air and then explore on your own. Road signs are far too sparse for strangers in these parts, though hotel signs help some. Four-wheel drive is advisable on some of the unpaved roads in the rainy season.

The road to Santa Cruz from Liberia is paved. There is bus service from San José (about 5½ hours) and from Liberia. A picturesque town (pop. 15,586) with streets of paving stones, Santa Cruz is a junction for a road to Playa Junquillal and beaches south. If you want to spend the night there, try the clean, modest Hotel Sharatoga, single $16, double $22; 40 rooms. Air-conditioning, pool in courtyard, credit cards accepted. The hotel offers tours to its beach recreation area at Junquillal, which has a restaurant/bar. This is marimba country, and the hotel has marimba music every night, folklore dances for large groups. Telephone 68-0011. Apartado 33-5150, Santa Cruz.

North about 4 miles (6 km) out of Paraíso, southeast of Santa Cruz, is the Lagartillo Beach Hotel. Single $20, double $40; 6 rooms. Fans, pool, restaurant, no hot water; accepts American Express. Boat, horse, and bicycle rental. Two minutes from ocean between Avellana and Negra beaches; trail on property. Telephone 57-1420, fax 21-5717. Apartado 1584-1000, San José.

Also out of Paraíso, on Playa Blanca, is Hotel Iguanazul. Rooms $70; 24 rooms. Fans, pool, restaurant; credit cards accepted. Arranges transport from San José. Tours to Ostional, Sugar Beach, Palo Verde. Horse and VCR rental. Telephone/fax 32-1423. Apartado 130-5150, Santa Cruz, Guanacaste.

Playa Junquillal is also south of Santa Cruz, just beyond Paraíso. The long, uncrowded, dark-sand beach invites long walks. After looking at the surf, I decided I would want to inquire locally about where safe swimming areas are. A few turtles also find their way here to lay eggs. Two hotels that cater to nature travelers are Villa Serena and Hotel Antumalal. English, French, and Italian are spoken at both, and both help arrange transportation from the bus in Santa Cruz or Tamarindo airport and accept credit cards.

Villa Serena. Double $100 including meals, taxes, tipping, and use of facilities; 10 bungalows. Fans, restaurant, pool, tennis, horses. As we ate a delicious lunch on the upstairs terrace looking out at the Pacific, we watched a bird of the oriole family feeding its young in a nest that seemed to hang by a thread from the tip of a palm branch. It is one of those terraces where you could probably sit happily for two or three years. Tours offered include a boat trip down a nearby river, visits to other beaches. German also spoken. Telephone/fax 68-0737. Apartado 17, Santa Cruz, Guanacaste.

Hotel Antumalal. Single $70, double $88; 23 rooms. Fans, pools, minigolf, tennis, horses, restaurant. The bathroom even has a bidet and hot water. Rocky areas at this end of beach good for tide pools. Howler monkeys visit. Boat rental, tours through Guanacaste Tours. Telephone/fax 68-0506. Apartado 49, Santa Cruz, Guanacaste.

I drove during the rainy season through the coastal hills from Junquillal all the way south to Playa Carrillo. Some of the stretches are gut-busters, and there are rivers to ford, but the landscape is interesting. Four-wheel drive is recommended; count on many 25-mile-per-hour (40-km-per-hour) stretches. The places mentioned are as you head south along the coast on this road, though travelers can reach specific areas by roads from Nicoya and Mansión or fly in to Sámara or Nosara.

Near Nosara is Ostional Wildlife Refuge (chap. 7), along with Nancite Beach in Santa Rosa, among the world's important nesting sites for olive ridley turtles. During the day, there is good bird-watching along the estuary. If you are there on an evening when the turtle *arribadas* begin, you may see horses with sacks of turtle eggs slung over them tied up in front of the local cantina. These eggs were taken legally in a managed harvest by the turtle cooperative that patrols the beaches against poachers.

Not far away is Hotel Playas de Nosara, one of those gracious beach hotels in harmony with its natural surroundings. Though room balconies afford a view of the sea, it is hard to spot the hotel among the trees from the beach just below. Expansive vistas of sky, sea, and

shoreline from the open-air dining room would surely bring a bit of balance to even the most restless mind.

Rock outcrops on the beach afford wonderful little pools at low tide which invite exploration. Tidal pools are good for swimming and snorkeling. Hotel arranges turtle nesting tours, river trips for birding, horse rental, and a day trip to a nearby ranch, led by local guides. There are trails on the property. Spanish, English, French, German, Greek, and Italian are spoken by owner John Fraser. There are 24 rooms, $55 each, and 2 suites, $90 and $100. Restaurant, fans, pool; no credit cards. Telephone/fax 68-0495. Apartado 4, Nosara, Nicoya, Guanacaste.

Rancho Suizo Lodge is just down the road. Single $23, double $35; 10 bungalows among the trees. Fans, restaurant; no credit cards. Hiking trips, horseback riding, tennis, car rental, nature films. Platform in tree for bird-watching. Swiss operated. Spanish, English, French, Italian, and German spoken. Fax 25-1493. Apartado 14-5233, Bocas de Nosara, Guanacaste. There is bus service from Nicoya to Nosara and 35-minute SANSA flights from San José three days a week. Travelair has daily flights.

Parrots and parakeets are among the many species of land birds that help travelers forget the rough and sometimes dusty routes from many of these beach areas to another. Howler monkeys rest in tree branches hanging over the roads.

Between Nosara and Sámara is Bahía Garza. Thatched bungalows and a towering thatched restaurant lend an exotic, romantic flavor to the Villaggio La Guaria Morada hotel. Located between the coastal hills and the sea, with forest along the beach stretching to Punta Guiones, the hotel offers tours to the Ostional refuge, horseback riding, sportfishing, and rental of diving and snorkeling equipment. The hotel can arrange transportation from the Nosara airport; there is a bus from Nicoya. Sounds of a group of howler monkeys, which the manager calls almost domesticated, drift to the bungalows at night and in the early morning. In this tranquil, natural setting, the hotel's casino and discotheque seem out of place. Restaurant, pool, fans. Rates: single $85, double $100, credit cards accepted. Telephone 68-0784, 33-2476, fax 22-4073. Apartado 860-1007, C. Colón, San José.

At Sámara, 22 miles (36 km) from Nicoya, there are some modest-looking places in town, but the Hotel Las Brisas del Pacífico is a first-class hotel on the beach, with 18 rooms, $60-$70, and 8 bungalows, $70. Pools, gift shop, restaurant, fans. Four-wheel-drive vehicles are for rent, as well as horses, boats, and equipment for windsurfing and waterskiing. Inquire about tours. English and German also spoken. Telephone 68-0876, 55-2380, fax 55-2380. Apartado 129-6100, Ciudad Colón.

Also outside town is the newer Hotel Marbella. Single $28, double $33; 14 rooms. Three furnished apartments rent for $46 each. Pool, restaurant for breakfast, fans; credit cards accepted. Horse and boat rental. Spanish, English, and German spoken. Arranges tours to Monteverde and Arenal, transport from San José, or pickup at Sámara airport. SANSA flies to Sámara three days a week; tickets are sold here. Telephone/fax 33-9980.

South of Sámara is Playa Carrillo and the Guanamar Beach Hotel and Resort. Five two-story villas rent for $290; double rooms $140. Pool, restaurant, fans and air-conditioning, TV; credit cards accepted. There is also a yacht for trips along the coast, waterskiing, and diving. Guided horseback tours are available. The setting high above the coast is spectacular. Telephone 20-0722, fax 20-2095; U.S. and Canada telephone (800) 245-8420, fax (305) 539-1123. Apartado 7-1880, San José 1000.

The best road access to Playa Carrillo is via Nicoya through Sámara. Another route, via Hojancha, was like a washboard when I was on it, but it is paved from Hojancha to Mansión, which is on the main highway.

Nicoya, about 7 miles (11 km) from Mansión, is a pretty town (pop. 23,205) with a nice colonial church. The Hotel Curime at the edge of town has 22 air-conditioned cabins with refrigerator, TV, and living area. Single $20, up to four persons $39. Pool, restaurant, gift shop. Telephone 68-5238. Apartado 51, Nicoya.

The small town of Guaitil is worth a visit if you are in the vicinity of Nicoya and Santa Cruz. Pottery in the Chorotega Indian style is available for sale. If you ask at the community gift shop, open 6:00 a.m. to 9:00 p.m., someone can probably tell you who is making pots that day so you can see the process. By the way, the shop will pack pieces so they are safe for travel. Pots are also sold in front of potters' houses. You will notice the outdoor ovens, used not only to fire pottery but also to bake bread or cook a pig.

From Mansión, you can head for the ferry across the Tempisque or a visit to Barra Honda National Park, or you can continue southeast to Playa Naranjo. When the pavement stops, it is slow going. Notice the salt beds near Lepanto. The car ferry from Puntarenas docks at Playa Naranjo, which is where some of you begin your journeys in the Nicoya Peninsula.

Oasis del Pacífico is a resort hotel not far from the dock. Hotel transport meets each ferry. Single $37, double $48; 36 rooms. Ceiling fans, restaurant, pools, ranchitos with hammocks by the water, private baths, hot water. Horses for rent for $5 per hour, boat charters and fishing trips. Half-day trips to San Lucas Island, site of a former penal colony, are $15 per person. Day trips in the Gulf of Nicoya are tailored to what people want, according to owners Lucky Wilhelm and wife, Agie, two of the world's truly nice people. A seven-day trip to Coco Island for four people runs about $1,800. By the way, Lucky also owns Piano Blanco Bar next to the Hotel Balmoral in San José.

Credit cards accepted. Telephone/fax 61-1555. Apartado 200-5400, Puntarenas.

For those who want the experience of crossing on the ferry but have no time to go farther, Oasis del Pacífico has a day rate: $2.50 entitles one to use of the pool, beach, and shower facilities.

Hotel del Paso is a motel-type establishment at the edge of Playa Naranjo on the way to Nicoya; the Nicoya bus passes in front. Air-conditioned singles are $25, doubles are $28; 14 rooms. Rooms with fans or shared bath are less. There is a pool and a restaurant that serves a delicious chicken sandwich and good *gallo pinto*. Credit cards accepted. Telephone 61-2610.

The road that goes from Playa Naranjo to Cabo Blanco is through the hills, up and down with occasional magnificent views of the coastline. Lots of birds. There is talk of paving the entire stretch, even beginning on the other side of Playa Naranjo at Lepanto.

Hotel Bahía Gigante sits on a bluff above the bay of that name. The hotel provides pick-up service at the ferry and will arrange transportation from San José. Rooms for two are $23, one- and two-bedroom condos are $40 to $60; 11 rooms, 2 condos. Fans, pool, restaurant, pier. The hotel owns a chunk of surrounding property with 9 miles (14 km) of road and numerous trails through forests and along the beach: birds, capuchin and howler monkeys, butterflies, armadillos, and deer may be seen. The hotel rents horses and offers a three-day package to Tortuga Island and a one-day horseback trip. English and French are also spoken. Telephone 61-2442; in Canada, (604) 926-8087. Apartado 1866, San José.

The launch from Puntarenas comes in at Paquera, where a bus waits to take passengers as far as Cóbano. South of Paquera is Curú National Wildlife Refuge, but to visit it, you need to make arrangements beforehand: access is through private property, and you will need directions (see chap. 8).

Bahía Ballena, which means Whale Bay, is down the road a piece. Waters lap on a long, curved beach with a very gentle slope. At sunset one July evening, two dogs and I were the only ones on the beach near the town of Tambor. A roseate spoonbill perched in a tree at the mouth of a stream, kingfishers darted back and forth, and howler monkeys sounded just out of sight. There are several places to spend the night and enjoy this tranquil setting. A large resort complex is going in, so you and the dogs may not have the beach to yourselves.

Hotel La Hacienda is a resort hotel that caters to the nature traveler. Rooms in the main hotel building look out at the bay and beautifully landscaped grounds. Thatched bungalows seem hidden among the trees and plants. La Hacienda has its own private airstrip and can help arrange transportation. Situated on a 17,300-acre ranch (7,000 ha), the hotel offers guided horseback tours, island visits, fishing, and a variety of area tours: a day trip to Cabo Blanco, visit to town of Montezuma and its beaches, visit to the Curú Wildlife Refuge. There are swimming pools, croquet, a lagoon good for birding, and a chance to visit the ranch's dairy. Single rooms are $53, doubles $64. Bungalows, which sleep up to six, are $88. Bungalow bathrooms have a kind of open skylight above and resemble a tropical greenhouse with all the plants. Fans cool the rooms; shower water is not heated, but its temperature is tepid, not cold. Remember this is a warm to hot climate. Telephone/fax 61-2980. Apartado 458-1150, La Uruca, San José.

Hotel Dos Lagartos is at the town of Tambor, on Playa Tambor. Room with private bath $16, with shared bath $12; 20 rooms. Can arrange a boat tour of the bay or to Tortuga Island, diving tours, and a visit to Montezuma or Curú. If the restaurant is not open (it may close at times in the low season), there is a typical restaurant nearby—Cristina's. Bicycle rental. Telephone 61-1122, ext. 236, fax 23-0093.

Tango Mar Beach Resort and Country Club, past Tambor, offers the traveler deluxe surroundings and a full range of activities. Resident naturalist guides lead sailing trips to Curú Wildlife Refuge and Cabo Blanco Nature Reserve and offer estuary tours expecially for birders. Turtles come ashore to nest on the beach in front. There is a pool with natural mineral water, a restaurant, a gift shop, satellite TV, nine-hole golf course, and tennis courts. The hotel rents mountain bikes, horses, canoes, kayaks, and equipment for tennis, golf, surfing, diving, and fishing. Inquire about air taxi service: San José is 20 minutes away by plane. The 125-acre (50-ha) complex includes pastures, primary forest, and beachfront. A waterfall graces one end of the property. Single $127, double $139; 16 rooms and 5 bungalows. Villas from $209. Credit cards accepted. Package tours available. Telephone 23-1864, fax 55-2697; Apartado 3877-1000, San José.

Past Cóbano is the interesting little beach town of Montezuma. It can't seem to decide whether to dress up and go for big-time tourism or just hang out and take what comes. So far, the latter prevails. There are a number of places to stay, all on the modest side. Some areas of the beach, especially to the north, have loads of gorgeous shells. The waterfall up a trail on the other side of the bridge at the south edge of town is worth the climb. Local fishermen will rent their boats. A local business has an open-air bus that offers direct service to and from the passenger ferry at Paquera for less than $3 per person. Phone 61-1122, extension 259. In Montezuma, inquire at Casa de Huéspedes Alfaro. Do not expect to use credit cards in Montezuma.

The Sano Banano, a macrobiotic restaurant, serves delicious food with a flair. Surely it has the only frozen yogurt machine on the Nicoya Peninsula. Lenny and Patricia Iacona, the owners, also show movies nightly on a big TV screen. They own Cabinas El Sano Banano, ranging from $30 to $40, some with equipped kitchen. Telephone 61-1122, extension 272, or ask for the Sano Banano. The cabins are in the forest near the beach.

Karen Wessberg has a small nature reserve with cabins—no electricity—up the beach; see chapter 8. She also runs Cabinas Karen (with electricity) where the road turns into Montezuma.

Hotel Montezuma is the largest, with 23 rooms. Single with bath $9, double $18, rooms with shared baths less. No hot water. Fans, restaurant, right on the water. Rooms across the street from the restaurant are quieter. Some English spoken. Will help arrange transportation to Cabo Blanco and Tortuga Island and horse rentals. Telephone 61-1122, extension 258.

Cabinas Mar y Cielo. Double $18.50; 6 rooms. Private baths (no hot water), fans; restaurant is Chico's Bar in front. Arranges Cabo Blanco tour by horseback or taxi. Telephone 61-2472, 61-1122, extension 261.

Casa de Huéspedes Alfaro. Room with bath $14, shared bath less. No hot water. Restaurant, fans. Telephone 61-1122, extension 259. Has bus and taxi services.

The road to the Cabo Blanco Strict Nature Reserve is worth the

trip. It eventually narrows to a one-lane track that can be quite muddy in the rainy season. There is one large river to cross. When I got
out of the car to photograph a thatched house with a television an-
tenna atop a bamboo pole, a small child ran up to advise me not to
venture too close to the water. "There are crocodiles in there," she
said. Spiny pochote trees and gumbo-limbo trees, in Spanish called
indio desnudo (naked Indian), with their peeling reddish bark, form
living fences along the road. A huge strangler fig stands at the road's
edge. See chapter 7 for information about visiting the reserve.

South

The Talamancas, the highest mountains in the country, are in the
region we are looking at here, along with beautiful mid- and southern Pacific beaches; plantations of pineapple, African palm, and
bananas; virgin forest; and some lands that knew only indigenous
peoples and a trickle of pioneers until the Inter-American Highway
to Panama pushed back the frontier in the 1950s.

Travel into the region from San José is mainly along two routes, the
highland route along the Inter-American Highway and the old Spanish road through Orotina and then south along the coast. Some of the
largest and some of the smallest national parks are attractions, along
with biological reserves, wildlife refuges, and some private nature
reserves.

The Highland Route

An early start is recommended for a trip on the Inter-American
Highway south from San José. Fog or rain at higher elevations is more
likely as the hours pass. After you pass through the colonial capital
of Cartago and turn at the sign for San Isidro de El General, the road
begins to climb out of the Central Valley. Fields of agave plants called
cabuya (hemp) grow on hillsides. Fiber from the plants is used for
rope or bags. Then small farms with dairy cows dominate the
landscape.

About an hour out of the capital is Bar y Soda Los Angeles. If you
did not have breakfast, a typical one awaits you here: gallo pinto and

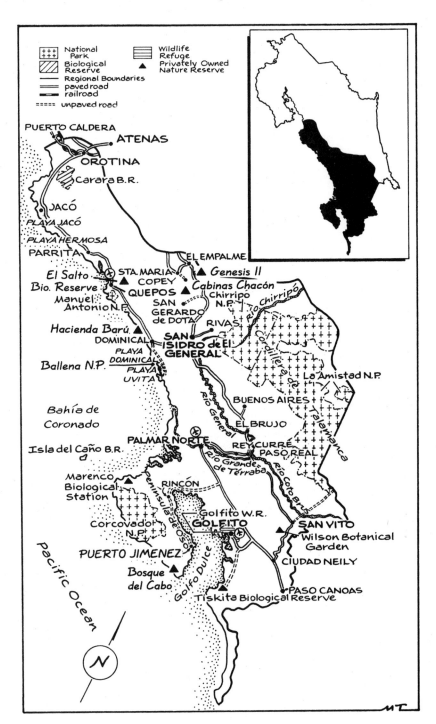

coffee or agua dulce, or you can order a papusa or a variety of *gallos* (tortillas filled with beef, cheese, chicken). This is your chance to try a typical restaurant. Several small roadside restaurants through here offer the same atmosphere. At kilometer 60, you'll find Chesperito, another one I like. If these places seem too rustic, Las Georginas on the other side of Cerro de la Muerte has good food. Buses stop there; it has a buffet.

Near the gasoline station at El Empalme, a road to the right takes travelers along what is called the Route of the Saints, visiting Santa María de Dota, San Marcos de Tarrazú, San Pablo de León Cortés, and San Cristóbal Sur. A four-wheel drive is recommended if you venture south of Santa María de Dota to Copey, where there is a graceful waterfall and a lake, plus rose nurseries. Inquire at ICT about the roads if you are interested in this day trip.

On the left near kilometer 58 on the Inter-American Highway is the little yellow church of Cañon. For a taste of the Talamanca cloud forest and a stay at the private nature reserve called Genesis II, take the unpaved road beside the church for about 2.5 miles (4 km). Genesis II is as intriguing as its name; read about it in chapter 8.

Albergue de Montaña Tapantí, named for nearby Tapantí Wildlife Refuge, is at kilometer 62, just before La Trinidad. Single $44, double $57, master suite $121. Birding tours with naturalist guides can be arranged with advance notice. Horseback riding (including classes), mountain biking, hiking. Restaurant, heaters (elevation close to 10,000 feet [3,048 m]). Telephone 33-0133, fax 33-0778. From U.S. and Canada (800) 344-1212. Apartado 26-1017, San José 2000.

If the day is clear when you get to Cerro de las Vueltas, you can see the peaks of Cerro de la Muerte ahead. Near kilometer 78 is a lake in a depression near the highway at Jaboncillo (park in a safe spot and take a look from the road or walk down a trail to the water). Nineteen miles (30 km) south of El Empalme, at kilometer 80, is the turnoff for San Gerardo de Dota, famous among natural history travelers in the know for its cloud forests and a chance to see the resplendent quetzal. Six bumpy miles (10 km) from the turnoff is Albergue de Montaña Saavegre, known everywhere as Cabinas Chacón. It is a delightful private nature reserve. See chapter 8 for specifics.

Just before the turnoff to San Gerardo de Dota, watch on the left

BANANAS

Bananas are in practically every backyard, sometimes planted between rows of coffee, and in huge plantations in coastal zones. More than 79,000 acres (32,000 ha) are devoted to bananas. Costa Rica is the second-largest exporter of bananas in the world, after Ecuador, and bananas are the leading crop in importance as a foreign exchange earner; coffee is second.

Bananas originated in the area of Asia, India, Malaysia, and the Philippines, brought to the New World in the fifteenth century. Both bananas and United Fruit Company got their start in Costa Rica in the 1880s. United Fruit was the company formed by Minor Keith, the builder of the railroad from Limón to San José, and his associates. Under the name of Chiquita Brands, it continues as a major foreign company in the banana business in Costa Rica, along with Standard Fruit and Bandeco (belongs to Del Monte).

Each trunk in a banana plant produces one bunch (a raicimo), and then it dies. But the plant has a continuous supply of new trunks that emerge from its base. Look at a banana plant in a commercial operation, and you will see the major trunk and two smaller ones. When the major trunk has fruited and been cut, trunk number two takes over, and another shoot at the base is allowed to grow. This way production from a plant is continuous.

It generally takes about nine months from the start of a trunk to cutting of the fruit, three months from flowering to harvest of a bunch. On a plantation, there may be 2,000 plants for every 2.5 acres (1 ha).

Blue plastic bags are put on a bunch at about two weeks, though this varies some.

The bags concentrate heat so that the fruit gets fatter and longer quicker, and they are also impregnated with insecticide and fungicide.

Here is what happens at harvest time at the plantation I visited. A cutter in the field removes the stalk of bananas (still green) from the trunk and places it on the shoulder of another worker, who carries it to a cable that goes to the packing plant. When 25 bunches are hanging on the cable, a runner pulls the "train" to the packing plant. (Some places use tractors now, pulling up to 100 bunches.) The plastic is removed, and workers cut "hands" of bananas from the bunch, tossing them into water, where they stay at least eight minutes to allow latex to drain out of the cut stem. The fruit that survives the selection process is washed again and stacked on trays in 42-pound lots (the amount that goes in each box), a fungicide is sprayed on, and each banana gets a label (Chiquita in this case). Bananas from a tray are loaded into a box lined with plastic and put aboard a container, which holds 800 to 900 boxes. Government inspectors do checks at the boxing stage, because once the doors on the container are closed, they are not opened until they reach their destination. Containers are trucked to the port for shipment by boat.

Costa Rica's bananas go mainly to the United States, with other important markets in West Germany, Belgium, Italy, and the Netherlands.

The banana industry has come under attack from those concerned about cutting of forests for plantations and about the ecological impacts of pesticides and plastic bags that sometimes end up in rivers and oceans.

for ruins of a refuge that once sheltered travelers on the trail through these mountains. Cerro de la Muerte got its name, Mountain of Death, from those who died in storms and frigid nighttime temperatures at these altitudes. Notice the change in vegetation: this is the northernmost true páramo in the hemisphere, containing plants associated with Andean climes. At this top-of-the-world vantage point, when conditions are right, it is possible to see both coasts.

The next part of the road offers one of the most spectacular drives in the country. In a distance of 28 miles (45 km), the road drops from its highest point at 10,938 feet (3,334 m) to 2,303 feet (702 m) at San Isidro de El General. You pass from páramo vegetation to oak forest with red bromeliads shining in the sun and then to tree ferns, vines, and sombrilla del pobre—walls of greenery on both sides of the road. As the vista of the General Valley opens up, you may catch a whiff of heliotrope from plants growing along the road.

Just below the statue of Christ above the highway on the right, there is a *trapiche* (sugar mill) on the left. If it is in operation, you can see oxen turning the press to extract liquid from sugarcane. Roadside stands sometimes offer wooden *bateas* for sale. You can occasionally still see a woman washing clothes on one in the countryside, but these small versions make beautiful trays or centerpieces loaded with fruit or flowers.

San Isidro de El General (pop. 36,973) is the commercial center for this rich agricultural area. It can easily be a hub for travelers as they visit Chirripó, Cerro de la Muerte, the Wilson Botanical Garden at San Vito, hot springs at Canaan de Rivas, the Savegre Caverns, or beaches at Dominical. Buses run frequently between San José and San Isidro, a distance of 85 miles (137 km).

San Isidro is a pleasant place to wander around in for the flavor of a small town in Costa Rica. I stumbled onto a double wedding when I entered the church on the plaza one evening. Shortly after, a dog ambled in through the open door, made his way down the aisle, sniffing and looking, and then ambled out again. Nobody got upset or even paid any attention. Since church doors stand open in this country, it is not uncommon to see a bird flying above the altar or to hear chirping from the ceiling in the quiet of the day.

This valley will be familiar to those of you who have read books by one of its most famous residents, naturalist and ornithologist Alexander F. Skutch. (See Practical Extras, Recommended Reading.) His farm and nature reserve is a few miles from San Isidro; it is open now principally to nature tour groups, not the general public.

Lodging in town is rustic to modest, but there is a comfortable hotel 3 miles (5 km) from the city center, Hotel del Sur, owned by an organization that trains people who work in cooperatives. Any weekend will find classes going on.

Hotel de Sur. Single $18, double $23; 43 rooms. Ten cabins, $30. Pool, restaurant, lighted tennis court, facilities for soccer, basketball, volleyball. Marimba on Monday nights, guitar or other music Wednesday and weekends; sometimes mariachis. Credit cards accepted. Bus from San Isidro passes in front. Telephone 71-0233, fax 71-0527. Apartado 4-8000, San Isidro de El General.

Entrance to Chirripó National Park is just a few miles toward the east of San Isidro, at San Gerardo de Rivas; see chapter 7.

Just 22 miles (35 km) west from San Isidro via a paved road are Dominical and lovely Pacific beaches. This route allows the traveler to make a loop, joining up with the southern coastal route discussed later in this chapter, a way to get to the middle Pacific without returning to San José.

Many choose the highland road to get to Dominical, combining a mountain experience with the coast. Near Dominical there are approximately 30 miles (50 km) of sandy beaches with names like Matapalo, Barú, Playa Hermosa, and Uvita. There is no bridge over the Uvita River, so unless you are in a four-wheel drive and truly adventurous, that may be the end of the road for you, though it does continue on to Cortés for a connection with the Inter-American at Palmar Norte.

There are a number of small hotels around the little beach town of Dominical. Do not count on using credit cards. Dominical is accessible by bus on the line from San Isidro to Quepos or from San Isidro to Uvita. Taxi fare from San Isidro is about $20.

Cabinas Río Mar. Doubles from $35, 6 cabins, some with living/dining area. Will stock pantry. Restaurant for breakfast only.

Fans, hot water, arranges horseback rides, tours. Fax 71-0441. Apartado 487-8000, San Isidro, Pérez Zeledón.

Albergue Willdale. Double $24; 6 rooms. Fans, hot water. Bikes, horses, and inflatable paddleboat available. Arranges nature hikes and birding tours. Owners also have two-bedroom mountain villa above Playa Hermosa for those who seek solitude, $125 a day, $700-$900 a week. Telephone 71-1903 (answering machine, leave message and will call back).

Centro Turístico Costa Brava. Cabin for three $16. Table fans, no hot water. Telephone 71-2552.

Pisces Pacific Boat Tours in Dominical runs day trips to the National Marine Park Ballena and overnights to Caño Island Biological Reserve and Drake's Bay. Half-day trip is $200, full day $325. Telephone for messages 71-1903. Apartado 239-8000, San Isidro, Pérez Zeledón. Most area hotels will make arrangements for you.

South of Dominical, situated high on the point at Punta Dominical, with the sea on both sides, is Cabinas Punta Dominical, a lovely retreat for nature lovers. Four cabins built of tropical hardwood are among the trees and have great views of the ocean, which you can enjoy from a hammock on the porch. Doubles are $40, including private bath, fans, screened windows. There is a thatched, open-air restaurant. Boat trips arranged. Telephone 25-5328, fax 53-4750. Apartado 196-8000, San Isidro de El General.

Cabañas Escondidas, a bed and breakfast, is between Dominical and Uvita. Three rustic cabins for up to four persons, private bath. Cove setting invites swimming, snorkeling, and tide pool exploration. Guided jungle walks. Two persons $30, $9 each additional. Telephone for messages 71-0735, fax 71-1903. Apartado 364-8000, San Isidro, Pérez Zeledón.

For the adventurous, visit Finca Brian and Milena out of Dominicalito. Getting there requires a one-hour horseback ride or 2-kilometer hike. Two cabins, one without running water, on a farm with virgin forest. Toucans and howler monkeys practically guaranteed. One day, one night $50, includes food and tours; $80 for two days, two nights. Horse rental extra. Contact via CB radio from Hacienda Barú.

Hacienda Barú is a private nature reserve just north of Dominical on the road to Quepos. It covers a variety of habitats, from beach to coastal range primary rain forest, with day visits or overnight camping possibilities. Jack and Diane Ewing are marvelous hosts. See chapter 8.

For those continuing south from San Isidro, the Inter-American Highway goes through farm and ranch country and then into mile after mile of pineapples. In less than an hour, you can be in the Buenos Aires area, where there is a Pindeco pineapple processing plant. The chamber of commerce in San Isidro can give you information on tours of the plant. Fresh pineapples at roadside stands sell for $.25 to $.35.

Past El Brujo a few miles on the right is a lovely waterfall that Indians in the area believe has a special quality. Healers use the water in medicinal preparations. Just before the Inter-American Highway reaches the Río Grande de Térraba is the junction to Paso Real and the road to San Vito and the Robert and Catherine Wilson Botanical Garden, operated by the Organization for Tropical Studies (see chap. 8). A bridge is being built over the mighty river, but in the meantime cars and buses to San Vito cross by ferry. The paved road passes through beautiful country, where travelers can come across cowboys and cows going down the road along with the usual menagerie of bicycles, dogs, chickens, and pedestrians. The Talamanca Mountains in La Amistad Park, an international biosphere reserve, rise up to the east. A four-wheel-drive vehicle is recommended to reach park headquarters at Las Tablas.

Italian immigrants helped settle the area around San Vito, arriving in the early 1950s to clear and farm the land. In this town of 11,111 people, you will find several Italian restaurants and hear the language spoken on the streets. (There is a gas station.) For lodging, there are modest cabins in San Vito and rooms at the Wilson Botanical Garden, ten minutes from San Vito. It is an easy day trip out of San Isidro as well. From San Vito and the gardens, there is a road to Ciudad Neily for travelers who want an alternate route to Golfito.

For those who continue on the Inter-American from the Paso Real cutoff, the road winds along the Térraba River. At the Indian village of Rey Curré, pull off for a visit to the local craft cooperative across from the school. If it is closed, go to the house next to the school. Children and adults carve plants, animals, and indigenous designs on gourds. It is much more fun to buy the gourds here than in San José. At the cooperative, each gourd has the name of the person who made it and the price they want for it—very inexpensive. Sometimes there are woven purses for sale. If you buy at the house by the school, where the chickens have more bravado than feathers, check to be sure there are no ants living in the gourds. You do not want to be cooped up in a car when the creatures decide to come out.

At Palmar Sur, SANSA flights land three days a week. From Palmar Sur it is 54 miles (87 km) to Golfito. The Inter-American, of course, continues past the Golfito turnoff to Ciudad Neily, Paso Canoas, and the border with Panama.

Golfito (pop. 19,095) is a port town on the Golfo Dulce and was a busy center for banana exportation when the Bananera Company, a subsidiary of United Brands, was operating in the area (1938-1985). Golfito was company headquarters. You will notice that African palms have replaced bananas on much of the land, though bananas are being planted again in the zone. The biggest news in Golfito in the last couple of years, however, has been the "duty-free" shopping complex known as the *depósito* that opened in 1990. Though some taxes are not imposed on goods and other restrictions have curtailed initial enthusiasm, people still come from around the country to shop, especially on weekends. The town itself is a narrow strip about 4 miles (6 km) between the water and the mountains. If you fly in, you may wonder as you approach where there is enough level land for a runway.

In Golfito, there are a number of hotels. Hotel Las Gaviotas is on the way into Golfito. There is a pleasant open-air restaurant and pools for children and adults right on the water of the Golfo Dulce, looking across to the Osa Peninsula. Private baths and hot water in each of the 18 rooms ($35) and 3 bungalows ($45). Mini gym, ceiling fans and air-conditioning, USA Direct telephone, video movies nightly, horse rental; credit cards accepted. In the garden, owners are adding markers with scientific names and common names in English and Spanish of the plants. Near the shore are remains of a mine sweeper used in World War II which now often serve as a picturesque roost

Hotel Las Gaviotas on shores of Golfo Dulce at Golfito (Photo by Ree Strange Sheck)

for land and sea birds. Telephone 75-0062, fax 75-0544. Apartado 12-8201, Golfito.

Hotel Sierra is a new hotel between the depósito and the airport at the opposite end of town. Single $70, double $84; 72 rooms. Adult and children's pools, TV, restaurants, small shopping center on premises; credit cards accepted. Arranges tours to Golfito Wildlife Refuge, Caño Island Biological Reserve, and Corcovado and Amistad national parks. Telephone/fax 24-9917, fax 24-3399. Apartado 5304-1000, San José.

Here are a few other possibilities.

Hotel Costa Sur. Doubles from $21 with fans, air-conditioning more; 25 rooms; no credit cards. Restaurant, nice private baths with hot water. In residential area near airport. Telephone 75-0871, fax 75-0832.

Hotel Golfito downtown near the dock. Rooms basic but clean, from $7, some with air-conditioning. Private baths, no hot water. Telephone 75-0047, Apartado 80-8201, Golfito.

Cabinas Castillo off the highway into town at kilometer 3. Residential neighborhood, 9 nice rooms, $7, shared baths. Restaurant.

Owners René and Jacinta Castillo have a car and a boat to take guests around in the area. Speak Spanish only. Telephone 75-0437.

Cabinas El Manglar. House in former United Fruit housing, residential area. Four rooms, $5, one with private bath. Hot water. Telephone 75-0510.

Both the Golfito Wildlife Refuge, which practically surrounds the town on its landward side, and Corcovado National Park across the gulf are good options for nature travelers (see chap. 7). Several private nature reserves on the Osa Peninsula draw travelers. See chapter 8 for descriptions of the Marenco Biological Reserve near Corcovado and the charming new Bosque del Cabo on the tip of the peninsula. Bus service is good to Golfito, and SANSA flies there every day except Sunday. Travelair has daily flights.

There are several lodges on the peninsula, among them, Drake Bay Wilderness Camp (telephone/fax 71-2436), La Paloma Lodge (telephone 39-0954, fax 77-0171), and Corcovado Lodge tent camp (telephone 57-0766, fax 57-1665). Package tours to these sites usually depart from San José, but charter air service from Golfito is available. Vuelos Especiales, for example, flies to Drake for $160 as well as to Sirena in Corcovado for $132. Captain Alvaro Ramírez does his bit to help Corcovado by carrying supplies when he goes empty to Sirena to pick someone up. With a week's notice, he will try to arrange shared rides on a charter. Telephone 75-0607, 41-1444; fax 75-0035, 41-2671.

At this time, the launch to Puerto Jiménez from Golfito has been discontinued. Check to see if it is again available. Air taxi service daily except Sunday takes about 10 minutes and costs less than $6. You can also get to Puerto Jiménez, where you find the headquarters for Corcovado National Park, by road from the Inter-American Highway.

If you need to spend the night in Puerto Jiménez, try Cabinas Los Manglares: 9 basic rooms, $8; good restaurant; telephone 78-5002. If you are backpacking, you might want to check out Tierra de Milagros on Playa Carbonera, south of town.

Surfers and nature travelers head south of Golfito to the Pavones Bay area—surfers for the big waves and nature travelers for Tiskita Lodge, a biological reserve and experiment station where exotic tropical fruits are grown (see chap. 8).

Boat travel common out of Golfito to nearby beaches and hotels (Photo by Ree Strange Sheck)

Coastal Route through Orotina

Part of this route was the old Spanish trail from San José to the Pacific. From the capital, take the highway for the international airport and head for Atenas, a town founded in the sixteenth century. This area is known for the quality of its fruits; ticos travel to Atenas and Garita on weekends just to buy. As you pass along the mountain road to Orotina, you pass through picturesque villages, farms, coffee fields, patches of forest. Notice the "living fences." A branch cut off a tree of certain species is stuck in the ground, and it grows. Besides serving as fence posts, the trees are windbreaks, and some of them offer fodder for cattle. *Madero negro* and *poró* (showy red flowers) are two of the species used. Sometimes the indio desnudo is chosen. Photosynthesis can take place through the bark of this species. It is easy to recognize: the smooth reddish bark peels.

Other trees with bright blossoms on this route are the *llama del bosque*, "flame of the forest" (with red flowers), and *cortesa amarilla* (with yellow flowers).

While you are in Costa Rica, you may hear talk of a dry canal, referring to a land route from coast to coast that Costa Rica can offer as an economical alternative to the Panama Canal. There are rail and road possibilities. As a matter of fact, the system is functioning already with containers trucked between Puerto Caldera on the Pacific and Moín, near Limón on the Caribbean. The missing highway segment that will streamline the route is between Ciudad Colón and Orotina, a straighter route farther south than this one.

Descending toward Orotina on the historic route, notice the almost perpendicular hillsides cleared for pastures. The terracelike appearance is created by the horizontal trails of grazing cows. Past Orotina is a turnoff northwest to Puntarenas and the Caldera dock, where cruise ships stop on a regular basis. Our route takes us to the Tarcoles River and Carara Biological Reserve. Get out your binoculars for a stop near the bridge over the river. Crocodiles usually bask in the mud along its banks; birds enjoy its waters. You might see a wood stork, blue heron, or American egret.

Because of one-day nature tours from San José, Carara has become a popular natural history destination. Seeing it with a guide is recommended. One disappointed young lady told me she had gotten off the public bus at the entrance to Carara and walked on the trail without seeing anything spectacular. I think she had expected the birds and animals to come out and greet her. Guides know animal territories, which trees are in fruit, and what to look for. They can point out orchids that a visitor might not even spot. See chapter 7 for information on Carara and chapter 9 for tour possibilities.

Hotels up and down the coast arrange tours to the reserve. The closest lodging is in Tarcoles, a little more than a mile (2 km) away. Cabinas Carara, near the beach, has singles for $10, doubles $20. Cabins for up to six are $28. Restaurant, pool, fans, credit cards. Accommodations simple but clean. Will pick up at the highway for bus travelers. Arranges birding tours on the Río Grande de Tarcoles, using local guides, and reserve visits. Telephone 61-0455. Speak Spanish only.

From Carara the road drops down to the coastal lowlands, with tantalizing views of the Pacific. Architectural variations appear, the most striking being the sharply pitched, thatched roofs on huts and open-air ranchos.

Between Tarcoles and Jacó is Hotel Punta Leona, a beach resort with 75 equipped apartments, most in the $75 range. Restaurant, pools, boutique, air-conditioning, tennis, skating rink. The 2.5-mile (4-km) drive from the highway passes through exquisite forest. This is scarlet macaw country. Perhaps you will see one. Telephone 31-3131, fax 32-0791. Apartado 8592-1000, San José.

Jacó, on the beach, is popular with Costa Ricans, and tour companies often take tourists there. There are hotels, cabins, restaurants, a disco, car rental, and rental of surfing and other water-sports equipment. Swimmers and surfers should read the tips on water safety; riptides are not uncommon.

Hotel Jacó Beach is on the water. It has a restaurant, a pool within view of the ocean, tennis, casino, and surfboard rentals. Rooms are air-conditioned; doubles are $64, triples $69. Credit cards are accepted. Telephone 32-5627, 64-3064; Apartado 962-1000, San José.

Hotel Jacó Fiesta. Standard rooms and studios with kitchenettes, $60 for up to four; credit cards accepted. On beach. Pools, restaurant, air-conditioning, cable TV, tennis, pedal boats, horses. Minibus transport from San José November to April. Tours to Monteverde, Poás/Sarchí, Carara, Arenal, Gulf of Nicoya. English, German, and Italian also spoken. Telephone 64-3147, fax 64-3418. Apartado 38, Jacó, Puntarenas.

Hotel Club del Mar is tucked away on a peaceful cove at the south end of Jacó Beach. Twelve air-conditioned, nicely furnished suites nestle among the trees with gorgeous ocean views, $70; rooms with kitchen and fans, $58; credit cards accepted. Hot water, gift shop, pool. Knowledgeable guides lead trips to Quepos, Isla del Caño, Corcovado, Monteverde. Mountain bikes and surfing equipment for rent. Trees and plants on grounds are marked with scientific and local names; bird list is available. English, French, and various African languages spoken by the Edwardes, who own the hotel. Telephone/fax 64-3194. Apartado 107, Jacó, Puntarenas.

Continuing south on the *costanera*, Playa Hermosa is a favorite with surfers and also is a sea turtle nesting site. Signs along the road advertise lodging. One of these is for Hotel Delfin on Esterillos Beach. Single $37, double $47, 15 rooms, all with balcony overlooking the sea. High-ceilinged restaurant with view of ocean, pool, gift shop, hot water; credit cards accepted. Hotel tours to Manuel Antonio and

Carara, and birding tours on nearby estuary. Local guides. Staff reports hawksbill turtles come ashore here between the end of July and December. Also speak English, German, Arabic, and French. Will pick up at highway for bus travelers. Telephone/fax 71-1640. Apartado 37, Parrita.

Going on south, waving fields of rice draw birds; there is a rice processing plant. Near Parrita, groves of African palm appear.

In 1945 the Bananera Company planted the first commercial plantation of the palms in this area, replacing banana plantations that were badly affected by Panama disease. By 1965, African palm plantations reached as far south as Golfito. Oil extracted from the plant is used not only for fat, margarine, and cooking oil but also in soaps and perfumes.

The town of Quepos is the gateway for visits to Manuel Antonio National Park. Express buses from San José make the trip in about three and a half hours, and there are daily flights. If you come by bus, you can get off at the Quepos stop and make reservations for your return trip before you continue on to Manuel Antonio. Just ask the driver to wait for you. There are also buses to Quepos from San Isidro de El General and Puntarenas. Call Transportes Morales in Quepos at 77-0318 for schedules; in San José, 23-5567. Car rental is available in Quepos and Manuel Antonio.

Quepos (pop. 11,936) was named for the Quepo Indians, who once roamed these parts. Artifacts turn up in surrounding pastures and fields. Mogote Island, a sheer-sided land with a crown of thick vegetation visible from Cathedral Point in Manuel Antonio National Park, was Quepo ceremonial ground. Today Quepos is the center of an agricultural area: cattle, rice, beans, sorghum, papayas, and mangoes.

The Kamuk Hotel in Quepos arranges tours to nearby Damas Island and to Dominical. The three-story, modern hotel faces the ocean. Rooms cost from $59 to $88, some with balconies; 28 rooms. Restaurant and snack bar, air-conditioning, gift shop, hot water; credit cards accepted. Telephone 77-0379, fax 77-0258. Apartado 18-6350, Quepos.

The Buena Nota gift shop, which also serves as an informal information center for the area, is run by Anita Myketuk. The shop may be moving from its Quepos location to near the Karahé Hotel on the road to Manuel Antonio within the year. Along with handcrafted items, including originally designed clothing, Anita has maps, books, the *Tico Times*, and patience to answer tourists' questions. A North American, she has lived here for more than seventeen years. She also has two houses for rent near the Mariposa Hotel, with a gorgeous view of Manuel Antonio: 1 bedroom $50, 2 bedroom $75, weekly rates. Telephone 77-0345.

At the far end of the road into town along the beach is the Nahomi, a tourism spot with restaurant and swimming pools.

The town of Manuel Antonio and the park are less than 5 miles (7 km) south of Quepos. A proliferation of small sodas in Manuel Antonio has unfortunately diminished the appeal of the place and raises questions about pollution, but the park itself continues to be a small jewel. It protects beautiful beaches as well as the flora and fauna of the tropical forest. Visitors must wade across an estuary to reach the entrance, an adventurous introduction to the special experience that awaits. Buses run about every two hours between Quepos and Manuel Antonio, passing in front of the hotels sprinkled along the road.

El Salto Biological Reserve is a private reserve (see chap. 8) perched on a mountaintop with fantastic views of the coastline and its own trails through tropical forest. Watch for the sign just out of Quepos.

The following hotels are along the road through the hills between Quepos and Manuel Antonio. Most arrange tours.

Hotel La Mariposa. Single $138, double $208, including breakfast and dinner; 10 villas. No credit cards or personal checks and no children under 15. Each villa has a sitting room, bedroom, spectacular bathroom in a greenhouse setting (hot water), and balcony. Pool, fans, restaurant. Arranges visit to park with naturalist guide ($25 for half day), horseback riding, snorkeling tours. Shuttle from airport and twice a day to beach. Telephone 77-0355, fax 77-0050; (800) 223-6510 (U.S.A.), (800) 268-0424 (Canada). Apartado 4, Quepos.

Albergue Turístico El Byblos. Bungalows begin at $148 singles, $197 doubles, breakfast and dinner included. Air-conditioning costs more. All hotel rooms are air-conditioned: single $148, double $185. Off-season rates are lower (meals not included). Pool, restaurant, cable TV, hot water; credit cards accepted. English, French, and Italian also spoken. Hotel has a 55-foot boat for cruises to park and islands ($80 per person), including a meal and snorkeling or fishing equipment. Inquire about trips to Caño Island Biological Reserve and Coco Island or Corcovado. Shuttle service. Telephone 77-0411, fax 77-0009. Apartado 112-6350, Quepos.

Bahías Hotel. Eight rooms for up to three persons, $93; two rooms with indoor Jacuzzi, $116. Restaurant, hot water, air-conditioning, sauna, mini gym; credit cards accepted. Day tours to nearby El Salto Biological Reserve. English, French, and Portuguese also spoken. Telephone 77-0350, fax 77-0279 or 77-0171. Apartado 186-6350, Quepos.

Hotel y Villas El Mogote. Single $76, double $87 (includes breakfast), two-story villas from $175. Restaurant, pool, art gallery, hot water, some air-conditioning, shuttle bus. Offers seven-day tour combining Tortuguero with Manuel Antonio. Half-day guided tours to park, $40, and Damas Island, $50. Telephone/fax 77-0582. Apartado 120-6350, Quepos.

Costa Verde. Eighteen rooms for up to three people start at $70. Kitchenettes, hot water, air-conditioning and fans, each room with ocean view and balcony. Two condos available. Squirrel monkeys pass through surrounding forest every day. Credit cards accepted. Ask about natural history slide shows and tours. Telephone 23-7946, fax 23-9446. Apartado 6944-1000, San José.

Karahé Hotel. Single or double occupancy $82; 9 independent cabins plus 7 rooms. Credit cards accepted. Pool across the road on land going down to the beach; cabins are up flights of stone steps from restaurant. Air-conditioning, fans, refrigerators. Telephone 77-0170, fax 77-0152. Apartado 100-6350, Quepos.

Hotel Divisamar. Single or double air-conditioned room $75; 25 rooms. No credit cards. Restaurant, pool, hot water. Offers horseback riding, tour to Damas Island, day trip to King's Beach ($35), including a canal trip through African palm plantation. Airport shuttle. Telephone 77-0371, fax 77-0525. Apartado 82-6350, Quepos.

Hotel El Lirio. Nine rooms, $70, including breakfast; accepts Visa. Air-conditioning, fans, hot water. English and Italian also spoken. Telephone 77-0403. Apartado 123-6350, Quepos.

La Quinta. With kitchenette $70, without $58; 4 cabins. No credit cards. Small pool. Down a dirt road off main highway. English, French, Hungarian also spoken. Telephone 77-0434. Apartado 76-6350, Quepos.

Hotel Arboleda. Single $64, double $76, breakfast included; 37 rooms. Credit cards accepted. Fans, pool, restaurant, snack bar on beach, shuttle service, tour agency (trips to Marenco Biological reserve and Rincón de la Vieja National Park). English and Spanish spoken. Trails in forest adjoining hotel. Rooms down flights of steps from restaurant toward beach. Telephone 77-0092, fax 77-0414. Apartado 55-6350, Quepos.

Villas Nicolas. Doubles start at $64, suites with kitchens at $90 and up to $163 for four. Pool, fans, hot water, some balconies opening onto forest. No credit cards. English and French also spoken. Telephone/fax 77-0538. Apartado 26-6350, Quepos.

El Colibrí. Ten bungalows, $58 double occupancy. Fans, refrigerators, hot plates, barbecue. Backs on national park. English and French also spoken. Telephone 77-0432. Apartado 94-6350, Quepos.

Hotel Villas Oso. Rooms from $58. Fans, ocean views from terraces, hot water. English and Scandinavian languages also spoken. Telephone 77-0233. Apartado 128-6350, Quepos.

Hotel Plinio. Double $50, including German buffet breakfast; 6 rooms. Restaurant well known in area for its Italian food; credit cards accepted. Pool, fans or air-conditioning, hot water, bike rental. English, German, and Italian also spoken. Hiking trails through almost 5 acres (2 ha) of primary forest around the hotel, plus an observation platform. Telephone/fax 77-0055. Apartado 71-6350, Quepos.

Hotel Los Charrúas. Rooms from $47. Restaurant, fans, hot water; credit cards accepted. View of Damas Island. Telephone/fax 77-0409. Apartado 38-6350, Quepos.

The following hotels are in Manuel Antonio, nearest the park.

Hotel Vela Bar. Single $29, double $38; 8 rooms. Credit cards accepted. Popular restaurant. Fans, with air-conditioning on request; no hot water. Adjoins park. English also spoken. Telephone 77-0413. Apartado 13-6350, Quepos.

Los Almendros. Rooms $33 with fans, $44 with air conditioning, for up to three persons; 18 rooms. No credit cards. Restaurant, no hot water. Telephone 77-0225. Apartado 68-6350, Quepos.

Cabinas Espadilla. Rooms with kitchenettes $37, without $32; 16 rooms. No credit cards. Fans. English also spoken. Telephone 77-0416. Apartado 30, Heredia.

Hotel y Cabinas Piscis. Room for up to four, $40. Restaurant December to April, fans, no hot water; credit cards accepted. Telephone 77-0046. Apartado 219-6350, Quepos.

Ríos Tropicales now has an office located near the Manuel Antonio school. There are sea kayaking tours with professional, bilingual guides. Beginners can kayak to the Damas Island estuary, great for seeing birds and perhaps even crocodiles and monkeys. Lunch is aboard the La Tortuga floating restaurant. Kayaking experience is necessary for tours to the park along its ocean side. Call the Osmans, who manage the Manuel Antonio operation, at 77-0574 for information or reservations.

Treasure Hunt Tours offers scuba diving and snorkeling tours. Call 77-0345 for information.

From Quepos, it is about 28 miles farther along the coast to Dominical, where the road to San Isidro de El General comes in, offering an alternative route back to San José or travels south on the Inter-American Highway. The private nature reserve Hacienda Barú just before Dominical is an easy day trip from Quepos or Manuel Antonio (see chap. 8). This area is mentioned in the earlier highland route section.

Caribbean

The Atlantic Coast is shorter than the Pacific and has a more extensive coastal plain. The area offers long, uncluttered beaches, high forested mountains, coconut palms, plantations of cacao and bananas, national parks and wildlife refuges, sleepy villages, and a commercial port.

The newer highway through Guapiles cuts travel time to 2½ hours by road from San José to Limón. It travels through Braulio Carrillo National Park. Even when you have left the park boundaries, keep your eyes peeled for sloths in trees along the way. One spotted here

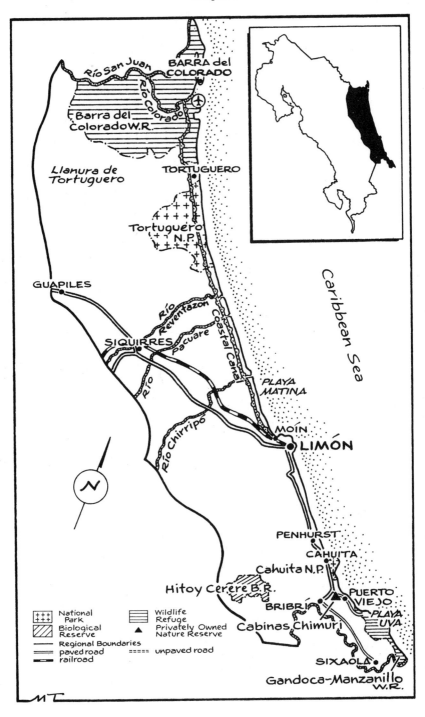

offers good photo opportunities. Be careful on this road if you are driving. It is subject to heavy fog and landslides, especially passing through the park. Beware also of speeding drivers.

The old highway through Cartago and Turrialba, mentioned in the Central Valley section, requires about four hours of travel time. The large pipeline you notice in places carries petroleum products from the port at Limón, following the old road to Siquirres. The railroad from capital to Caribbean no longer is a transportation possibility for passengers. The famous Jungle Train was discontinued in 1991. Some local lines persist in the coastal banana areas. Steel rails and both highway routes come together at Siquirres, where you are definitely in banana country. Signs point to towns whose names tie them to the railroad: Linea B, 28 Millas. Many short lines provided transportation in this area, some with rail cars pulled by burros until the 1950s.

About twenty years went into building the main line (1871-1890), with Chinese and West Indians brought in as workers. To help finance the project, bananas were grown for export (and to feed workers), and that brought in more blacks from British colonies, many from Jamaica. This is how United Fruit Company got its start in Costa Rica. Though only about 2 percent of the country's population is Afro-American, the percentage in the province of Limón is about one-third. Their cultural influence adds to the flavor of the Caribbean zone and broadens the monolingual English-speaking tourists' ability to communicate by leaps and bounds.

Limón, or more correctly Puerto Limón (pop. 67,784), is capital of the province. Christopher Columbus dropped anchor offshore near Uvita Island in 1502. Around October 12, which is a holiday about Columbus and his discovery that ticos celebrate as Día de la Raza, Limón throws a big party that draws about 200,000 people. It may not be Río, but this carnival is five days of music, parades, dancing, bullfights (the bull is never killed in this nation of peace), and local arts and crafts.

During the rest of the year, Limón is a center of commerce (with deep-water docking facilities at nearby Moín), of fishing, shipping, agriculture, and tourism. If sloths have so far eluded you, go to Vargas Park near the seawall, where several live. If you cannot spot the well-camouflaged mammal, a passerby will usually help. If you go to the Municipal Market, stop by one of the food stands to try rice and beans, or a fried cake, or *agua de sapo*, literally "toad water" but actually a kind of cold agua dulce with lemon.

North of Moín is an ICT park, and farther up there is a sanctuary for leatherback turtles at Barra de Matina Beach. These large turtles come ashore to lay eggs from February to July, with peak numbers in April and May. A joint project of public and private entities attempts to protect the eggs by patrolling the beach and placing some of the eggs in protected "nurseries," humble-looking contraptions on the beach that nonetheless turn out thousands of baby turtles each year. Green turtles and some hawksbills also nest here.

In Limón and south, you will probably still see signs of the April 22, 1991, earthquake that walloped the region, though reconstruction of buildings and damaged roads and bridges day by day whittles away at the physical evidence of the disaster. A courageous people have been digging out and are ready to share the natural beauty of the region with visitors. A positive note is that scientists predict no major earthquake here for about another one hundred years.

The quake, which registered 7.4 on the Richter scale, raised the Atlantic coast about 5 feet (1.5 m) at Limón, the elevation diminishing southward to about a foot (30 cm) at Gandoca near the border with Panama. So you will note some changes along the beaches.

Though several hotels exist in and near Limón, the following three would be my pick and offer a range of prices. At the Maribú Caribe on the ocean, sounds are of the sea; at La Matama, in the forest, birds break the silence; at Hotel Acón downtown, sounds are of the city. The first two are on the road to Portete, just north of downtown.

Hotel Maribú Caribe. Single $64, double $82; 56 rooms in 14 thatched bungalows. Air-conditioning, restaurants, swimming pools, bike rental, gift shop, parking, credit cards. Offers tours to watch turtle nesting during season plus one-day tours to Tortuguero for $65. There is a half-day banana tour as well as visits to Cahuita National Park for snorkeling and to Puerto Viejo and Gandoca-Manzanillo Wildlife Refuge. In the high season, you can learn to dance to Caribbean music in classes. Caribbean nights at the hotel present music and typical regional food. Situated on a hill, with grassy grounds going down to the Caribbean. Telephone in San José 34-0193; in Limón 58-4543, 58-4010; fax 58-3541. Apartado 623-7300, Puerto Limón.

Hotel Matama. Single $53, double $64; 16 rooms. The open-air restaurant/bar and rooms in scattered bungalows are nestled among the trees. Pool, air-conditioning, parking; credit cards accepted. The hotel offers a half-day walk on its own jungle trail for $30. Javier, the bilingual naturalist guide, knows just where the spectacled owl is likely to be and where a boa constrictor hangs out. The first part of the walk goes through a coconut plantation, where you can drink the liquid from a green coconut, or *pipa*. Passing by cacao trees, you can see where chocolate comes from. You may spot a black-cheeked woodpecker, yellow-tailed oriole, or three species of tanager, as well as a sloth, coati, or anteater. Tortuguero trips can be arranged. On weekends, guests are treated to Caribbean nights with music and typical food. Telephone 58-1123, fax 58-4499. Apartado 686, Puerto Limón.

Hotel Acón. Single $20, double $26; 39 rooms. Restaurant, private baths with hot water, air-conditioning, TV, discotheque. Arranges trips to Tortuguero. Telephone 58-1010, fax 58-2924. Apartado 528, Puerto Limón.

Buses for Limón depart from San José at Avenida 3, Calles 19/21, near the National Park.

Tortuguero and Barra del Colorado national parks on the northern Caribbean coast are popular destinations for nature travelers. SANSA flies to Barra del Colorado Tuesday, Thursday, and Saturday. Travelair flies daily. The most convenient way to get to either is by taking a prearranged tour. From San José, package tours include transportation by bus and boat or airplane, hotel, and meals. Some offer guided explorations of the waterways off the main canal. See chapter 9 for specifics. Hotels and travel-related businesses from Limón south also arrange tours to Tortuguero, many with one-day tours. You can do the trip yourself, arranging boat transportation from Moín outside of Limón, finding your own lodging, and hiring a boat and local guide once you arrive in Tortuguero or Barro del Colorado.

Green, leatherback, and hawksbill turtles nest in the area, with heavy concentrations on a long beach at Tortuguero. This is the home

CACAO

Cacao trees were growing in the New World when the Spaniards arrived. The plant, whose seeds provide us with cocoa, chocolate, and cocoa butter, is endemic to tropical America. The name it was given in Latin, Theobroma, means "food of the gods."

Indigenous peoples of Costa Rica cultivated cacao; fields were found by Spanish explorers at Matina in 1540. During colonial times, it was the most important cash crop until coffee was introduced, and cacao beans were even used as money up to the late 1700s.

Climatic conditions continue to make the Atlantic lowlands the major region for cacao plantations. You will notice the plantations on the road south from Limón to Cahuita and Puerto Viejo and between Braulio Carrillo park and Limón.

Cacao is a short tree, about 26 feet (8 m) in height. It has some interesting biological peculiarities. Leaves are both green (mature ones) and red (young ones). The leaves of this plant have the ability to go from a horizontal to a vertical position depending on the amount of sunlight—the more intense the sun, the more they droop. The fruits or pods (called mazorcas) grow directly from the trunk or branches, hanging like ornaments. As the pods ripen, they change from green to yellow or red. Seeds inside that oval-shaped fruit are the commercial cocoa beans, as many as twenty to sixty per pod. The one opened for me had forty-three, all covered in a slippery, soft pulp that is quite tasty.

Harvest is year-round, but it peaks in April and May and between October and December. Mature pods are handpicked and cut open. The seeds are fermented for a few days and then dried, either in the sun or by mechanical means. They are then shipped to factories—there are three large ones in Costa Rica—for processing. If you take a side road off the main highway in the Penhurst area, you will see platforms with cacao spread out to dry.

Costa Rica was once the leader in Central America in cacao export, but disease damaged many trees in 1978. Gradually, production has increased since that time. CATIE, the agricultural research center at Turrialba, has worked with disease-resistant strains and distributes hybrids.

Most of the cacao crop exported from Costa Rica goes to the United States, France, and West Germany.

of the Caribbean Conservation Corporation started by the late Dr. Archie Carr to carry out turtle research.

The canals that run parallel to the sea were built in the seventies to connect inland waterways from the Port of Limón to Barra del Colorado. Roads have yet to connect some of this area to the rest of the country, so this lifeline of canals and rivers is the highway. Canoes loaded with bananas and coconuts travel here, logs are floated south, barges carrying supplies head north. Families travel in tiny dugouts. Sometimes the narrow canals open into wide lagoons; signs give distances and directions. A trip on these waters is fascinating, and one notes a courtesy in traffic lacking in San José. Large boats propelled by motors slow down when small craft appear, to avoid swamping them. When our boat died between Tortuguero and Barra del Colorado, the first boat by took us on, luggage and all.

Fishing draws visitors to this area as well, especially for snook and tarpon. There is a fishing camp at Barra del Parismina and others at Barra del Colorado.

Roads do exist to take you south from Limón all the way to Sixaola and the border with Panama. The direct Sixaola bus from San José will take you by Cahuita National Park and to the Indian village of Bribrí. It does not go all the way to Puerto Viejo. Several tour companies now offer nature-oriented tours to the southern Caribbean region and lodges, and hotels in the area arrange visits to the parks and reserves. The mix of Indian and black culture in the area is unique in Costa Rica.

With the Caribbean on the left and forest remnants and farms on the right, there is much to take in. Some fields contain coconut palms, banana plants, and cacao trees together.

About 20 miles (30 km) south of Limón, just before the Estrella River, is a delightful destination for nature travelers: Aviarios del Caribe. Luís and Judy Arroyo own and operate a reserve of some 220 acres (85 ha). A 45-minute trail next to the lodge has an observation platform for good birding; more than 200 species have been identified. On the island across the tributary of the Estrella that flows through the reserve, black-crowned herons nest; howler, white-faced, and spider monkeys live there. The island is in the preliminary stages of being declared a wildlife refuge.

On guided night walks you may see caimans, raccoons, or a kinkajou. I saw river otters playing just offshore at midmorning. Canoes rent for $5 an hour, $10 with a guide to go to the mouth of the Estrella. You can also rent bicycles. The Arroyos offer a trip in the rugged Talamanca Mountains, for the hearty only.

Four rooms exist now, and more are coming. The earthquake necessitated starting over. Rates are $41 per person, including breakfast and dinner, private baths with hot water; credit cards accepted. Telephone 22-8974, fax 24-6895. Apartado 7-2030, San José 1000.

At Penhurst a road west goes through miles of cacao plantations. Platforms are covered with seeds, spread out to dry. You may see *guanábana* fruit covered with the same blue plastic bags impregnated with insecticide that you have noticed over bunches of bananas. The size of the guanábanas is astounding. Follow this dirt road through big banana plantations to the Hitoy-Cerere Biological Reserve. Little visited, it holds treasures for those who reach its forests.

A few miles farther back on the main road is the town of Cahuita and Cahuita National Park. A pedestrian entrance to the park lies at the edge of town.

Cahuita, 27 miles (44 km) south of Limón, is small—about 3,200 people. Tourism is increasingly big business here, but facilities are small. There is, however, a tour company, Cahuita Tours and Rentals; telephone 58-1515, extension 232 or 266. Snorkeling equipment is available, as well as bikes and scuba-diving gear. For $16 you can spend four hours in a glass-bottomed boat viewing the marvels of the coral reefs offshore. Other tours include late-afternoon guided nature walks, a half-day visit to the Bribrí Indian reserve, and visits to Manzanillo and the Gandoca-Manzanillo refuge and to Tortuguero National Park. A tour to Hitoy-Cerere Biological Reserve with a bilingual local guide is about $30 per person, minimum of two. Owner Antonio Mora sells locally made handcrafts and artwork.

Here is a sample of some of the hotels.

Hotel Jaguar. Rooms for $40 without meals or $27 per person including breakfast and dinner; 22 rooms. Meals are a treat, truly elegance by the seaside, with such delicacies as avocado omelets for breakfast and Basque-French cooking that uses fresh herbs and spices in ten different sauces served with fish, beef, or chicken. Paul and Melba Vigneault manage the hotel, which is across from the beach on the north end of town. Building design incorporates cross-ventilation and thermosiphoning, resulting in what Paul calls passively cooled rooms that have private baths and two queen-sized beds with orthopedic mattresses.

Nature trails on the 18 acres (7 ha) offer guests the possibility of seeing a crocodile, armadillo, sloth, kinkajou, agouti, or colorful frogs. A variety of fruit trees draw birds to hotel grounds. Trips can be

Hotel Jaguar at Cahuita (Photo by Ree Strange Sheck)

arranged to Aviarios del Caribe, Punta Uva, Manzanillo, or other area locations. A trip to Panama through Bribrí is another option.

If you cannot stay here, come by for a meal; the restaurant is open to the public. Credit cards accepted. Transport from Cahuita center is available if you come on the bus. Telephone 58-1515, extension 238, or 26-3775. Apartado 7046-1000, San José.

Cabinas Black Beach. Double $15; 4 rooms in two attractive bungalows. A short distance from town. No air-conditioning, but there are fans. Boat trips to the national park, to see coral reefs, or for fishing. English, Spanish, and Italian spoken; accepts Visa. Fruit trees draw birds. Restaurant serves some Italian dishes. Telephone 58-1515, extension 251. Will transport from Cahuita center.

Cabinas Vaz. Single $14, double $19; 14 rooms. Fans. Restaurant. In town. Telephone 58-1515, extension 218. Owner Charles Wilfred Vaz is opening another place at Playa Blanca. Single $12, double $15, private baths; 10 rooms. Telephone 58-1515, extension 284.

El Atlántida. Single $30, double $35, breakfast included; 14 rooms. Private bath with hot water, ceiling fan, restaurant, credit cards accepted. Offers horseback riding, first-run and natural history films. Telephone 58-1515, extension 213.

Puerto Viejo draws surfers, who enjoy the great waves along the beach. Small hotels and lodges are springing up right and left in this area. In Puerto Viejo itself, the Pizote Lodge is geared to the nature traveler. The 8 rooms (shared bath), $36, and six bungalows (private bath), $61, are tastefully decorated and seem in harmony with the surroundings. A three-bedroom casita rents for $110; no credit cards. It has a restaurant for guests and ceiling fans; no hot water, but the baths are otherwise modern.

Walks with a bilingual guide are offered on three nature trails, the longest a five-hour trek through primary forest in an Indian reserve. Guests also have the option of a trip to the Sixaola River, great for bird-watchers. Transportation can be arranged from San José, and the Limón-Puerto Viejo bus passes in front. Telephone/fax 29-1428.

For a homelike atmosphere, there is Hotel Pura Vida, 7 large, sparkling clean rooms, private baths with hot water, $12. Owners María and Karl can help you in English, Spanish, German, or French. There is no restaurant, but breakfast is available. Ceiling fans, no credit cards. Telephone 58-0854.

Cabinas Jacaranda has four small rooms, one with private bath. Single $8, double $12, no hot water. The restaurant, open to the public, specializes in Caribbean cooking and offers vegetarian plates. No telephone.

If you have not yet tried *patacas*, made of plantains, stop by Stanford's and order a plate of them. The person who serves you will probably be moving to the beat of the music.

For a thatch-and-bamboo experience, try Cabinas Black Sands located near the entrance to Puerto Viejo; turn at Pulpería La Violeta and go along the road parallel to the beach. Owned by Diane Applebaum and Ken Kerst, this rustic retreat has grounds sprinkled with banana, papaya, and other fruit trees, pineapple, and palms. There is an outhouse, and the outdoor shower is open enough to let you watch the birds while you bathe. A cabin consists of 3 rooms and a kitchen. Cost is $10 a room. Telephone 58-3844 and leave a message.

The privately owned nature reserve Cabinas Chimuri is near Cabinas Black Sands. Owner Mauricio Salazar, a Bribrí Indian, leads nature tours into the Indian reserves (see chap. 8).

Mauricio has been heading up a local group called the Talamanca Association of Ecotourism and Conservation (ATEC). *Welcome to Coastal Talamanca*, a booklet published by ATEC, is worth reading. It tells something of the history, traditions, and natural history of the zone and even tells you where you can get baked goods or a traditional Caribbean meal. The association promotes responsible tourist development, conservation of resources and traditions, and cultural interchange between visitors and local residents.

As you make your way south toward Uva Beach, one of the most beautiful on the coast, you will probably glimpse the brilliant flash of scarlet-rumped tanagers as they fly across the road.

Escape Caribeño has rooms beginning at $20 for a single. Two rooms with refrigerator and private bath go up to $45. Fans, breakfast available, but no restaurant. For reservations, call 58-3844 and leave a message.

Less than 3 miles (5 km) south of Puerto Viejo is Hotel Punta Cocles, an inviting place from which to explore the nearby parks and reserves or just sit and watch the toucans and parrots fly by. The complex of 60 rooms, open-air restaurant, and good-sized pool is surrounded by tall trees, with several well-maintained nature trails on the 25-acre (10 ha) property. Watch for small, brightly colored frogs, but do not touch them. Those bright colors usually warn of strong toxins. Guests can make one- to two-hour self-guided forays into the lush forest.

Nearby are white sand beaches where the hotel also has property. Local bilingual guides are available for regularly scheduled tours to Punta Uva, good for swimming and snorkeling; to Punta Mono (Monkey Point), land of howler monkeys, sloths, and a variety of birds; to Cahuita National Park; and for a walking tour of an Indian reserve.

Transportation can be arranged from San José, Limón, or Puerto Viejo, and bus service is also possible both from San José (on the direct Sixaola bus as far as El Cruce, where you can be picked up) and from Limón (the bus to Manzanillo passes the entrance). Rooms are in bungalows connected by covered walkways to the restaurant/pool area. Single $41, double $70, and bungalows for up to five persons, with kitchenettes, for $140. Private bath, hot water, private terraces, and both fans and air-conditioning. Credit cards accepted. Spanish, English, and German spoken. A nice feature is that the hotel rents binoculars as well as bicycles, rain ponchos, boogie boards, horses, and snorkeling equipment. Telephone 34-0306, fax 34-0014. Apartado 2692-1000, San José.

At Playa Chiquita, Miraflores Lodge, a bed and breakfast, has 8 rooms for up to twenty-five people, some with shared bath; $15 to $35 per person, including breakfast. Pamela Carpenter Navarro, the owner, is raising tropical flowers on an old cacao farm. She takes guests on trips to the Bribrí reserve and by boat into Panama and to the Gandoca-Manzanillo reserve and arranges visits that help guests learn about local culture, for example, to meet an Indian basket maker or to tour a cacao farm. English, French, and Spanish spoken. Telephone 33-5127, fax 33-5390. Apartado 155-2100, San José.

The Gandoca-Manzanillo Wildlife Refuge begins between Puerto Viejo and the town of Manzanillo, literally "the end of the line." No facilities yet exist to house visitors, but there is a restaurant in Manzanillo, and the lovely beaches can be enjoyed on a day visit.

▲ Orchids for sale outside of annual orchid show in San José (Photo by Ree Strange Sheck)

▼ Steam rises from hot waters at Balneario Tabacón near La Fortuna (Photo by Ree Strange Sheck)

Howler monkey, one of four monkey species in Costa Rica (Photo by Richard La Val)

▲ Author (a tall person) next to tree buttresses at Hacienda Barú near Dominical
(Photo by Jack Ewing)
▼ Gardens at private nature reserve Genesis II, where quetzals sometimes soar
(Photo by Ree Strange Sheck)

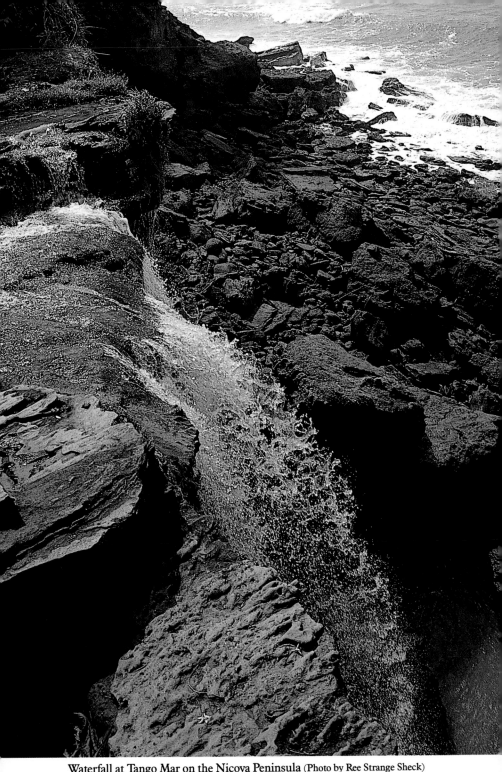

Waterfall at Tango Mar on the Nicoya Peninsula (Photo by Ree Strange Sheck)

▲ Silkmoth can flash its "eyes" to scare predators (Photo by Ree Strange Sheck)

▼ Gray fox, called *tigrillo*, in Monteverde (Photo by Ree Strange Sheck)

▲ *Guaria morada* orchid *(Cattleya skinneri)*—the national flower (Photo by Ree Strange Sheck)

▼ Scarlet macaw, called *lapa* in Spanish (Photo by Ree Strange Sheck)

This anteater, *oso hormiguero*, seems to wear a vest (Photo by Richard La Val)

▲ View of Ocotal Beach from Hotel El Ocotal in Guanacaste (Photo by Ree Strange Sheck)

▼ Golfito National Wildlife Refuge (Photo by Ree Strange Sheck)

7

National Parks, Biological Reserves, and Wildlife Refuges

After a breathtakingly beautiful multimedia presentation in which images of Costa Rica's flora and fauna inundated our senses from a giant screen, with three projectors going simultaneously, the ranger at Poás National Park asked if anyone in the audience had a comment. A middle-class Costa Rican in his fifties, there with his family, rose slowly from his seat. Persuaded by what he had just seen, he said, "With all the beauty and resources in this country, it must be the responsibility of every citizen to protect them."

In growing numbers, citizens of Costa Rica and the world feel the same. Today 12 percent of the country's land area is in parks and biological reserves; another 15 percent is legally set aside as forest reserves, protected zones, wildlife refuges, and Indian reserves.

Natural history travelers today follow in the footsteps of naturalists and explorers who have been drawn to the biological diversity of this small country since the mid-1800s. Five percent of all the plant and animal species known on the planet exist here, in a space that takes up three ten-thousandths of the earth's surface. The parks and reserves are showplaces for 10,000 species of vascular plants, 208 species of mammals, 850 species of birds, 160 species of amphibians, 220 species of reptiles, 350,000 species of insects, and 130 species of freshwater fish. Do not memorize these numbers; they are only mentioned to impress you. Even more impressive figures are coming over the next ten years with the efforts of the Biodiversity Institute to discover all the species of plants and animals in the country.

A new wrinkle in the conservation picture is the development of eight conservation areas that integrate the national parks, biological reserves, wildlife refuges, and Indian and forest reserves under a cooperative management program. The management committee for each also incorporates local and scientific interests, and that committee holds basic decision-making power. What this means to the natural history visitor is that administration is being decentralized, with more variation possible in the way parks and reserves are developed in each area, responsive to that area's needs and resources. The parks and reserves retain their names and identities.

The conservation areas are listed here so you will have an idea of which jurisdiction the parks, biological reserves, and wildlife refuges are in.

1. Amistad: La Amistad, Chirripó, Cahuita, Hitoy-Cerere, Gandoca-Manzanillo, Tapantí
2. Arenal: Caño Negro, Peñas Blancas
3. Central Volcanic Range: Braulio Carrillo, Poás Volcano, Irazú Volcano, Guayabo
4. Marine Parks and Reserves: Ballena, Caño Island, Coco Island
5. Guanacaste: Bolaños Island, Guanacaste, Santa Rosa, Rincón de la Vieja
6. Tempisque: Barra Honda, Lomas Barbudal, Palo Verde, Tamarindo, Pajaros, Negritos and Guayabo islands, Las Baulas, Curú, Ostional
7. Osa: Corcovado, Golfito
8. Tortuguero: Barra del Colorado, Tortuguero

The units also encompass private reserves such as Monteverde and La Selva along with forest reserves, Indian reserves, protected zones, and private landholdings. Some parks and reserves are considered satellite areas, like Carara, Cabo Blanco, and Manuel Antonio.

Emphasis since the park service was set up in the sixties has been on preserving areas before they are destroyed. Though money is still needed to purchase private holdings in the parks (about 17 percent is private), more attention now can be directed toward better protection of those areas and amenities for visitors.

No monorail systems transport people through this fantastic kingdom of plants and animals; a few parks offer roads, waterways wend through a handful, and trails are the primary access at the rest. Only Guanacaste National Park has overnight lodging built with nature travelers in mind, though travelers can sometimes stay in park ranger housing when space permits and in facilities built for researchers when there is an empty bed, such as at the Palo Verde Field Station or at the Sirena station in Corcovado. You usually need to bring your own bedding, towel, and soap; rangers are not in the hotel business. Some areas do allow camping. Housing from humble to fine may be available nearby. For day visits on your own, bring food and drink; there are no restaurants here or souvenir shops selling candy bars.

VOLUNTEERS IN PARKS

If you are open for a different kind of vacation—a working vacation—are eighteen years of age or older, and speak at least basic Spanish, the National Parks Service may have a deal for you. As a volunteer in the parks, you can work alongside rangers or in the San José office. Minimum time to volunteer is two and a half months.

Depending on skills and interests, you could lifeguard at park beaches during high tourist season, work on an archaeological dig, help fight forest fires, protect nesting sea turtles, cook, or maintain trails. Extra hands and minds are always needed in environmental education, from preparing materials to direct contact with school-children.

The work can be hard, the hours long, and living conditions rustic. You pay for your food and transportation (food about $4/day). You wash your own clothes in a pila. Small and remote areas are best for

those accustomed to a lonelier life—living with only one or two others. Some stations have no electricity, with the only contact by radio phone. Bring your own sheets. Both men and women are welcome, and there is no upper age limit.

What does a volunteer get out of all this? A rare opportunity to experience Costa Rica's parks in a way no tour or day visit can offer, to learn, to contribute to conservation efforts in a real way. Parks are understaffed and for the most part work within severe budget constraints.

If you are interested, write Stanley Argue-das, Asociación de Voluntarias de Parques Nacionales, Servicio de Parques Nacionales, Apartado 10104-1000, San José. He will send you information and an application. Allow at least three months for the exchange of letters necessary to arrange your stint. Telephone 33-4118, 33-4246. Fax 23-6963.

The men and women who work in the parks are delightful to know and will help you get oriented. However, staff is usually shorthanded, so do not expect a personal guided tour. If you call the park service or wildlife office in advance, tours with off-duty rangers can sometimes be arranged. You may be able to purchase a printed trail guide; if not, a map of trails is usually posted at the station where you pay admission.

Even parks where you will see the most people, like Poás or Manuel Antonio, are not usually crowded on weekdays except at Easter or Christmas. Your group may meet no one else on a trail through pristine country. Your chances of seeing the wildlife, of course, depend on you, too. Proceed quietly, be patient, and be alert. For safety's sake and to minimize impact, keep on the trails.

Hours vary a little, but most parks are open at least from 8:00 a.m. to 4:00 p.m. Admission is $1.60. The information center for the National Parks Service is at Parque Bolívar, the zoological park in San José, Calle 9, Avenida 11. Hours are 8:00 a.m. to 3:30 p.m.; closed Mondays. The center has maps, posters, postcards, and some pamphlets on the parks and biological reserves. It is scheduled to move to the parks office in 1992. Check. Call for general information at 33-5673. To contact individual parks and reserves about overnight space or availability of guides or horses, call 33-4160 or 33-4070. The staff person has radio contact with the parks and reserves. The National Parks Service is located at Calle 25, Avenidas 8/10, next to the Ministry of Natural Resources, Energy, and Mines.

For information on the wildlife refuges, call Vida Silvestre (the National Wildlife Directorate) at 33-8112. The Vida Silvestre office has no convenient street numbers, but any taxi driver can find it with these directions: behind the Santa Teresita Church, go 100 meters south and 150 meters east. There is a sign in front.

The region of the country where each park, reserve, or refuge is located is noted, so you can read about accommodations and the surrounding area in that region in chapter 6 or look up private reserves that offer accommodations in that area in chapter 8. Where scheduled tours provide access, that is mentioned; look for specifics in chapter 9 on companies specializing in nature tours.

To help you plan your trip, the brief descriptions here will let you know how easy or difficult it is to get to the site, what visitor facilities are there, and highlight some of the magic you will encounter.

Parks

La Amistad Costa Rica-Panama International Park (South)

La Amistad means "friendship," and it is designated an international park because it was created with an understanding between Costa Rica and Panama that a counterpart park would be established on the Panamanian side of the border. Though not much has happened on the other side, Costa Ricans are convinced of the soundness of the idea, so much so that the seed has been planted for a similar protected area on the northern border—a Peace Park along a part of the Nicaragua-Costa Rica boundary.

La Amistad is a gigantic national park, 479,199 acres (193,929 ha), big enough to sustain a healthy population of animals that require large areas for hunting and reproduction, such as the tapir, jaguar, puma, and harpy eagle. Probably the largest population of resplendent quetzals in the country resides in this refuge of rain forest, cloud forest, and páramo, along with at least 400 other bird species. Epiphytes abound in the tall cloud forests, where you can see oak, elm, magnolia, and sweet cedar. More than 130 varieties of orchids have been found in the southwest corner of the park alone. Spread across the rugged Talamanca Mountain Range, the highest range in Costa Rica, the park protects not only endangered plants and animals but important watersheds.

You will have to bring more than your binoculars to enjoy this fantasy land of geology and wildlife. This is backpacker territory, for adventure travelers. Much of the park has yet to be explored; trails are limited and unmarked. Camping is allowed. Contact the National Parks Service about a visit and inquire about the possibility of horse rental or hiring a local guide. If you are staying in the area (San Isidro, San Vito), a day trip would be a possibility, just to get a taste of it.

Elevation ranges from about 650 to 11,644 feet (200 to 3,549 m), and temperatures vary accordingly, with upper altitudes cool and rainy, sometimes cold.

Park administration is at Las Tablas, about 25 miles (40 km) northwest of San Vito de Coto Brus. When you call parks, also ask about the condition of that road. The highway is good to San Vito, which is about 5 hours from San José near the Panamanian border.

Ballena National Marine Park (South)

Created in 1990, the Ballena park was established to protect marine resources. It encompasses 10,378 acres (4,200 ha) of coastline, islands, and ocean. The coastal land is about 6 miles (10 km) long between Punta Uvita and Punta Piñuela on the Pacific coast south of Dominical. This area is rich in well-preserved mangroves.

Ballena Island and the smaller rocky protrusions called Las Tres Hermanas are nesting sites for frigate birds, pelicans, and boobies. The park gets its name, Ballena, from the hump-backed whales that visit here from December to March.

Park personnel have worked with local fishermen to change their methods to help protect the resources. It is the first marine park in Costa Rica to involve a fishing community. There is a guard station, but the park is not really developed yet for large-scale tourism. Visitors can, however, snorkel or dive in the protected area or visit by boat.

From the shore south of Dominical looking toward islands in Ballena National Marine Park (Photo by Ree Strange Sheck)

Barra Honda National Park (Northwest)

The main attraction at Barra Honda National Park is a network of caves through a peak that once was a coral reef beneath the sea. Located just west of where the Tempisque River flows into the Gulf of Nicoya at its northern end, Barra Honda still holds many secrets. Of the forty-two caves discovered, only nineteen have been explored. The human remains and pre-Columbian artifacts discovered have yet to yield their stories. But the exploration that has been done has revealed several large caverns adorned with stalactites, stalagmites, pearls, soda straws, columns, popcorn, and other intriguing formations. Nature's underground artistry is most profuse in the Terciopelo (fer-de-lance) Cave, so named because a snake of this species was found smashed on its floor by early speleologists. Terciopelo contains the Organ; when gently tapped, this columnar formation resounds with different tones. The deepest cave is almost 790 feet (240 m) beneath the surface.

The shafts into these caves are mostly vertical, and there are no elevators to carry you down or caverns lit with colored lights. This is not for the fainthearted or infirm. Descent to the caverns is straight down a metal ladder almost 90 feet (27 m). Back up the same way. If you want to descend into the caves, call eight days beforehand to make arrangements: 68-5580. A local community association conducts the tours on weekends and holidays. Charge for guide and equipment is about $45 for up to eight people. This community group has an agreement with the park to maintain the trails, offer tours, and operate a camping area located in the forest. Monkeys move through the trees around the small camp sites. The association has purchased property adjacent to the park entrance. It obtained a grant to build three cabins for visitors, a small restaurant, and store. This is an example of park neighbors protecting and benefiting from the area protected. The men and women in the association are enthusiastic, planning to open up trails on their property as resources allow and to add more cabins.

For noncavers, the 5,671-acre (2,295-ha) park offers aboveground trails that lead to a view point overlooking the Gulf of Nicoya and Chira Island to the east, a tall evergreen forest, and waterfalls over naturally formed travertine dams. The local guides reel off a list of fascinating trail names: El Hojache (a native tree), Las Cascadas (waterfalls), Los Mesones (goes to the springs), a la Cima Hedionda (Stinking Peak)—twelve in all. The summit of Barra Honda Peak (1,312 ft., 400 m), pocked with holes large and small and decorated with sculptured rock, hints of the artistry in caves below.

Below-ground wildlife includes bats, insects, blind salamanders, fish, and snails, while aboveground visitors might expect to see the white-faced monkey, Amazonian skunk, long-nosed armadillo, white-nosed coati, coyote, and orange-fronted parakeet. Vegetation corresponds to the tropical dry forest, moist province transition zone, with mostly deciduous vegetation.

Average annual rainfall is from 59 to 79 inches (1,500 to 2,000 mm) and average temperature is 81°F (27°C). The highest elevation is 1,886 feet (575 m).

To get to the park from San José, take the Inter-American Highway, turning off about 6 miles (10 km) before Cañas and taking the Tempisque Ferry. Go through Quebrada Honda and Tres Esquinas to Barra Honda. From Liberia, take Highway 21 south and turn north just before the town of Mansión to get to the park. There is a bus from Nicoya to Santa Ana, a little more than a mile from the entrance (2 km).

Braulio Carrillo National Park (Central Valley)

Braulio Carrillo is a symphony in green. Waterfalls, deep canyons, and raging rivers lend their tones. The exciting part is that the concert begins only twenty minutes from San José—and on a paved road.

While roads through virgin forest usually spell ecological disaster, this particular road spurred creation of a national park that now encompasses 108,969 acres (44,099 ha) of majestic beauty. Braulio Carrillo was born out of the conflict between the need for a new highway to the Atlantic and the determination to preserve the largely primary forest it would pass through. The park was established in 1978, and the road through this rugged, largely untouched land opened in 1987. Most of the traffic between San José and Limón now passes on a ribbon laid down through this awesome landscape.

The park offers many levels of enjoyment; just driving through is a thrill. View points provide safe places for vehicles to pull off. A five-minute trail I know leads from highway to primeval beauty, complete with waterfall and morpho butterflies that flutter up and down above the sparkling stream. A *tepezcuintle*, the wonderful name used in Spanish for the paca, once jumped from a cave hidden by vegetation into the pool where we had just been quietly swimming and disappeared behind the waterfall. It is a timeless, hushed place—one of nature's gifts. A park ranger at the administration center near the Zurquí tunnel told me about the trail; ask him to tell you. I trust you to treat its delicate beauty with respect.

At the other end of the spectrum is a trail that reaches from Barva Volcano, one of two volcanoes in the park, through a protected zone added in 1986 to join Braulio Carrillo with land protected by the Organization of Tropical Studies' La Selva Biological Station, all the way to Puerto Viejo de Sarapiquí. Refuges along the way offer a place to camp overnight on the multiday journey. Allow at least four days. The journey goes from 9,514 feet (2,900 m) to 112 feet (34 m), so perhaps how long it takes to do the trip depends on which end of the trail you start on. This is the only place in the country where an altitudinal variation of this magnitude is protected, which is extremely important for species that migrate, including some of the 347 bird species identified so far.

Braulio Carrillo is one of the beneficiaries of the Foresta project funded by the U.S. Agency for International Development in 1989 to lend a hand in development of some of the parks in the Central Volcanic Mountain Range and in improved protection for them. A major component of the $22.5 million project is to promote ecologically and economically sound forestry techniques and management in buffer areas around the parks as well as reforestation projects. For the visitor to Braulio Carrillo, the project means more trails, additional view points, and a genuine visitor center. With proximity to the burgeoning population in San José and nearby towns, the park offers a valuable opportunity for environmental education to resident and tourist alike.

Try to reach the park early to reduce chances of fog narrowing your views. Dropping into the lowlands, you may see a sloth in a tree alongside the road. Watch the *guarumo* (cecropia) trees in particular (see natural history information, below). Other animals that live in

LIFE IN A CECROPIA TREE

Discovery of relationships between trees, other plants, insects, and animals opens a window on understanding the intricacies of life in the tropical world. A symbiotic relationship that has evolved between the cecropia tree, called guarumo *in Spanish, and Azteca ants gives us a glimpse of one of these interrelationships.*

The cecropia tree, of the mulberry family, grows throughout the country at elevations up to approximately 6,500 feet (2,000 m). It is called a pioneer species because it is among the first to come back on cleared land or in a forest opening caused by the fall of a big tree. It grows rapidly and requires a lot of light. You will notice it along road cuts. Look for a tree with a ringed trunk that resembles bamboo; leaves are larged and lobed, resembling hands.

Because it is a relatively short-lived tree, maybe twenty years, the cecropia has not developed protection such as toxic leaves (longer-lived trees tend to have some form of chemical protection). Azteca ants, however, make their homes in its hollow stems. Some species of these aggressive ants, who tend to live in large colonies, swarm out

over the tree at the slightest disturbance, attack unsuspecting caterpillars, other ants, and even a lightly placed hand on the tree. (Azteca ants bite: they do not inject venom with a stinger.) Aztecas do not seem to bother birds, who eat the fruits and scatter the tree's seeds, but they zero in on epiphytes and vines—chewing off any vine that starts up the trunk. In return, the tree provides glycogen-rich food bodies at the base of each leaf stalk for the ants to feed on and hollow stems for them to live in.

The ant patrols are not effective against all predators. Sloths are among the animals that like cecropia leaves and fruit. You are more apt to spot them in a cecropia tree than others they feed on because of the openness of its growth. Apparently, the sloth's heavy fur gives him some protection. Howler monkeys also eat in cecropia trees.

Countless symbiotic relationships exist in the natural world. Some we know about; others remain to be discovered. Even in this tree-ant relationship, all the answers are not yet in on why the tree has developed lodging and food to attract these ants or the degree of protection the ants actually give.

the park include three species of monkey—also frequently spotted at lower elevations—tapir, jaguar, kinkajou, deer, and ocelot. You are not as likely to see these. The resplendent quetzal knows these forests, as do eagles, umbrella birds, trogons, hawks, curassows, and guans. Bromeliads and orchids, among the 6,000 species of plant life found here, adorn the trees. This is a good place to see the poor man's umbrella (*sombrilla del pobre*), a plant whose leaves grow up to 7 feet (2 m) across. People caught out in the rain in the countryside have used them for protection. But please do not cut one in a national park; it is prohibited. If you are caught driving in the rain, which averages 177 inches (4,500 mm) a year, enjoy the waterfalls that pour down the roadside and keep your eyes open for landslides.

Primary access to Braulio Carrillo is at the stations at either end of the highway through the park (Zurquí and Quebrada Gonzales). Some people start at the Barva Volcano station near Sacramento; there are nature travel companies in San José that offer hiking on Barva and day visits to the park. For the entrance near La Virgen, off the highway to Puerto Viejo de Sarapiquí, four-wheel drive is recommended. Since new trails are being developed, call the national parks office for current information on which entry point best suits your plans. Remember to stay on trails, and check with rangers before going into the backcountry; a guide is recommended. Vegetation is extremely dense in this rugged region. Experienced hikers have gotten lost; as one Costa Rican put it, the forest has eaten several small planes and a few people.

Cahuita National Park (Caribbean)

Take white sands, coconut palms, a coral reef, the wreck of an eighteenth-century slave ship just offshore, and clear Caribbean waters; add to these at least 123 species of fish, an abundance of bird life, and an assortment of other animals from monkeys to caimans. The winning combination is known as Cahuita National Park, with park headquarters just 27 miles (44 km) southeast of Limón at Cahuita.

The 593-acre (240-ha) reef encircles Cahuita Point, forming a rich undersea garden of 35 species of varicolored corals some 1,640 feet (500 m) from the shore. Brightly colored fish such as rock beauty, blue parrotfish, and angelfish swim among the formations. There are sea urchins, barracudas, moray eels, sharks, lobsters, sea cucumbers, and green turtles that feed on the expanse of turtle grass.

There is trouble in paradise, however. Increased erosion from deforestation in the Talamanca Mountains has had an impact on Cahuita. Silt carried to the sea by the Río Estrella is affecting the reef, a vivid reminder of the distance trouble can travel from a mismanaged forest.

Snorkeling and scuba diving are allowed (the park does not rent equipment), and tours out of the town of Cahuita offer glass-bottomed boats. Damage from the 1991 earthquake forced closure of the

Puerto Vargas station. Check at the park entrance in Cahuita to see if camping and hiking in Puerto Vargas are once again possible. Ask also about the possibility of guided walks. The park has a 4-mile (7-km) nature trail where visitors can experience the exuberance of tropical moist forest vegetation. The abundance of land and sea birds makes it a bird-watcher's delight. Troops of up to twenty-five howler monkeys roam the area, and coatis and raccoons are abundant. You might also encounter a three-toed anteater, an otter, a four-toed armadillo, or a three-toed sloth. Total area of the park is 2,639 acres (1,068 ha).

Colors of the sea on a sunny day run from almost transparent near the white sand to bright green, turquoise, and aquamarine. At some points, it is possible to wade quite a distance in water not above knee level. Some areas have strong currents where swimming is not safe; rangers can advise you. In general, the first 400 meters after the park entrance are the most dangerous.

The park receives just less than 118 inches (3,000 mm) of rain a year, and the distinction between the wet and dry seasons is not as clear as in the Central Valley. Visibility around the reef, however, is better from December to April.

Tour companies in Cahuita and San José offer both day trips and multiday options. Lodging is available along the route from Limón to the towns of Cahuita and Puerto Viejo and south; see chapter 6.

Chirripó National Park (South)

Geologists, botanists, mountain climbers, biologists, adventure seekers, and just plain nature lovers make their way to Chirripó National Park, 94 miles (151 km) south of San José near San Isidro de El General. The park contains the highest peak in the country, Chirripó Peak at 12,529 feet (3,819 m), glacial lakes, rivers, and habitats from mixed forests, fern groves, and swamps to oak forests and páramo.

On a clear day, the visitor can see both oceans from the peak. There are cloudy and clear days throughout the year, but the driest time of the year in this region with an annual rainfall of up to 276 inches (7,000 mm) is February and March. Some longtime visitors say, however, that they cannot resist trips in the rainier times when the exuberance of the vegetation defies description.

At whatever time of year, take warm clothes. Though maximums in the 80s (°F) are possible, count on cold at night in upper elevations. Extremes between day and night can vary by 43°F (24°C); the lowest temperature recorded is 16°F (−9°C). You can wake up to a frosty world, finding ice on lakes and stream banks.

Marked trails traverse the 123,921-acre (50,150-ha) park. A few cabins offer bunks, a wood-burning stove, and a table to hikers along mountain trails. Be sure to carry enough liquids; while the ascent to the summit appears daunting, it is not so difficult if taken slowly and carefully. Allow at least ten hours to get to the top.

Endangered species protected at Chirripó include margay, puma, ocelot, jaguar, tapir, and quetzal. Birds and animals are more abundant in the forest zones, though there are hummingbirds even in the high páramo. Plants seem to cover every inch of trees in the cloud forest—orchids, bromeliads, mosses, ferns. On the way to the summit you pass through seven distinct forest types. The higher you climb, the more stunted the vegetation.

Names like Savanna of the Lions, Valley of the Rabbits, and Moraine Valley hint of what early explorers found when they scaled these heights (the lions being pumas). Discovery awaits today's visitor to Chirripó National Park, a place where you can look down on rainbows.

The entrance to the park is 9 miles (15 km) northeast of San Isidro through Rivas to San Gerardo. Buses run from San Isidro to San Gerardo. The hardy inhabitants of San Gerardo have been known to actually run up the mountain and are often sought out as guides. If you are going independently, call the park service for information about guides or pack horses and to reserve space in a shelter. No open fires are allowed.

Coco Island or Isla de Coco (South)

A small green island in the Pacific, more than 370 miles (500 km) off the Pacific coast of Costa Rica, Coco was an early haven for explorers, privateers, pirates, and whalers because of its abundant fresh water supply and its coconuts; *coco* is Spanish for coconut. Today, it attracts treasure hunters, scientists, and natural history travelers.

More than 500 expeditions have uncovered only a few tantalizing pieces of three treasure caches believed to lie hidden on Coco Island.

Some believe that stories of these treasures fired the imagination of Robert Louis Stevenson for his *Treasure Island*.

Scientists and tourists come in search of other riches: many endemic species have evolved on this isolated piece of land; its wild beauty encompasses both spectacular inland waterfalls and waterfalls that plunge into the sea, dense vegetation, and underwater caves and coral gardens. Endemic species, those that occur nowhere else, include 70 of the 235 plant species identified so far, 2 species of lizards, 64 of its 362 species of insects, and 3 bird species: Cocos finch, Cocos flycatcher, and Cocos cuckoo. There is an endemic palm named for Franklin Roosevelt, who visited the island four times. The island is an important nesting site for seagulls, noddies, and boobies. Another nesting bird is called in Spanish the *Espíritu Santo*, or Holy Spirit. A small white bird, it often hovers in the air, unafraid, a few feet above a visitor's head. Its more prosaic name in English is white tern.

A fragile environment maintains this living laboratory for the study of evolutionary processes. Species introduced by man, such as pigs, deer, rats, coffee, and papaya, endanger the delicate ecological balance. Historically, the island's isolation minimized human impact; its inclusion in the park system is aimed at its protection in a shrinking world. Today fishing in its waters and increased tourism are having an impact on this special place.

A rugged coastline of high cliffs make access possible at only two bays, Chatham and Wafer. Inscriptions dating back to the 1600s on the rocky coast at Chatham provide evidence that sailors sought safe harbor here as well. Visitors are urged to stay on the trails through the rain forest. Though the island is small (4.7 by 2 miles, 7.5 by 3.3 km), its rugged terrain and dense vegetation call for caution. In 1989, a tourist became separated from her tour group and has never been found.

There is a park station on Coco Island with radio contact. Permission from the parks service is necessary for a visit. Most travelers come as part of an organized tour; see the chapter on tour companies. There are no overnight facilities for visitors on land.

Rainfall averages up to 276 inches (7,000 mm) a year. Highest point on the island is Iglesias Peak, 2,080 feet (634 m), and upper elevations are cloud forest; epiphytes abound. Of volcanic origin, the island con-

tains volcanic rocks that are two million years old. It is the only out-
crop of the Cocos Ridge, a chain of volcanoes that reaches from Costa
Rica almost to the Galápagos Islands. Total area of the park, sea and
land, is 5,930 acres (2,400 ha).

Corcovado National Park (South)

Corcovado, on the Osa Peninsula in southwest Costa Rica, is a remote
park. It is a big park—103,260 acres (41,789 ha). And it is a fantastic park, one of the most biologically diverse in the world.

The administrator of the park told me he had once counted 150
scarlet macaws flying in two groups near the Madrigal River. Herds
of white-lipped peccaries have sometimes treed visitors along trails.
Five hundred species of trees, one-fourth of all those found in Costa
Rica, live here, including probably the tallest in the country, a ceiba
or kapok tree that soars to 230 feet (70 m). Eight different habitat
types exist, including montane forest, cloud forest, alluvial plains forest, swamp, palm forest, mangrove, and rocky and sandy vegetation.

When you visit, you are likely to encounter scientific researchers
studying everything from how jacamars know not to eat toxic butterflies to the life habits of the squirrel monkey to why certain species
from South America are found here when they are absent in Panama
and the Atlantic side of Costa Rica. Researchers often work out of the
Sirena Station, which is where overnight tourists generally lodge on
a space-available basis. If you are on trails in the park, you may not
see anyone else. Three trails from Sirena offer 1- to 2-mile (2.5-3.5
km) forays into the forest.

The beach along the Pacific adds a marine component to the park.
Sperm whales have been sighted offshore and marine turtles nest on
its beaches. There is a live coral reef at Salsipuedes. Among endangered species protected are 5 species of cats (including the jaguar),
giant anteaters, sloths, and the harpy eagle, the largest bird of prey
in the world (last seen in 1977). Identified so far are 400 species of
birds and 139 species of mammals.

Though its remoteness and heavy cover of vegetation protected the
area now encompassed by the park, Corcovado does have some interesting human history. Local lore holds that Cubans trained along the
beaches before the Bay of Pigs and that Sandinistas sought its isola-

tion for training for a brief period before President Somoza of Nicaragua was overthrown in 1979. Miners in the 1980s have invaded its confines to pan for gold, and though evicted in 1986, they continue to trickle in to seek their fortunes. Small farms and a forestry operation had made inroads in the virgin forest before the park was established in 1975.

Much of the terrain is hilly, rising from sea level to 1,932 feet (782 m). December through March are the driest months; rainfall is 197 inches (5,000 mm) a year in the mountains. The average temperature is 77°F (25°C).

Park headquarters are in Puerto Jiménez across the Golfo Dulce from Golfito; you can call there directly at 78-5036, fax 78-5116. Camping is allowed, and space is sometimes available at Sirena or one of the other park stations. Bring mosquito netting. Overnight tours frequently fly into Sirena or Carate, and day tours of the park are offered by several private nature reserves or lodges in the area. Bridges have brought year-round access to Puerto Jiménez via road: turn off the Inter-American Highway for Rincón. From park headquarters, access is still some distance away. You can walk or ride to La Palma and then take the trail to the Los Patos Station on the eastern edge of the park, about a two-hour trek. Once inside the park, trails between the stations range from 4 to 12.5 miles long (6 to 20 km). A nice booklet on Corcovado for less than $1 contains maps and trail information and is available at park headquarters.

Guanacaste National Park (Northwest)

Established in 1989, Guanacaste encompasses dry tropical forest to rain forest and stretches from lowlands along the northern Inter-American Highway to mountains of the Guanacaste Range. It contains 80,337 acres (32,512 ha). It is a crucial piece in a puzzle of ecological interdependence being fitted together in northwestern Costa Rica.

Preservation and restoration of one of the last remaining tropical dry forests, protected in adjoining Santa Rosa National Park, was an impetus for forming Guanacaste National Park. Tropical dry forests once stretched along the Pacific from central Mexico to Panama, but most have fallen prey to agricultural and residential use. Studies at

Santa Rosa on the forest's seasonal patterns, distinct life forms, and interactions between plants and animals helped determine the size and habitats necessary to sustain healthy populations of species. Seasonal migration of some of the animal life from Santa Rosa to rain forest in mountains to the east meant protecting that forest as well. Animals are a crucial component in the life cycle of the forest as seed dispersers. As the story unfolds, even the place of insects in the food chain cannot be overlooked.

The idea grew from preservation to regeneration, allowing the original dry forest to reinvade large areas cleared for agriculture and pasture, a long-term project its initiators will not see completed in their lifetimes. But they and natural history visitors can measure the progress of this innovative experiment with each season. Environmental education programs for visitors, who range from local schoolchildren to foreign travelers, communicate what is being learned.

Guanacaste is big enough to maintain the needed habitats for plants and animals that have historically lived in the area and to open up areas for intensive use by visitors and researchers. The good news for nature lovers is that three biological stations inside the park offer accommodations for tourists as well as researchers.

Cacao Biological Station sits in cloud forest at 3,609 feet (1,100 m). Cacao Volcano, 5,443 feet (1,659 m), looms above. Accommodations are rustic: no electricity, cold-water showers. Five dormitories can house forty people; bedding is provided, but towels are not. Access involves a one-hour trek by foot or horseback. Lodging is $5 per person, and meals cost $12 a day. From the high station there is a clear view of Santa Rosa and the coast. Virgin forest behind holds tapir, cats, bellbirds, orchids, bromeliads. One trail leads to the top of Cacao. Another leads to a second biological station, Maritza, about three hours away by foot, less on horseback.

Maritza is also accessible by a road that so far is best for four-wheel-drive vehicles. I can personally attest to that, having slid the entire 10.5 miles (17 km) after a serious downpour. Maritza lies on the skirts of Orosí Volcano in a windier, cooler area. A modern facility, the station can house thirty-five people, both tourists and researchers, with shared baths. Lodging is $12 a day, meals $15.

Carlos de la Rosa, resident biologist researcher, has established a well-equipped laboratory for water studies here: the rivers are pure in this high, remote place. He is studying aquatic insects in these unpolluted waters, gathering data that will help us understand what changes take place as purity decreases.

In forests around the rivers, wildlife is abundant: toucans, bellbirds, peccaries, sun bitterns, monkeys. Jaguars have been known to kill cattle in the area. I arrived too late to see a band of fifteen peccaries that had appeared on the trail near the laboratory that morning. Coatis frequently visit the station. Less than two hours from Maritza by foot is Llano de los Indios, an open pasture with petroglyphs carved in volcanic stone. The more than eighty pieces of rock art are both abstract and representative.

In the Atlantic watershed, Pitilla Biological Station can lodge thirty-two people. Both the facilities and the road leading to it are rustic; there is no electricity, and four-wheel drive is necessary. Lodging is $5 per day, and meals are $12. Views from Pitilla include the Lake of Nicaragua, Orosí Volcano, and the rain forest around it.

All three stations have radio contact, and horses are usually available at $5 per hour. The fee for camping is less than $1 a day. Call the Guanacaste Conservation Area for information: 69-5598. Transportation can sometimes be arranged from Santa Rosa.

Volunteers from the University of Costa Rica are working with park staff to create an ecological museum at Agua Buena near the highway that turns off the Inter-American for Santa Cecilia. Located in the old customs house once used to check cattle coming in from Nicaragua, the museum will give a view of life and culture in the province of Guanacaste.

Visitors are also welcome at a nursery for native species at Pocosol. While much of the open parkland will be reforested naturally, some sites demonstrate reforestation technology with native species.

Nearest lodging outside the park would be at Liberia or some of the private nature reserves in the area. Some one-day tours are offered by hotels in Liberia and along the north Pacific coast, and nature tour companies in San José offer Guanacaste trips. Access is via the Inter-American Highway north of Liberia. Several buses a day run from San José to Liberia, a trip of about four hours; the bus from San José to La Cruz passes in front of the park. However, you will not see

Carved monolith at Guayabo National Monument (Photo by Ree Strange Sheck)

much from the highway. Trails for visitors are mainly from the stations located inside the park.

Guayabo National Monument (Central Valley)

Guayabo is the blue morpho butterfly, the yellow flash of a Montezuma oropendola flying through the tall trees, flowing water, patches of profuse pink impatiens, ancient carved stones. It is the quiet of centuries-old ruins hidden in the rain forest.

The only archaeological park in the country, Guayabo protects the remains of a city that flourished and disappeared before the arrival of the Spaniards. People may have occupied the area as early as 1000 B.C.; at its peak, Guayabo is estimated to have had a population of as many as 10,000 people. Small rural villages perhaps supplied labor and revenue to this religious and political center. There was little new building after A.D. 800, and the site was abandoned by A.D. 1400.

Visitors today see cobbled roads (*calzadas*), stone-lined tanks to store water, open and covered aqueducts that carried water through the site (many still in use), and mounds (*montículos*) with stone-covered bases. Information signs at the park depict conical houses believed to have been built of wood and palm leaves on the mounds. Trails lead past covered and open tombs, plundered before the park was established. Stylized forms of a jaguar and caiman decorate a striking monolith. Petroglyphs (46 so far) picture birds and animals as well as art whose meaning has yet to be deciphered.

A five-year conservation and excavation project begun in August 1989 may shed light on some of the mysteries of people and place. While only 10 acres (4 ha) of the archaeological site have been excavated to date, the project will increase the excavated area to half of the almost 50-acre (20-ha) site.

Among items found in the area are golden bells, carved stone tables, roasted corn kernels, beautiful pottery, a copper and gold frog, and a sacrificial stone. Some of the works of art are exhibited at the National Museum in San José. In 1991, four fragments of Nicoya pottery were discovered which allowed precise dating—A.D. 1350. According to park administrator and archaeologist Rodolfo Tenorio, the find indicates contact between Guayabo and Nicoya at that time which perhaps went beyond commercial interchange. One hypothesis is that the contact was at a diplomatic/political level.

In addition to the archaeological site, Guayabo protects the only remaining primary forest in the province of Cartago, accounting for 22 percent of the park's 538 acres (218 ha). Orchids—more than 80 varieties—and other epiphytes adorn the trees; toucans are present, as are chachalacas, woodpeckers, and brown jays (ticos call them *piapias* and say they are the scouts of the forest, their warning cries signaling that an intruder is near). Notice the abundance of long, hanging nests built by oropendolas. Mammals include sloths, coatis, rabbits, squirrels, and armadillos.

Local guides have been trained to accompany visitors on Sendero de los Montículos, the interpretive trail that leads through the archaeological site and to a mirador with a fantastic view of the ruins below, the valley where Turrialba lies, and mountain peaks. Their English is limited but improving, and their enthusiasm and knowledge about natural history and the ruins comes across in any language. Guides are required on this trail; the fee is less than $.50. Guayabo is open from 8:00 a.m. to 4:00 p.m. daily, but the last

MONKEY BUSINESS

Four species of monkeys live in Costa Rica; the white-faced capuchin (called cara blanca *in Spanish), the howler (*congo*), spider (*mono colorado *or* araña*), and the squirrel (*tití *or* ardilla*). The word for monkey in Spanish is* mono. *Howlers, the most abundant, are fruit and leaf eaters, as are the acrobatic spider monkeys, while the capuchins and squirrel monkeys eat everything from fruits to insects to lizards.*

The small squirrel monkey, or tití, is found only in the southern Pacific lowlands of the country. At Manuel Antonio National Park, Grace Wong, a student in the wildlife program of the National University in Heredia, is doing a study of the titís in this area, which are a subspecies endemic to Costa Rica. Another subspecies, farther south, is endemic to Costa Rica and Panama, though few remain in Panama.

So far she has identified nine troops of about thirty individuals each. Her primary study group of twenty-eight monkeys forages and moves over an area of about 150 acres (60 ha). From May to October, when fruit is abundant, the titís have more time to rest and play, but by November they spend most of the day looking for food. They are up at 5:00 a.m. and retire for the night about 6:00 p.m.

The young are born from the end of February to end of March, one birth per pregnancy. Females have young every two years. Babies are carried for their first three months, with other adults helping the mother by taking a turn. In Grace's study group, there are four male adults, six female adults, and the rest are young.

When food is scarcer, there is some competition between capuchins and titís. Grace says that when there are clashes, the smaller tití leaves; she has seen a capuchin grab a tití and throw it to the ground. When food is plentiful, they eat together. In Manuel Antonio, natural enemies of the tití are mainly boa constrictors and tyras, minklike animals.

Though human activity does not seem to drive titís away, Grace is concerned about tourism development in areas outside protected Manuel Antonio National Park. Monkeys do not recognize those man-made boundaries. Part of her project is to work with owners of land the monkeys travel through and forage from, asking them to leave patches of forest—corridors—so healthy populations of the monkeys can continue.

---

guided walk begins at 3:00 p.m. A new trail that is open Monday to Friday allows visitors to watch excavation of a road that ran from Guayabo to an outlying area. The trail requires about one and a half hours. Visitors can walk alone on the nature trail, which makes a short loop or a longer one down to the river. It can be muddy in the wet season. Rainfall averages 138 inches (3,500 mm) and the average temperature is 68°F (20°C). Highest point in the park is 3,609 feet (1,100 m).

Do not miss the visitor center across the road from the park entrance. The nearby camping area is revamped to provide ten individualized camping sites scattered among the trees and one group camping area. There are bathrooms and potable water.

Nearest lodging outside the park is a ten-minute walk away in the town of Guayabo; hotels in Turrialba are thirty minutes away (11 mi., 18 km) by paved road. Tour companies in Turrialba and San José offer trips. Bus service from San José to Turrialba is frequent and good—just over two hours for the 86 miles (138 km). There is bus service from Turrialba to Guayabo once a day six days a week. Taxi fare between the two runs about $16 one way.

Irazú Volcano National Park (Central Valley)

Irazú Volcano has a history of showing off. Its awesome power is evident long before one reaches its impressive craters. Near Cartago, notice the devastation from the most recent major eruptions, which occurred from 1963 to 1965. Whole areas were buried in mud, floods were significant, and volcanic rock still peppers the countryside. As you travel along the paved road to the park, give the volcano credit for the rich soils that now produce cabbages, potatoes, onions, and grasslands for dairy cows.

The highest peak in the Central Volcanic Range, Irazú reaches 11,260 feet (3,432 m). It has been known to send ash as far away as the Nicoya Peninsula; steam clouds have billowed 1,640 feet (500 m) high and debris has shot up 984 feet (300 m). The rumbling giant in 1963 tossed boulders weighing several tons from its innards and sent earth tremors to rattle buildings miles away.

Today, with Irazú in a sometimes restless resting phase, visitors can ride right to the top to a lunar landscape that muffles its fiery nature, thin streams of steam or gas and occasional earth tremors reminding us that it is not dead; it only sleeps. People walk along the rims of the craters, peering down into a bright green lake at the bottom of one, almost 1,000 feet (300 m) below. Volcanic grays and blacks are highlighted by swatches of reds and oranges in the steep sides. The diameter of the main crater is 3,445 feet (1,050 m).

Tenacious plants dot the largely empty areas around the craters,

Lunar landscape at Irazú Volcano National Park (Photo by Ree Strange Sheck)

some bravely sporting bright flowers. On slopes, where the green of secondary growth gives testimony to nature's powers of recovery, old, barren branches rise like ghostly fingers above the new forest.

Animal life is scarce at the park as a result of both human activity and eruptions. Where cougar and jaguar once thrived, today you may see rabbits, coyotes, armadillos, or even a tiger cat. Hummingbirds are numerous, and you might spot a volcano junco, mountain robin, ruddy woodcreeper, or ant-eating woodpecker.

For clearest views and a chance to see both oceans from that lofty place, go early. I have a memory of Irazú at sunset, however, that I would not trade. Buffeted by a cold wind, I stood on a narrow path between two craters and watched as the setting sun lit swirling clouds of mist with rich tones of orange and gold.

Whatever time of day you visit, take a jacket and something for rain, just in case. The average temperature is 45°F (7.3°C), with the lowest recorded temperature 26°F (−3°C). When it is cold, it is very, very cold. Frost is possible from December through February. Annual rainfall is 85 inches (2,158 mm). Park area is 5,706 acres (2,309 ha).

Irazú Volcano is an easy 1½-hour drive from San José, taking the main highway to Cartago. Watch for signs in Cartago telling where to turn for the park. Up on the mountain, there is a pleasant view point with picnic facilities where you can safely pull off the road and drink in the expansive view of the valley below and peaks beyond. Most tour companies in San José offer trips to Irazú, some in conjunction with a visit to the Lankester Gardens, Cartago, or the Orosi Valley.

Las Baulas de Guanacaste National Park (Northwest)

Protection of nesting areas for the big leatherback turtles (*baulas*) spurred creation of this park in 1991. Leatherbacks are the largest sea turtles; female adults can be 6 feet (1.8 m) long and weigh more than 1,300 pounds (590 kg). Peak nesting months along the beaches in the park are November through January, when as many as 200 females may come ashore per night. I spoke with a woman who had personally counted 198 sets of tracks from one night. Protection here gets a boost from Boy Scout and Girl Scout groups that camp on the beach and protect it to discourage egg poachers.

These beaches attract one of the largest populations of leatherbacks in the world. Smaller numbers continue to arrive until April. Females lay as many as sixty eggs per nest, and the turtles hatch in about seventy days. This species has a tough skin or hide instead of a true shell.

Major dangers to survival of these sea creatures are not only loss of habitat, egg poaching, and accidental catch by fishermen but also plastic pollution. Plastic resembles jellyfish in the water and may be ingested by the turtles, who love the jellyfish most sea animals steer clear of, the Portuguese man-of-war.

Olive ridley turtles also sometimes come ashore on Playa Grande to lay their eggs, though not in the massive *arribadas* found at Nancite or Ostional. Ridleys also nest in small groups or singly.

Las Baulas park, 277 acres (112 ha), encompasses not only Playa Grande and Playa Langosta and the territorial waters offshore but also what was Tamarindo National Wildlife Refuge. There are estuaries where the American crocodile can be found, a fragment of tropical dry forest, and lowlands that attract the wood stork, white ibis, jacana, roseate spoonbill, and American egret. All five species of mangrove found in Costa Rica are here: black, white, buttonwood, tea, and red, with its stilt or prop roots. You may be surprised to see what can decorate the woody plants: orchids, bromeliads, termite nests. There are more than 117 species of trees and bushes, some of them endangered species. A large pochote tree at Langosta is 9 feet in diameter (2.8 m). Crabs abound: ghost crabs, hermit crabs, and mouthless crabs, those garish creatures with black bodies, orange legs, and purple pincers.

Access to the park is easiest at Tamarindo and Playa Grande. Lodging exists at each, and several hotels and tourist businesses in the region operate tours. Boats can be rented for trips in the estuaries. There is a daily bus from San José to Tamarindo (109 mi., 308 km) that takes five and a half hours. SANSA flies Monday, Wednesday, and Friday, a forty-five minute flight. Travelair flies daily.

Manuel Antonio National Park (South)

This park is special. White-faced monkeys leap from tree to tree along the beach in dazzling displays of aerial skill. Shier squirrel monkeys, found only in this area and the Osa Peninsula, peek from behind leaves along trails. Slow-moving sloths turn a lazy look at visitors from their high vantage points. I had my first close-up look at a coati and an agouti in the wild on the forest trail in Manuel Antonio. Large iguanas rustle through leaves on the forest floor or sun themselves on logs along the beach.

The warm waters of the Pacific are home to a variety of marine life;

snorkelers, skin divers, and even watchers at the tide pools see brightly colored fish. Do not miss the tiny bright blue ones in pools among the rocks at the western end of Manuel Antonio Beach. Whales pass by, and those of you who venture out into the sea may come across dolphins. There are 10 species of sponge, 17 of algae, 78 of fish, 19 of coral, and 24 of crustaceans.

A 1989 study lists 353 species of birds and 99 species of mammals, 59 of which are bats rarely seen by visitors. Among marine birds are brown pelicans, magnificent frigate birds, and brown boobies. Land birds include parrots, Baird's trogon, green kingfisher, gray-headed chachalaca, and golden-masked tanager.

The fun begins at the entrance to the park, across an estuary from the community of Manuel Antonio, an estuary that can be waist high on a short adult at high tide or barely cover the feet at low. There is no bridge, so wear shoes and clothes you do not mind getting wet. Carry whatever you want to eat or drink as well.

Once inside the park, you can choose a wide trail through the tall forest or walk along South Espadilla Beach. Toward the far end of the beach, you can enter the forest and cross over to gentler Manuel Antonio Beach or take the path to Cathedral Point, which separates these two beaches. From Cathedral Point, you can see Mogote Island, one of twelve islands included in the park, rising up sharply from the sea, its high cliffs crowned with vegetation. Both Mogote and Cathedral Point were sites of prehistoric Indian activities by the Quepo tribe. The trail on the point is steep; among rewards are the primary forest, monkeys who live there, and breathtaking views.

These two white sand beaches are lined with lush vegetation almost to the high-water line. The clear waters are warm. Espadilla is steeper with bigger waves. Two other beaches lie farther down a trail through the low mountains; Puerto Escondido has a beach that disappears at high tide, so do not get cut off. Check with rangers before you start out. Playa Playita is the southernmost beach. These last two are rockier, not as kind to the feet.

Allow time for a leisurely walk along Perezoso Trail, named for the sloths you may see there. At Manuel Antonio Beach, face the sea and look at the far right end near the rocks for a prehistoric turtle trap built by the Quepo Indians. Most easily visible at lowest tides after a full moon, the trap is a semicircular rock barrier that forms a pool at the beach's edge. Low and high tides vary about 11 feet (3.4 m) here. Female turtles would come in on high tide over the rock walls. Some would be caught in pools when they tried to return to the sea as the tide went out and water level dropped below the enclosure. Both green and olive ridley turtles lay eggs here, though not in mass nestings.

The park, which covers 1,687 acres (683 ha), does have a dry season from December to March, but rains are possible then and clear days, especially mornings, in the rainier months permit hours of quiet enjoyment on the beach. Annual rainfall is 150 inches (3,800 mm), and average temperature is 81°F (27°C).

In addition to primary and secondary forest and beaches, there are marshes, a mangrove swamp, lagoons, and woodland. More than 346 plant species have been identified. Warning signs point out the manzanillo tree along the beach; its leaves, bark, and applelike fruit secrete a white latex that stings the skin and is toxic.

The park is open from 7:00 a.m. to 4:00 p.m. It is crowded at Easter, Christmas, and during the two-week school vacation in July. Even though it is one of the most-visited parks, it is possible on a midweek visit to have the beach practically to yourself.

To protect both vegetation and animals in this small park, camping is no longer allowed. Accommodations are available in the adjacent town of Manuel Antonio and along the road to Quepos, less than 5 miles (7 km) away.

Daily express buses travel between San José and Manuel Antonio. The trip takes about 3½ hours. SANSA makes the trip in twenty minutes, flying every day except Sunday. Travelair flies daily.

Palo Verde National Park (Northwest)

Palo Verde National Park, which includes what was formerly known as the Dr. Rafael Lucas Rodríguez Wildlife Refuge, covers 32,686 acres (13,228 ha). Lying along the east bank of the Tempisque River above where it empties into the Gulf of Nicoya, the area encompasses lakes, swamps, grasslands, savanna woodlands, and forest—probably fifteen habitats in all. It is one of the most important sanctuaries for migrating waterfowl in Central America. Along with the thousands of migratory birds that arrive every year, there are many resident species. So far, up to 300 species of migrating and resident birds are believed to inhabit this land.

Herons, ibis, ducks, storks, and jacanas are among those that descend on the lowlands to feed and mate. Six pairs of the rare, endangered jabiru stork nest here. The largest stork in the world, the jabiru has a white body, gray neck and head, and a rose-red necklace. The only scarlet macaws left in the tropical dry forest of the Pacific live here.

In the rainy season, flooding of the plains is widespread. In the dry months of December through April, some waterholes disappear, and those that remain attract birds as well as other wildlife, allowing the patient visitor a good chance to see them. An observation tower open to visitors is near a marsh.

Approach the mango trees near headquarters quietly for another chance to see some of the many mammals that make their home in the region. Peccaries, iguanas, deer, monkeys, and coatis feed on the fruits. The white-tailed deer who watched us while we watched him did not seem the least frightened.

Because the Organization for Tropical Studies (OTS) has a biological station here, a good trail system takes visitors into the forest past flowing springs that attract wildlife, past a natural cactus garden, to a superb lookout over the Tempisque floodplain, through a marsh (a printed guide recommends this as the best place to see a tropical rattlesnake or a boa constrictor), through second-growth forest that is reclaiming pasture, and to possibly the largest single intact tropical dry forest in the province of Guanacaste.

Another trail leads to the Tempisque River and a view of Isla de los Pájaros in the middle of it, an important nesting site for herons, ibis, and egrets. If you are not content to view it through binoculars, you may be able to arrange a boat trip with park guards; you will not be permitted to land but can circle it. Since crocodiles live in the river, you have a good chance of seeing one. Many boas inhabit the island, feasting on bird eggs and nestlings. The river has a 13-foot (4-m) rise and fall with the tide. Sometimes it flows backward.

At the park you may see cattle grazing; it is part of a management plan to keep the marshes open. The park administrator told me they may plant rice in some areas as a good-neighbor gesture. Nearby farmers lose more of their crops than they like to birds, who do not recognize boundaries.

Elevation ranges from 33 to 689 feet (10 to 210 m) above sea level. Annual rainfall is 90 inches (2,295 mm), and average temperature is 81°F (27°C).

In the dry season, most trees lose their leaves to conserve water, but many wear bright flowers. Temperatures can reach 105°F (41°C) at midday, but nights and early mornings are cool. While it is windy in the dry season and insects are scarce, the rainy season brings humidity, little breeze, and mosquitoes and gnats: pack the repellent.

If the Palo Verde Biological Station belonging to OTS is not full up with researchers, visitors are welcome. Contact OTS at Apartado 676-2050, San Pedro Montes de Oca. Telephone 40-6696. Room and board for natural history travelers is less than $50 a day. Lunch is provided on a day trip with prior reservation. Facilities are rustic. Camping is allowed at the administrative center. You may want to write or drop by the OTS office (450 meters west of Lincoln School in Moravia just outside of San José) to purchase a marvelous naturalist's guide to the field station written by Douglas E. Gill and OTS staff. It also has interesting tidbits about what you see on the drive to the park from San José.

Tour companies offer natural history visits, including a kayaking trip. The main route is by the Inter-American Highway to Bagaces, between Liberia and Cañas. Look for the sign and turn west. The pavement ends but the road is passable year-round. Just follow the signs. Keep your binoculars and cameras handy, because birds are everywhere. The trip takes about 1½ hours from Bagaces, depending on how often you have a binocular stop. The public bus will also get you from San José to Bagaces. From there you will need to get a taxi.

The second route is to turn off the Inter-American for the Tempisque Ferry; once across the river, head for Puerto Humo. There you can hire a boat to take you along the meandering Tempisque to a dock at the park. From there it is a little more than a mile (2 km) by foot to park headquarters.

Poás Volcano National Park (Central Valley)

At Poás Volcano, you can stand at the edge of a multicolored crater almost 1 mile (1.5 km) in diameter, look down 984 feet (300 m), and watch geyserlike eruptions that leave no doubt this mountain still has something to say.

Its message was so clear in 1989 that the park was closed. The intensity of eruptions, the gases, and the ash made visits too dangerous. Agriculture, especially coffee on the slopes below, and forests suffered from acid rain. Some residents were evacuated. One woman told of the effects of the fallout on family laundry: holes appeared overnight in clothing. Today the park is operating on a reduced schedule, 8:30 a.m. to 3:00 p.m., and no camping is allowed. Check with the park service for an update.

Vulcanologists cringe when they hear Poás called the largest geyser in the world, but the fact that it is not takes nothing away from the beauty and power of this 8,884-foot (2,708-m) giant. There are actually five craters on the mountain, but two get most attention from visitors: the newer active crater responsible for the lava, rocks, ash, and steam in historical times, and an extinct one now called Botos Lake, a twenty-minute easy climb through dwarf forest from the active crater.

From the view point constructed along the edge of the active crater, you have a spectacular view of the greenish hot-water lake. The earlier you go, the better chance you have of an unimpeded look. Clouds that drift in as the day progresses can completely obscure the bottom. While waiting for a column of mud and water to shoot into the air, notice the fumaroles, and look for small measuring devices scattered around the crater. Costa Rica has a fine Vulcanological and Seismological Observatory at the National University in Heredia; its staff keeps a close watch at Poás and at other sites around the country. Depending on wind direction, you may get a good whiff of sulfur.

The park, with 13,838 acres (5,600 ha), has even more to offer than volcanic craters. Trails lead through shrubs, dwarf forest, and cloud forest covered with epiphytes. Because of volcanic activity, hunting, and deforestation outside the park, few mammals remain. Coyotes, rabbits, frogs, and toads are common, and at least 79 bird species are at home here. A park ranger told me he has seen resplendent quet-

POETRY ON ESCALONIA TRAIL
POÁS VOLCANO

I am light and shadow
Shining sun
Cold kiss of clouds
Fertile home of ancient trees
Of flowers just born
And of the red-green hummingbird
All pass their days
In my arms
Free
I am the cloud forest
That crowns Poás
We have much to share.

Poetry on Escalonia Trail, Poás Volcano National Park (Photo by Ree Strange Sheck)

197

zals fly over the road between the park entrance and administration building in early morning. Hummingbirds are easy to see, and if you take some of the lesser-traveled trails, you might spot an emerald toucanet, brown robin, black guan, or masked woodpecker.

The trail to Botos Lake, named for the Botos Indians who lived on the north slope when the Spaniards arrived, begins near the view point. At this altitude, take your time, enjoy the tangled vegetation, and try to figure out the birds you are hearing but may not be able to spot.

My favorite is the Escalonia Trail, which begins at the picnic area. Trees soar overhead, bromeliads are everywhere, and trail markers full of poetry do justice to the forest's magnificence. They are only in Spanish; I have translated one of them for you.

If you visit on Sunday, inquire about the audiovisual presentations offered in the auditorium. Flora and fauna from all over the country flash across the big screen; the beauty brings tears to the eyes. Unscheduled showings can happen during the week. If you are going with a group, ask about the possibility. You may have to bring your own projector bulb. The lack of one has prevented the presentation twice when I have been there.

Bring a jacket and rain gear. Rainfall is 138 inches (3,500 mm), and though temperatures average between 48° and 55°F (9° to 13°C), a minimum of 21°F (−6°C) has been recorded. On a bright, sunny day, it can be 70°F (21°C).

Poás lies about 1½ hours from San José through Alajuela and San Pedro de Poás. The drive is spectacular, through coffee farms, nurseries where ornamental plants are grown for export (that is what is under those huge expanses of black shade cloths), strawberry fields, and dairy farms. If you are going by tour, check to see if they get to Poás by 9:30 a.m. at the latest and how much time they allow there. Some give you thirty minutes, barely enough to peer into the crater. Some nature tour companies offer more time or even a naturalist guide to take you on a day trip to the area.

Public bus is not the easiest way to get to Poás. The only direct bus is on Sunday, and it is crowded. Daily buses go from Alajuela to San Pedro de Poás, and you can hire a taxi from there. If several persons are going, you can hire a taxi from San José for about $45 and split the cost.

Rincón de la Vieja National Park (Northwest)

From the porch of the century-old ranch house that now serves as park headquarters, I watched a doe and fawn at the edge of the clearing. They walked without fear. On the way to Rincón de la Vieja, a morpho butterfly had fluttered across the road; four species of this brilliant butterfly live in the park. Tapir roam here, as do howler, capuchin, and spider monkeys. The armadillo is so abundant it could practically be the symbol of the park. Peccaries are common, and there is evidence that jaguar and puma stalk this 34,801-acre (14,084-ha) preserve.

The white-fronted Amazon parrot and spectacled owl are among 270 species of birds. Doves are everywhere; you have a good chance of seeing the curassow at lower elevations. The park ascends from 1,968 to 6,545 feet (600 to 1,995 m). There are kites, toucans and toucanets, redstarts, and motmots. A small cicada with the voice of a frog lives under the ground, its imitation fooling even the experts.

The park, 14 miles (23 km) northeast of Liberia in the Guanacaste Mountain Range, is the source of thirty-two rivers. As much as 197 inches (5,000 mm) of rain falls at higher elevations, practically year-round. The park's forests are important not only in preventing rivers that flow to the lowlands from disappearing in the dry season but in keeping them from flooding in rainy months. The area's importance as a water source is one reason the park was established.

Not one, but two volcanoes crown this mountain mass: Rincón de la Vieja, active, and Santa María, currently dormant. In fact, Rincón de la Vieja has two craters. The dormant one has a crystal clear coldwater lake, while the lake in the other crater steams. The best time to climb to the craters is in the driest months, February through April.

A short trail beginning at park headquarters is called Enchanted Forest, and indeed a walk through that fairyland of tall trees, delicate orchids (the national flower, the *guaria morada* orchid, thrives in the park), ferns, and mosses touches a primeval chord within. A small waterfall makes it picture perfect.

A 5.6-mile (9-km), three-hour trek takes you to Las Pailas, a magic land of bubbling mud pots, pools of hot water, and steam and gas vents near the southwestern edge of the park. Less than 2 miles (3 km) from headquarters are sulfur waters that many claim are medicinal.

Visit the exhibit room in the adobe hacienda that is now park headquarters. (The story has it that the last owner was former U.S. president Lyndon Johnson.) Call the Guanacaste Conservation Area, 69-5598, to find out if overnight space is available. Bring warm bedding and a towel. Average temperature is 59° to 79°F (15° to 26°C), but it gets cold at night. Camping is permitted; horse rental is available. Bring rubber boots for hiking.

The road from Liberia via Colonia La Libertad to the ranger station has been improved. There is no bus from Liberia, but a jeep-type taxi will make the trip for about $45 one way. Contact the park service to see if park personnel have a trip scheduled; sometimes you can arrange transportation with them.

It is possible to visit Las Pailas by taking the Inter-American Highway north of Liberia, turning east to Curubandé, and continuing to Guachipelín, a private ranch at the end of the line. From there, you can walk to Las Pailas in half an hour. See chapter 6, the northwest section, for information about Guachipelín, which also offers lodging.

Santa Rosa National Park (Northwest)

In times past, Indians have walked this land, and hunters, woodcutters, cowboys, and soldiers. Footprints today belong mainly to researchers, park rangers, and a whole variety of nature lovers. What had been virgin tropical dry forest, cleared pastures, and a battlefield now is Santa Rosa National Park, a piece of property where history is still being written.

The historical significance of Santa Rosa was the primary reason it was protected by the government, first as a national monument and then a national park. Soon, however, the ecological importance of its flora and fauna and of the habitats that exist in this dry Pacific region was recognized.

It is the ecological battle that is making history now, an effort not only to protect but to restore some of these habitats. Research at Santa Rosa is shedding light on plant and animal interrelationships and how forests regenerate themselves—discoveries that make a difference here and around the world.

A young park ranger told me that most Costa Ricans who visit Santa Rosa National Park come initially because of its history, but they leave excited about the intricacies of nature. She carries the park's environmental education program to nearby village schools and walks with the children when they come on tour.

The historical drawing card is the site of the Battle of Santa Rosa, March 20, 1856, which pitted a well-trained and well-armed invading army against a ragtag band of Costa Rican peasants who had become soldiers overnight. The patriots won, routing the forces of the adventurer William Walker in fourteen minutes. The battle took place around La Casona, the house at Hacienda Santa Rosa. Visitors today can walk through the big house and see the historical displays, stand on the wide wooden veranda and look toward the 300-year-old stone corrals, or step into the kitchen and see where cheese was hung over the wood stove to preserve it.

A stately guanacaste, national tree of Costa Rica, stands nearby. A sign explains that its wood is good for construction and its ear-shaped fruit, which gives the tree its English name of ear fruit, has been used to wash clothes and is food for horses, cows, and small forest mammals.

Climb the short view-point trail behind La Casona or take the short, well-marked nature trail. Keep your eyes open: I was within spitting distance of a handsome 5-foot (1.5-m) boa constrictor before I could discern it draped over a tree root by the path. Its natural camouflage is remarkable. The trail is called Indio Desnudo for the gumbo-limbo tree. You can identify it by its reddish-brown bark, which inspired the popular name—*indio desnudo* means "naked Indian." Since the reddish skin has a tendency to peel, ticos sometimes irreverently refer to it as the "tourist tree."

Two of Santa Rosa's beaches are famous as sea turtle nesting sites: Naranjo, about 8 miles (12 km) from park headquarters, and Nancite, 11 miles (17 km) away. Though three species come ashore to lay eggs, it is the hundreds of thousands of Pacific or olive ridley turtles on small Nancite Beach that get the most attention. From July to December, mass nestings, called *arribadas*, occur periodically, while single turtles come ashore every night in this peak season. The other two species are green and leatherback turtles. Nancite is in a study area, so permission to visit is required. You will likely need a four-wheel-drive vehicle to get to Playa Naranjo in the rainy season.

The park does have a pronounced dry season from December to May. Rainfall for most of the 91,719-acre (37,118-ha) park is about 63 inches (1,600 mm). Average temperature is 79°F (26°C).

Entrance to this part of Santa Rosa, which also includes park headquarters, is 27 miles (43 km) north of Liberia via the Inter-American Highway, paved all the way to La Casona. At the entrance booth, you can buy a map of the park, and the ranger can help you decide what you can see in the time you have.

Entrance to the Murciélago section of Santa Rosa is farther north on the Inter-American, turning off to Cuajiniquil at the rural guard station. If you do not see a sign for Murciélago when you get to the village, ask for directions. The road is unpaved, and a couple of rivers must be forded to reach the ranger station. I did it in the rainy season in a standard pickup, but I would have worried less in a four-wheel drive: lots of mud.

Stop along the narrow road and take a close look at the acacia tree for a lesson in plant and animal relationships. The tree provides food for acacia ants, and the ants protect it from animal predators and foreign vegetation. They even keep a circle cleared around the tree. Find the small hole near the base of one of its thorns and watch what happens when the tree is disturbed. Do not get your fingers in the way of the ants rushing out: their stings are painful. If you unwittingly brush against an acacia branch along a trail, you will find out for yourself.

Murciélago ("bat" in English) belonged to Anastasio Somoza when he was president of Nicaragua. Talk to the delightful cook at the ranger station there; she can share stories from those days. She can also tell you about the coyotes and monkeys that come into the

Butterflies—part of the intricate web of life in the rain forest (Photo by Ree Strange Sheck)

yard. You can travel on to the coast at Playa Blanca or Santa Elena Bay or walk on the trail to the Pozo El General, which has water year-round, important for animals in the dry season.

Santa Rosa National Park has capuchin, howler, and spider monkeys, deer, armadillos, coatis, raccoons, and even some cats—115 species of mammals in all, though about half are bats. Studies have identified 3,410 species of moths and butterflies among more than 10,000 of insects. Magpie jays and parrots make lots of noise, while some of the 253 species of birds get attention with their coloring: look for orange-fronted parakeets, elegant trogons, and crested caracaras.

No lodging is available in the park, but camping is allowed. There are hotels in Liberia as well as some private nature reserves that offer day trips to Santa Rosa. Several nature tour companies have trips to Santa Rosa, and it is easy to find on your own if you drive. Buses to La Cruz will let you off at the park entrance, though you will have a 4-mile (7-km) walk to headquarters. Or you can take a bus to Liberia and hire a taxi for a day trip to the park. Santa Rosa is 4½ hours from San José. The information booth at the entrance is open from 7:30 a.m. to 4:30 p.m. Telephone 69-5598.

Tortuguero National Park (Caribbean)

With very little imagination, you can see yourself as Hepburn or Bogart on the *African Queen* as you wind your way through the rivers and canals of Tortuguero National Park on the northern Caribbean coast. Flora, fauna, and the condition of the boat may differ, but the feeling is there—you and the water, vegetation, and wildlife in an intimate and solitary encounter.

If you travel to Tortuguero by boat from Limón, the contrast of settled lands along the water with these protected lands vividly portrays the difference a park can make. From the air, the park is a mass of greens from the coastal plain to the Sierpe Hills, broken only by narrow ribbons of water.

However you get there, to explore Tortuguero is to discover a crocodile along the bank, a small turtle sunning on a trunk in the water, a monkey or sloth asleep in a tree, vultures peering down from a lofty perch. Perhaps a river otter will slip into the water as the boat approaches. Water and land birds keep your binoculars busy: at least 309 species live here. Watch for the green macaw, herons, egrets, parrots, kingfishers, oropendolas (notice their large, hanging nests), tanagers, toucans, and bananaquits.

Tortuguero is tall forest and palm groves, lianas trailing into the water, and floating gardens of water hyacinths. The endangered West Indian manatee feeds on these and other aquatic plants. This large sea cow can be 13 feet (4 m) long and weigh about 1,300 pounds (600 kg).

Tortuguero is also beaches, important nesting sites for sea turtles (*tortugas*), which gave the place its name. Green, leatherback, hawksbill, and occasionally loggerhead turtles return to these beaches every year to lay eggs. Some come in massive arribadas; others singly. Though you could possibly see a turtle any night during the year, there are peak times. The best time to see a hawksbill is from July to October, leatherbacks from February to July with a peak in April and May, and green turtles from early July into October, peaking in August. Rangers from other parks are brought in to help patrol the beaches during peak months to prevent eggs from being stolen. Researchers at the nearby Caribbean Conservation Corporation have been tagging nesting turtles since 1955. The female green turtle comes ashore to lay eggs an average of two or three times during her season there, staying not far offshore in between. It may be three years before she returns to Tortuguero, or two years, or four.

There are many crustaceans (prawns also feed under the water hyacinths), eels, 30 species of freshwater fish (including the gar, considered a living fossil because species of that genus lived 90 million years ago), and sharks.

Trails take off from park stations on the water at either end of the park. There is also a station at Río Frío. On foot in this zone of tropical wet forest, perhaps you can spot small, brightly colored frogs that live here. Some of the mammals include peccaries, raccoons, kinkajous, giant anteaters, tapirs, ocelots, pacas, cougars, and skunks. Rain gear and rubber boots come in handy.

Rainfall averages about 197 inches (5,000 mm), but it can get up to 236 inches (6,000 mm) in parts. Elevation reaches from sea level to 1,020 feet (311 m) in the Sierpe Hills. It is hot and humid, with an average temperature of 79°F (26°C). The park covers 46,818 acres (18,947 ha).

Camping is allowed in the park. Nearest lodging is in the village of Tortuguero, at the park's northern end. It is possible to visit Tortuguero park in a day trip from Limón, but I do not recommend it. Take time to savor the adventure. Being there overnight allows for an after-dark boat ride to see nighttime animal life on the river or for a chance to see the turtles. You can also make your own arrangements for boat and hotel, but you save yourself that hassle by going with one of the tour companies, leaving from either San José or Limón. Tour companies offer boat or plane trips or a combination of the two; see chapter 9.

Traditionally, boats have left from Moín, a few miles north of Puerto Limón, a trip that can take from three to four hours. However, the 1991 earthquake caused changes in the depth of canals, so that some tour companies at this time depart from Hamburgo. The plan is to dredge the problem section, but you can still do the trip from Moín either on a local tour or by hiring your own boat.

Even before the earthquake, canals sometimes got low and boats would have to proceed slowly. I have heard tales of passengers getting out to push; I myself have seen the captain do it. If you choose not to take a tour, check with the JAPDEVA (Atlantic Port Authority) office to see if there is room on their launch (58-1300), or hire a small boat to take you. You can sometimes get a ride on a cargo boat. Planes land in Barra del Colorado, where you can hire a boat for Tortuguero.

Biological Reserves
(Administered by National Parks Service)

Cabo Blanco Strict Nature Reserve (Northwest)

Here is a trip for the adventurous. A visit to Cabo Blanco Reserve can require a ferry or launch trip across the Gulf of Nicoya from Puntarenas and then slow miles by car or bus toward the tip of the Nicoya Peninsula. Part of the road is paved, but my memories are of the unpaved portion between Cóbano and the Cabo Blanco Nature Reserve. Even guests of privately operated nature reserves near Tambor who fly in and go to Cabo Blanco for a day trip face that stretch of rough road. The key is to go slow, enjoy the magnificent scenery of coast and mountains, and remember that a beautiful wilderness area waits at the end of the road.

And the road, which piddles down to a one-lane track before you reach the reserve, does end here. It is a muddy track in the rainy season, and since you must also ford a river en route, a four-wheel drive is recommended for those months.

The reserve is a treasure, with a small museum, picnic area, latrines, and well-maintained trails. A plaque near the museum honors Nils Olaf Wessberg, a man who loved nature and who saved this virgin forest and sanctuary for seabirds in 1963, before Costa Rica had a park service.

Visitors often see howler monkeys and an admirable assortment of birds and butterflies from the picnic area. A 1½-hour trek through the low mountains (the trail is steep in places) leads down to Balsitas or Cabo Blanco beaches, two sand beaches on a mostly rocky shoreline. Perhaps you will have the beach to yourself, except for colored crabs and seabirds. A trail links the two beaches, which are on opposite sides of the point. If the tide is right, you can return along the beach; be sure to ask the rangers before you start out. This 2.8-mile

(4.5-km) loop trail is marked on a brochure you can purchase at park headquarters. Park hours are 7:00 a.m. to 5:00 p.m.

Cabo Blanco (White Cape) got its name from the small island a short distance off the point. There seems to be some dispute about whether the white comes from deposits of bird guano or a white cliff or the light-colored soil. Pelicans, frigate birds, and brown boobies hang out there. The area is rich in marine life: octopus, starfish, sea cucumber, lobster, giant conch, and fish such as snapper and snook.

Though the park is only 2,896 acres (1,172 ha), wildlife is plentiful: deer, white-faced and howler monkeys, agoutis, pacas, margays, ocelots, coyotes, coatis, tamanduas, and raccoons. The reserve claims 119 tree species and possibly the largest pochote tree in any park. The administrator told me it is 115 feet high (35 m) and almost 10 feet (3 m) in diameter. Because rainfall is higher here than on the rest of the peninsula—91 inches (2,300 mm)—more of the trees are evergreen. Predominant species are gumbo-limbo, lemonwood, frangipani, dogwood, trumpet tree, and cedar. Birds are abundant—one birder counted 74 species in four hours. Land species include manikins, woodpeckers, trogons, crested caracaras, parakeets, and chachalacas.

No camping is permitted inside the reserve, though some neighbors have sites. Nearest lodging is 7 miles (11 km) away in Montezuma. The only entrance to the park is from this eastern side. Check in Montezuma about limitations on visitation. Guidelines being developed now will set a maximum number of persons who can enter per day, probably beginning during 1992. Remember that this is a small reserve, a place that could be loved to death. The study on carrying capacity will define safeguards to prevent that.

See chapter 6 for transportation possibilities: launch, ferry, bus. There are no buses between Montezuma and Cabo Blanco, but a local taxi can take you. Some private reserves nearby offer day trips to Cabo Blanco Reserve; see chapter 8.

Keep in mind that the average temperature is 81°F (27°C).

Caño Island Biological Reserve (South)

Located 12 miles (20 km) west of the Osa Peninsula in southern Costa Rica, Caño Island is of interest largely as an archaeological site and for its marine life. About 494 acres (200 ha) rising to 361 feet (110 m) above the Pacific, the land today contains tall evergreen forest, a prehistoric cemetery, and mysterious round stones sculpted by the Indians who once walked here. Unfortunately, many graves were plundered before the island came under the protection of Corcovado National Park.

The crystalline waters are a snorkeler's delight. Five coral reefs, containing 15 species of stony coral, create a marine wonderland. Lobster and giant conch live in these waters, as do eels, octopuses, sea urchins, brittle star, and countless fish—jacks, grunts, triggerfish. Manta rays, sailfish, sea turtles, humpback whales, and dolphins have been seen near the island.

Wildlife on the island is scarce, consisting mainly of pacas, opossums, boa constrictors, a few species of bees, moths, butterflies, and beetles. There are also frogs, bats, rats, lizards, and ants. Among the birds are ospreys, brown noddies, brown boobies, terns, and egrets.

The forest is largely made up of locusts, wild figs, rubber trees, wild cacaos, and milk trees, which exude a white latex that can be drunk as milk.

Rangers are stationed on the island, and there is a trail. High cliffs rise from the coastline, with only a few small, sandy beaches that largely disappear at high tide.

Most visitors to Caño Island arrive as part of a tour. Private nature reserves in the area offer optional day trips to the island (see chap. 8) as do several coastal hotels (see chap. 6). Advise Corcovado National Park in advance to arrange an independent trip (telephone 78-5036, fax 78-5116). Visitation is limited to fifteen persons a day.

Carara Biological Reserve (South)

You can spot the Carara Biological Reserve before you see any sign as you come from San José through Orotina toward the Pacific coast. Its green forest stands tall against the eroded hillsides—land whose soil, once the trees were cut, tired out quickly when turned into fields for crops or pastures for cattle. In a transition zone between the dry north Pacific and the more humid south, Carara has an average rainfall as high as 126 inches (3,200 mm) in the interior and as low as 79 inches

(2,000 mm) near the coast. A large lagoon and rivers and streams supply life-giving moisture.

The reserve has archaeological importance, with Indian sites dating from 300 B.C. to A.D. 1500. Artifacts include gold objects, pottery, and large rectangular stones. The early inhabitants lived there and buried their dead there.

Most of the 11,614-acre (4,700-ha) reserve is in primary forest, with regal giants that spread their branches in a tall canopy. Some plants live up in the trees and send their roots to the ground, vines wind up trunks toward the light. Epiphytes, ferns, and palms soften the setting.

Because of the lush vegetation and relative ease in seeing the abundant wildlife, Carara Biological Reserve can be an excellent choice for a traveler's first experience in a tropical forest—especially when accompanied by a naturalist guide. Let me share with you what we saw in about three hours: a fiery-billed araçari, blue-gray tanager, spectacled owl, boat-billed heron, crested guan, anhinga, brown jay, white-tailed kite, wood stork, blue heron, orange-bellied trogon, roseate spoonbill, yellow-headed caracara, chestnut-mandibled toucan, dotted-winged antwren, blue-crowned motmot, great kiskadee, scarlet macaws, crocodiles, white-faced monkeys, iguanas. We saw squirrels, leaf-cutting ants, and lizards. We did not see the snakes that live there, the morpho butterfly, or a sloth, coati, agouti, peccary, porcupine, anteater, coyote, or howler and spider monkeys. Perhaps you will.

Near sundown, dozens of the red, blue, and gold scarlet macaws fly from the reserve over the Tarcoles River to nighttime resting places in mangroves along the ocean. Our guide told us the macaws come in June and July to feed on fruiting palms at the entrance to the reserve near the Tarcoles bridge; this entrance is unmarked, but rangers at the main entrance can direct you to it. Check in at the administration building before you venture into the reserve.

The dry season is from December to April. Terrain is hilly, and though the maximum altitude is only about 3,576 feet (1,090 m), you may find yourself huffing and sweating—average temperatures are from 77° to 82°F (25° to 27.5°C). Take it easy.

A parataxonomist working with the National Biodiversity Institute was collecting insects at Carara the last time I was there. He showed me cases of insects so tiny they can barely be seen, as well as flashy butterflies and bizarre-looking beetles. This multiyear project aims to identify all of the species in this biologically diverse country.

Carara is 68 miles (110 km) from San José along the old Spanish highway. No camping is allowed. It is an easy day trip from the capital or a stopping place on the way to Jacó or Quepos. See chapter 9 for nature tour options. I had crossed the Tarcoles River there a dozen times and never knew crocodiles wallow in the mud along its banks until the guide pointed them out. Naturalist guides know where the wildlife is, which trees have fruit, and when the orchids are blooming.

Guayabo, Negritos, and Los Pájaros Biological Reserves (Northwest)

These small islands in the Gulf of Nicoya are havens for large populations of resident and migratory birds, mainly seabirds. No visitor facilities exist; in fact, along with protection of the birds, another reason for making them biological reserves was to spare their "development" for tourism or other purposes—to keep at least some of the gulf islands in a natural state.

Guayabo welcomes peregrine falcons in the winter and holds the largest of the four nesting colonies of brown pelicans found in the country. Located 5 miles (8 km) southwest of Puntarenas near San Lucas Island, Guayabo is also home to brown boobies, frigate birds, laughing gulls, lizards, and crabs. It has cliffs, a small beach, and sparse vegetation.

Two islands make up the Negritos, separated by a narrow channel that harbors whirlpools. Brown pelicans, frigate birds, boobies, and gulls live here, too, along with parrots, doves, raccoons, and iguanas. Artifacts indicate that Indians came ashore at some time, whether to live or to bury their dead is uncertain. Coral reefs make access difficult, but their waters support dolphins, giant conch, and oysters. Forests of palm, cedar, gumbo-limbo, and frangipani survive. The Negritos are almost 11 miles (17 km) south of Puntarenas near the

Nicoya Peninsula. The Guayabo and Negritos reserves cover 355 acres (144 ha).

Isla de los Pájaros means "island of the birds." Less than 550 yards (500 m) from the coast, 8 miles (13 km) north of Puntarenas, it has some low-growing forest and fresh water. Again, seabirds, mainly pelicans, are the predominant species. It is the smallest of the four, 10 acres (4 ha).

There are no facilities at these reserves, camping is prohibited, and permission to visit is required. Look at them as you pass by on a cruise of the Gulf of Nicoya on one of the popular day trips several tour companies offer.

Hitoy-Cerere Biological Reserve (Caribbean)

Visitors are welcome at the Hitoy-Cerere reserve. So few arrive that park guards are really glad when they see a new face, though area hotels and businesses are beginning to promote tours that will bring more people.

Off the beaten path, Hitoy-Cerere is not a stopping-off point on the way somewhere else but a destination in itself. The most recent map I have does not even show a road in, but there is one, passable even in the wettest months. The reserve is 37 miles (60 km) southwest of Limón, 1 ½ hours from Cahuita.

The real adventurer will thrill to know that parts of this rugged portion of the Talamanca Mountains have yet to be explored. We do know some of the animals that live on its 22,622 forested acres (9,155 ha): tapirs, jaguars, peccaries, pacas, porcupines, weasels, white-faced and howler monkeys, agoutis, anteaters, armadillos, kinkajous, sloths, squirrels, otters, and deer. Among the 115 bird species identified so far are the blue-headed parrot, keel-billed toucan, squirrel cuckoo, spectacled owl, green kingfisher, and slaty-tailed trogon. Frogs, toads, insects, and snakes have not been counted yet. Perhaps you will spot one of the remarkable Jesus Christ lizards, so named because they can walk on water. Their secret is quick movement and large hind feet with flaps of skin along each toe that allow them to skip over the surface of streams and ponds.

The forest canopy hovers at about 100 feet (30 m), but some species protrude through the top, reaching more than 160 feet (50 m). Buttresses from the trunks of these giants widen their base of support. Some begin as high as 7 feet (2 m) up from the ground and have a horizontal reach of almost 50 feet (15 m). There are black palms with spiny stilt roots, tree ferns, orchids, and bromeliads. Mosses and lichens cushion trunks and branches.

Trails in this perpendicular place are difficult, but visitors can follow the paths rangers and Indians use. (The reserve is surrounded by legally protected Indian lands.) One researcher found it easier in this steep landscape to stick to the rivers, though moss-covered rocks make streambeds slippery.

Water flows through the spirit of the reserve. "Hitoy" in Bribrí refers to moss- and algae-covered rocks in the river of that name; "Cerere," to another river's clear waters. Pools surrounded by exuberant vegetation invite a solitary dip, while waterfalls of up to almost 100 feet (30 m) inspire awe. Bring rain gear—there is no defined dry season. Yearly amounts average 138 inches (3,500 mm). Humidity is high year-round; temperatures average 77°F (25°C). Elevation goes from about 650 to 3,363 feet (200 to 1,025 m).

To stay overnight, check with the park service about space in the ranger station. For day trips, lodging in Limón, Cahuita, Puerto Viejo, or spots in between would serve. Parks can also give current road status. The bus from Limón to Valle de Estrella comes within 6 miles (10 km) of the entrance to Hitoy-Cerere (stay on until the end of the line at Finca Seis, one of several stops in a big banana plantation); a taxi from there costs less than $5. Taxi fare from Cahuita to the reserve is less than $30 one way. If you stay overnight, you may want to arrange with the driver to pick you up for the return trip.

Lomas Barbudal Biological Reserve (Northwest)

My impression of Lomas Barbudal was birds—birds everywhere. We could hardly make progress driving along the dirt road for stopping to peer through binoculars. The species list is up to 205; the sheer quantity is overwhelming. Three species particularly important because they are disappearing in other areas are the king vulture, great curassow, and yellow-naped parrot. The man on the street will tell you that yellow-naped parrots are the best talkers in the parrot family.

Blue-crowned motmot (Photo by Ree Strange Sheck)

Trapping is no doubt a factor in their disappearance, along with loss of habitat. Curassows make for good eating. Located just north of Palo Verde National Park, Lomas Barbudal can also play host to its residents, such as the scarlet macaw.

Enthralled with the birds, we had little time for the bees, one of the reserve's claims to fame. About 250 species are thought to live here, some found nowhere else in the country. Moths, butterflies, and wasps are also abundant. Congo and white-faced monkeys move about the reserve, as do coatis, peccaries, white-tailed deer, armadillos, and raccoons.

Four species of endangered trees survive here, only three of which are familiar to most people: mahogany, Panama redwood, and rosewood. Deciduous forests, those with trees that seasonally lose their leaves, make up 70 percent of the 5,631-acre (2,279-ha) reserve. One of the species that flowers profusely in the dry season, when its branches are bare of leaves, is the yellow cortez, *cortesa amarilla*. With a profusion of yellow blossoms, the trees resemble giant bouquets. Flowers in a single tree last only about four days, but it may bloom two or three times during the dry season. A curious tree is the cannonball. You will know it when you see it. The fruit look like big balls hanging on strings down the trunk and on lower branches.

Water sources are plentiful in this region classified as tropical dry forest. Rainfall averages 59 to 79 inches (1,500 to 2,000 mm). Rivers such as the beautiful Cabuya flow year-round; its natural, sandy-bottomed pools are ideal for a swim under big trees along its banks, where monkeys and birds escape afternoon heat. Natural springs number more than fifteen.

Lomas Barbudal, which means "bearded hills" in Spanish, is three hours from San José on the Inter-American Highway toward Nicaragua or half an hour south of Liberia. The turnoff is 6.8 miles (11 km) north of Bagaces. Turn west and continue about 9 miles (15 km). Ranger headquarters is on the north end of the reserve, where there are picnic and camping areas, a visitor/community center, a lookout, and a place to swim in the river. Guide service is available, and there is a good trail system. Lodging is available in Liberia or at nearby privately owned nature reserves.

Wildlife Refuges
(Administered by National Wildlife Directorate)

Barra del Colorado National Wildlife Refuge (Caribbean)
The Barra del Colorado refuge is located the farthest north one can go on the Caribbean and still be in Costa Rica. On the other side of its northern border along the San Juan River is Nicaragua. Access within the park is by its waterways. Virtually no land trails exist. Part of the western region has yet to be explored.

What is happening on that western edge illustrates the pressures on protected areas in Costa Rica. Logging and roads to bring the trees out are cutting into the virgin forest. It is a remote area, and wildlife staff are spread too thin to control it.

Travelers get to Barra del Colorado by air or by boat. Boats come through Tortuguero park or the Sarapiquí-San Juan-Colorado River route. There is plenty to see from the network of rivers, channels, and lakes in the reserve. Among the endangered species are the West

Indian manatee, tapir, cougar, jaguar, ocelot, and jaguarundi. Species you are more likely to see are caimans and crocodiles, white-faced and howler monkeys, red brocket deer, and sloths. Birds include the great green macaw, great curassow, herons of various kinds, the red-lored Amazon parrot, great tinamou, cormorant, and keel-billed toucan.

A very wet rain forest, the area averages from 158 inches (4,000 mm) of rain on the western edge to 221 inches (5,600 mm) at the town of Barra del Colorado. However, my two-day visit in one of the rainiest months was sunny and beautiful. Go prepared for rain, but take your sunscreen just in case.

You will see swamp forests, swamp palm forests, and mixed forests growing above the swamps in this 242,158-acre (98,000-ha) refuge. *Caña brava*, a wild cane, grows mainly along rivers. Its stiff, solid stems are used in building—they make decorative ceilings—and to prop up banana plants. Another forest species with commercial value is cativo, used in plywood. If you come via the canals, you may see lumber being floated down to Moín; supposedly it is all being cut outside of park lands.

A variety of fish live in the lakes, rivers, and estuaries, among them snook, tarpon, mackerel, snapper, gar, and *guapote* (a tropical rainbow bass). The area draws many sportfishermen.

Lodging is available inside the reserve at private hotels near the town of Barra del Colorado. Tour companies offer one-day or multiday trips to the reserve. See the description of Tortuguero National Park in this chapter for some ideas on boat travel from Moín if you want to do it yourself. You can easily combine a trip to Tortuguero and Barra del Colorado, either with a tour or on your own. Scheduled airlines fly from San José to Barra del Colorado; you can hire a boat to Tortuguero. The flight takes thirty minutes; the canal trip to Barra from Moín takes six hours.

Bolaños Island National Wildlife Refuge (Northwest)

This rocky mound rises 266 feet (81 m) out of the Pacific on a little bay whose waters lap on both Costa Rican and Nicaraguan shorelines. Bolaños Island, all 99 acres (40 ha) of it, is a wildlife refuge because of seabirds who live and nest there. Magnificent frigate birds and American oystercatchers nest there, and this is one of four nesting sites in the country for brown pelicans.

Winds seem to be an important factor in where frigate birds build a nest: they need help landing and becoming airborne because of

THE RESPLENDENT QUETZAL

The name is exotic. The bird is exotic. A member of the trogon family, the resplendent quetzal was a symbol of freedom and independence to some indigenous Central American peoples. It thrives in Costa Rica. Travelers are more likely to see it here than in Guatemala where the quetzal is the national bird because of the protected forests at elevations where they live: 5,000 to 10,000 feet (1,524 to 3,048 m) in the Central and Talamanca ranges, above 4,000 feet (1,219 m) in the Tilarán Cordillera.

Though Monteverde Cloud Forest Reserve is the more famous site for seeing the fantastic iridescent bird with its blue-green head, neck, and body and its crimson stomach, Braulio Carrillo, Poás, and Chirripó national parks are also home to the quetzal as well as other forests in the Talamanca Mountains. Some birders say the easiest place to see it is near San Gerardo de Dota off the Inter-American Highway before Cerro de la Muerte. Dr. Alexander F. Skutch, who wrote a classic descriptive account of the natural history of the quetzal, lives near San Isidro de El General. He says in the 1970s he often saw quetzals at 7,000 to 8,000 feet on the road from San José to San Isidro.

The birds are endangered because of the destruction of their habitat. Though they eat many kinds of fruits and such other things as insects and lizards, they depend

heavily on fruit from the laurel family, a relative of the avocado. At Monteverde, quetzals move seasonally, apparently following the fruiting patterns of the different species and migrating from Monteverde to unprotected land. As reserves such as Monteverde become isolated by deforested land, the survival of migrating species is endangered.

Not only do quetzals depend on laurels, laurel trees depend on the quetzals to distribute their seeds. Swallowing the fruit whole, the bird coughs the seed up after the nutritious part is digested in its stomach.

Breeding period is from March to June, peaking in April and May. This is the easiest time to see quetzals because they come down lower in the trees to nest, making do with a hole already hollowed out by a woodpecker or excavating in rotting limbs or trunks of dead trees. The female generally lays two blue-colored eggs, which hatch about eighteen days later. As soon as the first babies fly from the nest, she lays eggs again. Both male and female take part in building the nest, incubating eggs, and feeding the young. The end of the male's longer tail streamers (up to 25 in., 64 cm) can sometimes be seen protruding from the hole when he has a turn on the nest.

The main predators of eggs and chicks at Monteverde are short-tailed weasels and perhaps snakes.

their small bodies, short feet, and long wings and tails. Wind on Bolaños during the dry season, which is nesting time, is consistent and strong. Wildlife personnel estimate there are as many as 1,000 of these birds, which are called *tijeretas* (tea-hay-RAY-tahs) in Spanish, referring to their scissorlike tails. During mating season, the male blows out a bright red throat pouch to attract a female. The female lays a single egg.

Rainfall averages 59 inches (1,500 mm). Vegetation is low-growing, dense, and deciduous. Vultures and lizards like it here because of the supply of eggs and the pieces of fish chicks drop.

Since Bolaños is a bird sanctuary, visitors are not invited to drop by. There are no facilities. Watching through binoculars at a tactful distance, however, is not against the rules. The island is less than 3 miles (5 km) from Puerto Soley, southwest of La Cruz, which is on the Inter-American Highway. You can see it well from the Mirador in La Cruz.

Caño Negro National Wildlife Refuge (North Central)

The Caño Negro reserve is a sleeper as far as natural history tourism goes. You may want to see it before it is "discovered." The centerpiece of the 24,633-acre (9,969-ha) reserve is Caño Negro Lake, which covers 1,977 acres (800 ha) with up to 10 feet (3 m) of water in the rainy season, diminishing to a few pools, streams, and an arm of the river that feeds it as the dry season progresses.

A refuge for resident birds, Caño Negro is also on the flight path for large numbers of birds migrating from the north. This is a good place to see the roseate spoonbill, jabiru stork, wood stork, anhinga, species of ducks you have never seen before, and the neotropic olivaceous cormorant (largest colony in the country).

A number of endangered mammal and reptile species live here: tapir, jaguar, ocelot, cougar, and crocodile. Other animals include white-faced, howler, and spider monkeys, sloths, river otters, peccaries, white-tailed deer, silky anteaters, bats, and tayras. What is a tayra? you ask. It looks like a large mink, colored chocolate brown to black, with a long, furry tail. It lives in a den under the ground but searches for food both on the ground and in trees. Tayras probably include bird eggs and nestlings in their diets. In the dry season, visitors who wait patiently and discreetly in sight of remaining waterholes can watch a variety of animals come for water.

From January to April less than 4 inches (100 mm) of rain falls, with only 1 inch (25 mm) of that in March and April. Since the year's total rainfall averages 110 inches (2,800 mm), you can see that the other months are damp. South and west of the lake, where the land rises from the plain abruptly to the Guanacaste Mountain Range, rainfall can reach 158 inches (4,000 mm) a year.

One of the aims of the wildlife entity is to work toward improving the economic well-being of those who live around the refuges. Through environmental education and management programs, residents are taught sustainable use of resources, especially of the many species of fish. Opening up the area for research and tourism also brings development to the area when carefully planned.

Camping is allowed at the refuge, and there is limited space in rustic facilities for overnight visitors. Bring your own sleeping bag. Call Caño Negro at 46-1301. Cost for a bed is about $2; for meals, $5. In the dry season, visitors can explore on foot or horseback (horse rental is possible), but in the rainy months, a boat will be necessary. Boat rentals can also be arranged. Refuge personnel will be pleased to show you around as time permits and local guides are available.

The Upala-Caño Negro bus runs daily; the trip takes about forty-five minutes. Los Chiles to Caño Negro is 14 miles (23 km). When you look at the map, you can see that a visit could be combined with a trip to Guanacaste parks and private nature reserves, taking the road east at La Cruz for Santa Cecilia and Upala and returning to San José through Ciudad Quesada, or combined with a visit to Arenal.

Curú National Wildlife Refuge (Northwest)

The Curú refuge has a deserted island kind of feeling about it, even though it is on the Nicoya Peninsula. Perhaps it is the coconut-strewn beach, or the mangrove swamp, or the jungled hills that rise up at the end of the bay. Walking through the tall forest behind the palm-fringed beach, one senses the wildness of the place.

Boa constrictors are at home here, as are paca, agouti, ocelot, white-faced and howler monkeys, rattlesnake, iguana, white-tailed deer, mountain lion, and margay (a small, spotted cat with a long tail). Waters along the beach host giant conch, lobster, and oyster — good snorkeling. Hawksbill and olive ridley turtles come ashore to nest. The magnificent frigate bird soars overhead. Parrots squawk. Hummingbirds, trogons, hawks, swallows, egrets, motmots, tanagers, roseate spoonbills, and fish eagles are among the 190 species of birds.

Small islands jut up in the Pacific in front of Curú Beach, one of three sand beaches in the refuge. On the distant horizon is the mainland.

The refuge is small, only 185 acres (75 ha). It is private property belonging to the Schutz family, Doña Julieta and her three grown children. They have 3,000 acres in all (1,214 ha), of which two-thirds is forest and one-third is pasture. Visitors may explore eleven trails, some marked with scientific names of plants. The Finca de los Monos trail has a printed guide for walking on your own. Lists of plants and trees, birds, and mammals are available.

Besides running their place, the family manages Curú as a living laboratory for high school and university students on directed projects. To walk with Doña Julieta or her daughter or sons is to walk with the best guides around. Doña Julieta took me to the corral to see baby white-tailed deer. Captured by a nearby landowner on private property, the deer were brought to be cared for until they can be relocated on protected land. She had predicted that white-faced monkeys would be at the corral at that time of day to get bananas, and they were. We climbed a ladder to the second floor of a barn to look at a makeshift museum of shells and bones and rocks and other research projects. Near the forested mountain, she told of a leader of the Costa Rican conservation movement who got lost overnight in that dense jungle; he shall remain nameless.

Walking with daughter Adelina, I received an introduction to the forest, to the swamp, to the life she has in this wonderland, where boas can be found in bedrooms and dinner can be for family or for hungry hordes of researchers.

Though the rustic cabins along the beach are primarily for researchers, you can inquire if space is available for an overnight stay. Meals, served family-style, are ample and tasty. Cost of lodging and meals is $25 per day. Day tours are $5. Doña Julieta requests a call in advance even for a day visit: 61-2392, 26-4333. Nice T-shirts for sale.

The entrance is unmarked and may be locked if you have not called beforehand. The dirt road passes through numerous fenced and gated pastures. If you are on your own, Doña Julieta can give you directions. A bus from Paquera to Cóbano passes on the highway, and taxis are available in Paquera. The sea offers another route—either by rented boat or on a kayak tour. One way to visit Curú is as a guest of one of the area hotels that offer day trips. They make all arrangements. See appropriate chapters for tours and hotels in the southern part of the peninsula.

Gandoca-Manzanillo National Wildlife Refuge (Caribbean)

The coastal reserve of Gandoca-Manzanillo, which touches the border with Panama on the Caribbean, is a mixed-management reserve. That means its goal is not only to conserve the rich biological resources but to work with the community in sustainable use of those resources to promote economic development. Though tourism is one of the components in the development formula, no facilities for visitors exist yet.

Nature, however, has spread a visual feast at the most accessible part of the reserve. Go and enjoy. Take the road south from Limón past Cahuita and Puerto Viejo. Since the tourism bureau and roads people are adding more signs, perhaps there will be one to tell you where the refuge starts by the time you get there. If not, know you have arrived when you get to Punta Cocles. If you do not recognize that landmark, you will recognize the end of the road at Manzanillo, which is definitely part of the refuge.

Some call the beaches around Punta Uva the most beautiful on Costa Rica's Caribbean coast. They are often pictured on postcards. And gorgeous they are: white sand, graceful palms with jungle-looking vegetation beneath, just the right amount of logs and coconuts washed up on the shore. Coral reefs about 650 feet (200 m) out create a snorkeler's paradise: blue parrotfish, green angelfish, white shrimp, red sea urchins and long-spined black ones, anemones, sea cucumbers, lobsters, sponges. Turtle grass sometimes attracts Pacific green turtles; they feed on it.

If you want to explore the rest of the land portion of the refuge, it will be by foot from Manzanillo or by boat to a more southern shore where you can then go by foot. It is about a four-hour hike to the Gandoca Lagoon. The refuge is flat to rolling country with small, forest-covered hills. You might discover a freshwater marsh, the only natural banks of mangrove oysters in the country, the place where larvae of the tarpon fish grow to adulthood. Endangered species protected include the manatee, crocodile, and tapir. There are also paca, caiman, opossum, five species of parrots, sloth, ocelot, margay, otter, bats, falcon, hawk, frigate bird, pelican, chestnut-mandibled toucan, and collared araçari.

As for weather, forget the Costa Rican rule of thumb for wet and dry seasons. Rain falls year-round, though the driest months are March, April, May, September, October, and November. Expect cooler temperatures with wind and rain in December and January. The temperature averages 82°F (28°C). Total area of the refuge, land and sea, is 23,348 acres (9,449 ha).

Check with the wildlife office about camping on the refuge. Consider Limón, Cahuita, Puerto Viejo, or places along that road for lodging. Buses and taxis will get you to Manzanillo. Several hotels, lodges, and tour agencies along the Caribbean coast offer tours to the refuge.

Golfito National Wildlife Refuge (South)

Virgin forest covers most of the 3,336 acres (1,350 ha) of Golfito National Wildlife Refuge. Preservation of that forest is the reason the refuge was created, not only for the species of plants and animals that live in it, some of which are endangered, but for the community of Golfito it surrounds. The tall evergreen forest on this rugged terrain safeguards water sources for today's population and future generations at the same time that it reduces danger of landslides that would affect the town.

Rainfall is heavy in this area of southwestern Costa Rica, almost 196 inches a year (4,976 mm), and temperatures are warm, averaging

82°F (28°C). The combination creates a marvelous tropical wet forest where mosses, lichens, bromeliads, and orchids (31 species) make a veritable greenhouse on the limbs of a single tree. Heliconia plants splash their exotic, showy flowers of reds, oranges, and yellows against the vibrant greens of the understory. Eleven of the 30 or so species of heliconia found in the country are here. Pollinated by hummingbirds, their berry fruits are food for many birds. Indigenous peoples used the bananalike leaves for building and thatching and to wrap food in. The leaves have also been used medicinally.

Some tree species reach almost 165 feet high (50 m). The purple heart tree grows here; you see its beautiful purple wood made into salad bowls and earrings in souvenir shops. There is manwood, whose wood can lie on the ground for more than thirty years without decomposing, ceiba, and bully tree, whose red leaves stand out against the canopy.

Among the 146 bird species identified so far are the endangered scarlet macaw, great tinamou, parrots, herons, pelicans, ibis, owls, parakeets, and trogons. All four species of monkeys found in Costa Rica (including the squirrel monkey, or tití) live in the Golfito refuge, as do cats such as jaguarundi and margay, anteaters, bats, pacas, and agoutis. A number of trails, short and long, crisscross the refuge. A visit to the Naranjal on the other side of the airport may allow you to see monkeys who come to eat the exotic fruits planted here by the banana company. It will certainly allow you to see a variety of birds.

Driest months are January through March, but bring your rain gear even then. Check with the wildlife office in San José about camping in the refuge. Since it is at the edge of the town of Golfito, lodging is nearby. Some Golfito hotels offer guided tours to the refuge. By bus from San José, the trip takes eight hours for the 213-mile trip (342 km). There is scheduled airline service daily between San José and Golfito.

Ostional National Wildlife Refuge (Northwest)

The night was very dark. A young man led us across the beach of the Ostional National Wildlife Refuge to the high-tide line, where a Pacific or olive ridley turtle was patiently digging a hole in the sand with her back flippers. She dug as far as the flippers would reach,

Olive ridley turtle ashore to lay eggs (Photo by Mayra Bonilla, courtesy of Audiovise, S.A.)

flinging sand out behind her shell. Holes can be as deep as 1.6 feet (50 cm) according to researchers.

Practically as soon as the flying sand had settled, soft eggs began to drop into the hole—one at time, or two or three at a time—plopping on top of each other until there were about a hundred. Once the egg-laying began, we could briefly use flashlights without any danger of disturbing the creative process. We could hear the whishing of sand off to the left, another hole begun.

Within twenty-five minutes, the digging and laying were done, and the turtle began methodically to push sand back in, using both front and back flippers. Then she pounded her body against the surface to pack it down and moved around in a circle, scattering sand and leaves and other beach debris over the spot to obliterate any evidence of her buried treasure. Within an hour of emerging from the sea, she was back in it.

Nesting turtles can be found on this beach practically any night of the year, though massive arrivals, called arribadas, peak from July to December, when as many as 120,000 ridleys nest over four- to eight-

SEA TURTLES

Six of the eight species of sea turtles in the world nest on Costa Rica's coasts. Though it is possible to see a turtle laying eggs on a beach somewhere in the country almost any night of the year, there are times when turtles arrive in large numbers (arribadas) at particular sites. Some of the most important nesting sites are in protected areas: Tortuguero and Santa Rosa parks and Ostional, Las Baulas de Guanacaste, Wildlife Refuge.

The turtle species and their Spanish names are green (verde), leatherback (baula or canal), hawksbill (carey), olive ridley (lora or carpintera), Pacific green (negra), and loggerhead (cabezona). The Pacific green, green, hawksbill, and leatherback are found on both coasts, while the ridleys are only on the Pacific. The loggerhead is mainly in the Caribbean, though it may also be on the Pacific side. Hawksbills, loggerheads, and leatherbacks usually are solitary nesters; the greens come ashore in concentrated colonies to lay eggs; and the ridleys come singly, in small colonies, or in massive arribadas.

Following are the most important nesting beaches and months of most activity.

Tortuguero: green turtles nest from early July to October, with August the peak month; hawksbills are also easiest to see here at this time, though they nest year-round on both coasts.

Playa Grande in Las Baulas de Guanacaste National park: peak nesting for leatherbacks, the largest sea turtles, is from November to January, though nesting continues until April.

Ostional Wildlife Refuge: July to December are peak months for olive ridley turtles, though there are nesting turtles or hatchlings almost all year.

Santa Rosa Park: July to December brings arribadas of olive ridley turtles, especially on Nancite Beach. Two other species nest at Nancite and Playa Naranjo: leatherbacks and Pacific greens.

Barra de Matina Beach, north of Limón: leatherbacks come ashore from February to July, with peaks in April and May; green turtle nesting peaks from July to September; hawksbills also come ashore.

Green turtles are prized for their meat, especially in the Caribbean area. Hawksbills are hunted for their shells (tortoiseshell jewelry) along both coasts. While eating turtle meat is not a tradition on the Pacific, the eggs are prized as aphrodisiacs. Turtle protection and conservation programs in Costa Rica range from patrolling beaches and public education to egg hatcheries, controlled harvesting of eggs at Ostional, and setting of legal catches of turtles to be sold for meat near Limón.

---

day periods. Arribadas are usually about two weeks apart, but they can stretch to a month apart.

Harvesting of turtle eggs for food (there is a false idea circulating that they are aphrodisiacs) along with the killing of adults for their meat or the leather trade threaten this and other species of sea turtles around the world. The Ostional refuge was set up to protect the nesting sites of ridleys and the leatherbacks and occasional green turtles who also come ashore. In an innovative program, local inhabitants, who once plundered the nests and now live mainly from subsistence agriculture, harvest some of the eggs from the first arrivals on the beach and patrol it to prevent illegal egg taking. About 30 percent of the eggs deposited during an arribada are lost anyway when turtles dig up eggs laid earlier, so everybody is happy with the arrangement. Visitors who come for the nesting should report to the rancho at the upper edge of the beach; a member of the turtle cooperative will act as guide.

Ridley eggs hatch in about fifty days, with many hatchlings picked off on their way to the water by vultures, crabs, or frigate birds, while others become food for predators in the water, including other turtles. Survival rates are small, making the protection of eggs all the more important. Ostional and Nancite in Santa Rosa Park are the major nesting sites for olive ridleys in Costa Rica.

The 395-acre (160 ha) refuge also has a few patches of forest that contain howler monkeys, kinkajous, coatis, and basilisks. The estuary of the Ostional River offers good bird-watching—190 species have been identified.

You may notice a sign for a University of Costa Rica laboratory at Ostional. Under an agreement between the university and the refuge, scientists are conducting turtle research as well as carrying out education programs on rational use of eggs.

Rainfall averages almost 67 inches a year (1,700 mm); temperature averages 82°F (28°C). Ostional is on the west coast of the Nicoya Peninsula. Nearest towns of any size are Nicoya, Santa Cruz, and Liberia. See chapter 6 for hotels in the area. Unpaved portions of the road are slow going and rough. Your best bet is to rent a car or take a tour to Ostional.

Peñas Blancas National Wildlife Refuge (Northwest)

The Peñas Blancas refuge located northeast of Puntarenas off the Inter-American Highway protects important watersheds. The steep terrain is covered mainly by forests, some of which show man's penchant for altering the natural landscape. In deep river canyons, however, and more rugged terrain, nature has had the upper hand and forests are almost intact.

No tourist facilities exist on this 5,930-acre (2,400-ha) refuge, but a couple of trails exist along the Jabonal River, which flows through its heart. The visitor can find vegetation typical of the tropical dry forest near the south end, with deciduous forest of both dry- and moist-zone species in the lower middle region. Premontane moist forest species grow in the upper part.

At least 70 species of birds have been identified and butterflies are abundant, but wildlife in general is scarce. You might see howler or white-faced monkeys or a paca, opossum, kinkajou, or raccoon. It is hoped that protection of the area as a refuge will increase the wildlife as well as preserve forest land and protect the watersheds of several rivers.

Elevation of the refuge goes from about 1,970 to 4,600 feet (600 to 1,400 m), and the crumpled topography requires stamina for hikes. Contact the wildlife office in San José about access and overnight camping. The nearest large town is Puntarenas.

Tapantí National Wildlife Refuge (Central Valley)

"Dripping forest" is not a scientific term, but it describes for me the Tapantí National Wildlife Refuge in the Talamanca Mountain Range. Inside the forest, raining or not, the air is moist, plants seem wet, the earth smells fresh. The sound of running water can be pervasive: 150 rivers and rivulets run here, important sources for hydroelectric projects.

The wildlife department reports average rainfall in the zone at about 128 inches (3,240 mm), but the refuge itself must get more. One account says up to 276 inches (7,000 mm). (Such discrepancies drive a writer crazy.) What is clear is that even in the drier months of January through April, wise travelers bring rain gear. Average temperature is 70°F (21°C).

A number of marked trails near the entrance lead through the extravagance of rain forest vegetation. Tree crowns form a leaky umbrella under which grow delicate ferns (including 18 species of tree ferns), orchids, bromeliads, lianas that tempt one to take a swing, mosses, and multicolored lichens. Along the road and on forest slopes grows a plant with immense leaves and a tall reddish flower that Costa Ricans call "poor man's umbrella." I have seen its leaves used in the countryside by people caught in the rain.

Tapantí is a favorite with bird-watchers. To accommodate them, it opens at 6:00 a.m. Closing time is 4:00 p.m. Among the more than 200 species identified here are the ones everybody wants to see: quetzals, exotic hummingbirds, toucans, parakeets, parrots, great tinamous, and squirrel cuckoos. Endangered mammals live here: jaguar, ocelot, tapir. Animals you are more likely to see are squirrels, monkeys, raccoons, opossums, coyotes, agoutis, and red brocket deer. There are porcupines, silky anteaters, otters, and lots of toads. Butterflies are everywhere. Your day may be blessed by the appearance of a blue morpho.

An exhibit room at the entrance is a good place to start, to orient yourself and talk with a friendly ranger. A map and booklets on forest fauna (in Spanish) published by the wildlife service can be purchased here. About half a mile (1 km) from the ranger station is the Oropendola Trail, with covered picnic shelters, popular swimming spots in frigid river water, and a place designated for fishing. Two and a half miles (4 km) farther is a vista point marked by a sign with a large eye. Climb the short trail for a splendid view of a waterfall on the densely forested mountains across the river. In all the refuge covers 15,024 acres (6,080 ha).

The graveled road is excellent because the Costa Rican Electric Institute (ICE) has a dam about 9 miles (15 km) from the entrance. You can continue along it for views of magnificent virgin mountain forest.

Tour companies offer day trips to Tapantí. If you go by the Orosi-Río Macho bus from Cartago, you still end up more than 5 miles (9 km) from the refuge entrance, though you can hire a taxi to go the rest of the way. If driving yourself, take the highway to Cartago, and continue to Paraíso and Orosi, taking the bumpy road for Purisil. Watch for the Tapantí sign.

8
Privately Owned Nature Reserves

Privately owned nature reserves catering to natural history tourists are springing up around the country. These are more than hotels. They encompass tracts of protected ecosystems that range from large areas of virgin forest to river habitats to ribbons of primary and secondary forests surrounded by pastures. These reserves offer not only a chance to spend the night where monkeys live and toucans fly but to learn about the ecosystems on guided walks or horseback rides. Some have bilingual biologist guides, others use local people with varying commands of English who are naturalists by life experience. Accommodations range from bunk beds and ''bring your own gear'' to comfortable lodges with hot water and fine dining. Some provide transportation; others help arrange it from San José or other locations.

Some people thrive on adventure: tromping along muddy trails through a jungle miles from nowhere is bliss. Others prefer to view plant and animal life from a shady veranda or to stroll along a quiet beach. These reserves run the gamut. There is something for everyone. This chapter is designed to indicate which offers what, with details on how to get there, costs, and some idea of what you may see. Reserves are in alphabetical order in the regions where they are found. Only those personally visited are described. Other reserves are mentioned in chapter 6.

If you call from outside Costa Rica to make reservations, first dial the international area code (011) and then the country code (506); for example, 011-506-00-0000. Places that accept credit cards are noted. Most do not.

Central Valley

Rancho Naturalista

Fields of cane and coffee spread out below this mountain retreat called Rancho Naturalista, while Irazú and Turrialba volcanoes dominate the skyline to the northwest across a vast valley. Tropical forest is steps away from the lodge. Tranquillity is the key word.

Located southeast of Turrialba, 1.5 miles (2.4 km) up a dirt road from the village of Tuis, the ranch belonging to Kathy and John Erb caters strictly to nature travelers. "Anybody else would probably be bored," said John. Boredom does not seem likely, however.

Daughter Lisa is an enthusiastic, knowledgeable guide on the trails and farm roads that visitors may take to look for the birds, butterflies, and moths that abound in the area. More than 330 species of birds have been seen within a two-mile radius of the lodge. Lisa likes to help visitors start a bird list and is extremely patient with beginning bird-watchers who find it difficult to spot birds in dense forest foliage, much less zero in on them with binoculars. With her encouragement, neophytes experience the thrill of seeing something first— maybe even a rare bird. Noticing a blue-crowned motmot, she points out the telltale tick-tock motion motmots make with their racket-tipped tails. You are likely to see toucans, manakins, trogons, tanagers, and a world of hummingbirds. Lisa speaks English and Spanish. Husband Arnoldo also guides.

If you have yet to see the gorgeous morpho butterfly, this could be your chance. Several of the six Central American species of this butterfly live near the lodge. The blue flash of one of these against the greens of the forest is a treasure that glows forever in the mind's eye.

The Erbs don't claim to have all of the 12,000 species of moths found in Costa Rica, but they believe they have enough to keep you occupied. Just ask, and they will put up a sheet and plug in a lamp outside at night to attract moths. The variety is awesome.

A neighbor down the road has a trapiche, the old-style sugarcane press operated by oxen. As a guest at Rancho Naturalista, you are welcome to stop by. Horses are available at no extra charge, and you may want to explore the part of the 125-acre (50-ha) ranch under cultivation—in coffee, black pepper, and pineapple.

If you stay a week, the Erbs offer you a complimentary all-day field trip to an area with a different elevation, so you may see different flora or fauna. Popular choices are the Tapantí Wildlife Refuge, Irazú Volcano and the Lankester Gardens, or a cloud forest in the Talamanca Mountains. Tours can be arranged to volcanoes, beaches, or national parks at an additional cost, as well as for white-water rafting on the nearby Reventazón River.

The two-story main house has seven comfortable bedrooms, four with private bath. All baths have hot-water showers. A cabin with private bath is near the house. Meals are family-style, and food is plentiful and delicious, ranging from filet mignon to Mexican food, with some Costa Rican cuisine as well. The Erbs are gracious hosts who have lived in Costa Rica for many years and are pleased to share their knowledge with you.

Because of the personal service Rancho Naturalista offers, a minimum stay of three days is required. The Erbs say most guests stay at least a week. Laundry service is part of the package—no extra charge.

The lodge is at 2,953 feet (900 m) and is in the transition zone between premontane wet forest and premontane rain forest. Daytime temperatures are usually in the 70s (21°-26°C), nights in the 60s (15°-20°C). Afternoon rain is common, especially from May through November. Rubber boots are recommended. The almost 2 miles (3 km) of trails are well-maintained and are not difficult. You will find three shelters and benches along the way where you can sit and wait for nature to reveal its treasures.

Transportation: The Erbs provide transportation to and from San José as part of the package. You can arrange for pickup at the airport if you wish or at another location you agree upon. There is a moderate charge for transportation on optional tours.

Rates: From December to May, costs are $90 a day per person or

$550 a week double occupancy; from June to November, $80 per day, $450 for one week. Rates include meals, lodging, guided walks, and horseback riding.

Reservations: Rancho Naturalista, Apartado 364-1002, San José. Telephone/fax 39-7138.

North Central

Arenal Volcano Observatory

At 4:30 in the morning, a thunderous explosion brought us from our bunks to the door in one swift leap. Outside, the cone of Arenal Volcano, about 1.2 miles (2 km) away, was sharp against the dark blue of the night sky. Stars were brilliant. A huge cloud of smoke and ash, reddish at the bottom, billowed from the crater. Red rocks and thin streams of lava began to make their way down the slopes.

Arenal Volcano Observatory has a front-row seat for viewing eruptions of one of the most active volcanoes in the world. Built in 1987 to give scientists carrying out long-term geological and biological research a laboratory and a base, the facility is now also open to non-scientific visitors.

Arenal Volcano Observatory (Photo by Ree Strange Sheck)

The small group I was in had already jumped up twice during dinner to pay homage to the spectacle in a steady rain. Later, two of us sat patiently on the elevated, covered observatory platform trying to elicit a command performance, but Arenal seemed uninterested in our schedules. The real show began after everyone was in bed. In all, I jumped up for four explosions, saluting two rumbles from underneath the covers.

After a four-hundred-year dormancy, Arenal devastated more than 4 square miles (10 km²) the last three days of July 1968. It has been continuously active since then. The direction of the flow is from a horseshoe-shaped crater, one of four, that is open to the northwest, west, and southwest. The observatory is south of the volcano. Arenal is young as volcanoes go—about four thousand years young—and relatively small—5,358 feet (1,633 m) high. It is in the Tilarán Mountain Range.

The observatory continues its scientific role. Scientists from the Smithsonian Institution stay here while monitoring the volcano, and Earthwatch groups have used it as a base.

When you are not watching eruptions, you can turn your eyes to the tranquillity of Lake Arenal, just down the hill, site of Costa Rica's largest hydroelectric project. Visitors may want to arrange optional tours for fishing, windsurfing, or kayaking on its waters through Costa Rica Sun Tours, which operates the Arenal observatory. John Aspinall, who is president of the company and whose family owns the observatory, says Sun Tours can provide the gear you need.

Visitors to the observatory have access to almost 300 acres (120 ha) of primary forest reserve on the property, a 75-acre (30-ha) reforestation project of pine and eucalyptus, and almost 250 acres (100 ha) in a macadamia plantation. Trails through the lush forest lead to Cerro Chato, an extinct crater near Arenal and its green-colored lagoon. Trails as well as roads through the farm offer excellent bird-watching as well as a chance to see the spectacular morpho butterflies. Walking is easy around the farm and along roads, but the trail to the crater is for the physically fit.

Being on the farm allows a firsthand look at agricultural operations. You can watch macadamia nuts being harvested and husked. You can also rent horses to explore the area.

The eleven rooms are rustic, but each has a bath with hot water, and there is electricity. Maximum capacity is thirty people. In the dining room/main lodge, guests sample fruits from the area and such typical meals as *olla de carne* (a meat and vegetable soup) or *arroz con pollo* (chicken and rice).

Elevation at the observatory is 2,428 feet (740 m) and annual rainfall is 197 inches (5,000 mm). The drier months are from December through May, but rain can occur anytime, so bring your rain gear.

Day trips are also available to the observatory from San José. If time and weather permit, the tour includes a dip in nearby hot springs.

Transportation: If you are driving, you can go through either Varablanca or Zarcero to Ciudad Quesada, continuing to Fortuna and the observatory, south of the volcano across the Agua Caliente River. The road is paved to the turnoff at the lake. For the day trip or the two-day, one-night tour, transportation is part of the package.

Rates: The one-day tour to the observatory is $69 per person, including breakfast, lunch, a bilingual guide, and round-trip transportation from San José. Fixed departures are Tuesday, Thursday, and Saturday. Cost of the two-day, one-night tour is $150, including meals as specified, lodging, transportation, a guided walk to an old lava flow and a hike to Cerro Chato, and a tour of the macadamia plantation. These tours depart from San José Monday and Friday. Other packages incorporate a visit to Caño Negro Wildlife Refuge, Monteverde, or a cruise in the Gulf of Nicoya. Lodging only is $40 single, $25 each for a double. Meals are $20 per day.

Reservations: Costa Rica Sun Tours, Apartado 1195-1250, Escazú. Telephone 55-3418, 55-2011. Fax 55-4410. The office is located at Avenida 7, Calles 3/5 in San José.

EcoAdventure Lodge, Lago Coter

You will learn about such things as flying sticks and why some tropical trees shed their bark (to keep epiphytes from getting a hold). You can see a huge mound built by busy little leaf-cutter ants and marvel at the free-form sculpture of a vine called monkey ladder.

On the thirteen marked trails that wind through the EcoAdventure Lodge property, bilingual, well-trained naturalist guides can help guests appreciate that tropical forests are more than monkeys jumping from branch to branch, than coatis darting across a trail, than the turquoise flash of a scarlet-thighed dacnis as it flies against the rich greens of the trees and plants. It is these things, but it is also the tiny flower almost hidden among fallen leaves, an insect disguised as a dried leaf, an animal track in the mud, the elegant tree fern, thousands of species of plants and animals intertwined in a web of life.

In the distance Arenal Volcano rumbles. It seems to rise out of Lake Arenal from some vantage points on the property, though it is not visible from the lodge itself.

EcoAdventure Lodge, new in 1991, is a comfortable place from which to wander forest trails or go horseback riding, bicycling, fishing, windsurfing, canoeing, or sailing either on Lake Arenal or Coter Lake. Those who want to can plant a tree native to the area in an ongoing reforestation project. It can be the base for trips to the volcano (even an overnight camping trip), to caverns at Venado, 90 minutes away, to Guanacaste beaches. Rubber boots and rain ponchos are provided.

The lodge has a spacious living/recreation area with a big fireplace, conversation areas, television with a supply of videos, billiard table, bar, and restaurant. Ample meals are served buffet style. The twenty-five rooms are in two wings off this area, maximum capacity of fifty persons (no one under twelve). Each wing has a bath for women and for men, among the nicest shared baths I have seen: sparkling clean, light, and with a degree of privacy.

Guests are invited to record which animals they have seen and where. More than 350 birds have been sighted. Leafing through the book, one finds monkeys, brocket deer, keel-billed toucans, the bare-necked umbrellabird, squirrel cuckoo, and coatis, among others.

Interesting photographs of an earlier Costa Rica adorn hallways. Probably one of the most intriguing photographs at the lodge is of a flying saucer near Arenal Volcano. The friendly staff can show you books commenting on the authenticity of that photo.

The dry season is not as pronounced here as in some other places in the country: rainfall amounts to about 152 inches a year (3,857 mm). Elevation varies, but the lodge is at about 2,329 feet (710 m). The forested slopes have characteristics of rain forest and cloud forest.

Transportation: EcoAdventure Lodge is located 17 miles (28 km) from Tilarán above the northwest section of Lake Arenal. Buses between Tilarán and Ciudad Quesada (San Carlos) pass by on the highway less than two miles (3 km) below. Transportation can be arranged from San José or Tilarán.

Rates: A new package offers a one-day, one-night trip including meals, lodging, taxes, and guide service for $72 per person. A three-day, two-night package for one person is $294, for a double, $269 per person. The eight-day, seven-night package is single $819, double $699. These packages also include tours and other activities offered by the lodge for those days. People staying in the area can take part in lodge activities; for example, trail walks are $21 for half a day, $33 per day; tours to the caves or volcano, $69; horseback riding, $30 a day; sailing, $59 for half a day.

Reservations: EcoAdventure Lodge, Apartado 60, Tilarán, Guanacaste. Telephone 21-4209, fax 69-5579.

La Selva Biological Station

La Selva Biological Station near Puerto Viejo de Sarapiquí offers a marvelous opportunity to see a variety of habitats: besides the virgin tropical wet forest, there are swamps, creeks, rivers, pastures, agricultural lands, and secondary forests in various stages of growth. Tropical biologist Dr. Leslie R. Holdridge began La Selva as an experimental farm in the fifties and sold his plantations of peach palm (*pejibaye*), cacao, and laurel along with virgin forest to the Organization for Tropical Studies (OTS) in 1960. Primary use of La Selva is for biological research, for education (many of the leading tropical biologists in the the hemisphere today have studied or worked at the biological station), and for linking the research with rational use of natural resources that will allow man to make use of the rich biological diversity without destroying it.

Visitors are guaranteed to get a taste of that diversity even if they never get farther than the main dining hall. The panorama from the porch may include flocks of parrots flying overhead or the red flash of a scarlet-rumped tanager. As you sway across the long suspension bridge over the Puerto Viejo River, look down. Machacas leap up to grab leaves floating down to the water's surface. You could be lucky enough to see a caiman or a river otter. La Selva is home to more than 100 species of mammals, including the howler, spider, and white-faced monkey, peccary, agouti, coati, sloth, jaguar, and tapir. There are more than 2,000 species of plants in this tropical rain forest, 400 species of birds, and thousands of species of insects.

The bala, or bullet, ant is one species it pays to look out for. Researchers tell tales of its powerful sting. You can't miss it, as it is the largest ant in Costa Rica, up to an inch long. It looks big when you see it on a leaf next to you.

Brightly colored poison dart frogs may jump in the leaf cover at the side of the trail. Toxins secreted from their skin glands were used by Colombian Indians to poison blowgun darts—hence the name. Because of their toxic skin, these frogs have no need for drab coloration; in fact, their colors warn predators. As the life history of these tiny creatures is being discovered, we learn that they lay eggs on the ground, with adults transporting the tadpoles on their backs to water in a bromeliad in the trees. Studies of one genus show that the female feeds the tadpoles unfertilized eggs.

Trails meander through the 3,707-acre (1,500-ha) reserve. Don't miss the arboretum, where a keel-billed toucan perched patiently while a group of us drew near, admired his splendor, and photographed him. We spotted a purple-throated fruitcrow, collared araçari, crested owl, and yellow-billed cacique within a few yards. Armed with a trail map and a delightful printed guide (written by Beth Farnsworth and Héctor González) to the natural history trail, one can set out for an experience in a tropical forest in relative safety. Snakes do live in the tropics, however, and can appear as you make your own foray into their world. As the trail guide suggests, watch where you walk, stay on the trail, and give any snake you see plenty of breathing room. The trail takes about an hour.

La Selva is open for day visits from 6:30 a.m. to 5:00 p.m., but reservations are recommended because there are limitations on the number of visitors per day. Local naturalist guides trained in an intensive natural history course at the biological station will accompany individuals and groups on La Selva's trails. The charge is less than $7 for a half day, $15 for a whole day. Completely bilingual guides cost 15 percent more, but all of those trained receive rudimentary English instruction to enable them to communicate the essentials. These guides have formed a cooperative whose activities include environmental education in the communities, ongoing education for members, and conservation and sustainable management of natural resources in the area. This project is an example of an ecotourism-related activity around a forest reserve that involves the community and presents an alternative to deforestation and unemployment.

Overnight facilities are open to visitors as space permits. The new buildings have four beds per room, with a shared bath (hot water) between two rooms. Each bed has its own reading lamp, and there is a ceiling fan. Since the rooms are primarily for researchers who may stay awhile, there is ample storage/closet space. A modern dining room is set up for cafeteria service, where you may find yourself rubbing elbows with leading tropical scientists. Mealtime conversations are fascinating, but remember that the time these researchers have in the field is precious to them, so don't expect one to lead you on a tour.

There is a small gift shop in the dining hall, with a great selection of T-shirts, and a visitor center with exhibits.

More than 4 inches (100 mm) of rain falls even in the drier months, from February to April, and the yearly total is almost 158 inches (4,000 mm). Average temperature is 75°F (24°C). Elevation ranges from 115 feet (35 m) to 656 feet (200 m). The reserve is adjacent to Braulio Carrillo National Park.

Transportation: La Selva has van transportation from San José three times a week, so check when you make your reservation to see if space is available. There are two routes from San José by public bus—through Braulio Carrillo and Las Horquetas to Puerto Viejo or through Varablanca, Chilamate, and Puerto Viejo. Tell the driver you want to get off at La Selva. Buses leave from Calle 12, Avenidas 7/9. There are no doormen at La Selva; you will be carrying your own luggage, so pack lightly.

Rates: For a bed and three meals per day, the charge for natural history visitors is $76 per day per person. Charge for a day visit is $15.

Reservations: For individual travelers who want to visit for the day, there are two ways to reserve. You may contact the OTS office in San José, telephone 40-6696, fax 40-6783, open Monday through Friday. Under this arrangement, lunch is provided and you are not required to walk with a naturalist guide. You may use the trail guide and maps and go on your own. The second option is to reserve through La Selva, telephone 71-6897, fax 71-6481, open daily. For this option, La Selva needs forty-eight hours notice to arrange for the naturalist guide who must accompany you on the trails. Lunch is not provided. For overnight stays, contact the office in San José: Organization for Tropical Studies, Apartado 676-2050, San Pedro Montes de Oca.

Rara Avis

Visiting the beautiful Waterfall Lodge for the first time, a local tour operator remarked to Amos Bien, founder of Rara Avis, "You know, Amos, most people would have put the road in first." But Amos Bien is not most people, and Rara Avis is not your ordinary country inn.

Actually there is a road of the sort that allows your adventure to start at Las Horquetas. The 10 miles (16 km) into Rara Avis from there can be a three-hour horseback ride plus a one-hour walk or four hours in a tractor-pulled cart, fording two large rivers and lurching along the miles of slippery clay, mud, and corduroy road. Planned road improvements will shorten the trip, but, one hopes, not the adventure. There is a chance to see the great green macaw as you bump along, to hear about a nearby *achiote* plantation (the plants are grown in Costa Rica both as ornamentals and as a source of red dye), to observe the pasture lands clear-cut from tropical rain forest, to see reforestation projects and secondary forest. Amos spins tales about a horse who died along the way and a budding student of the tropical world who lugged the bones for miles in the belief that they represented a giant tapir.

Amos himself first came to Costa Rica in 1977 as a biology student. He returned to found Rara Avis, not only for nature/adventure tourism but as a biological research center and a conservation proving ground to show his neighbors they can make more money by maintaining the forest than by clearing it for ranches or farms.

The road leads to Albergue El Plástico, a former prison colony barracks rehabilitated into a rustic lodge with four to six bunk beds per room and shared baths, with hot-water showers. Visitors who come to enjoy the tropical forest sit at dining tables on a hard-packed dirt floor where the prisoners sent in to cut the forests once ate. Food, served family-style, is tasty and includes typical black beans and rice as well as more exotic fare such as fried chicken or tuna croquettes. Lighting is by kerosene lantern. There is good bird-watching even from the upstairs porch/library; a rushing stream down the open slope invites a dip on sunny days. At the edge of the clearing, forest beckons on all sides.

Two miles (3 km) farther into that forest is the impressive, two-story Waterfall Lodge, built of beautiful tropical hardwoods. Each of the eight spacious rooms is a corner room with chairs and a hammock on a wraparound balcony and a private bath complete with both shower and bathtub. A longtime birder saw five birds he had never seen before from his balcony one afternoon. A breathtaking 180-foot double waterfall is a two-minute walk away. The dining room is in a separate structure, where a spectacular variety of hummingbirds feeds on flowers at the porch rail.

Five hundred feet from the Waterfall Lodge is Donald Perry's motor-driven cable car, which moves horizontally and vertically through the forest canopy, allowing researchers access to the mysterious upper reaches of the forest largely unexplored until now. Though the canopy tramway is not normally available to the public, if you are lucky enough to be there on a day when it is not being used by scientists and you are willing to sign a forbidding document that washes its hands of your fate if you step aboard, you may be able to arrange a thirty-minute flight of fantasy that takes you into the treetops for about $25. The experience? Unforgettable.

For those who prefer to keep their feet on the ground, there are miles of trails through virgin rain forest, with emphasis on the rain. There's virtually no dry season at Rara Avis; rubber boots are essential. A fellow visitor, after an hour on the wet, slippery trail between El Plástico and the Waterfall Lodge, commented, "This must be the only trail in the world with an undertow." In a four-day period, we explored Rara Avis in 4.5 inches (114 mm) of rain. Annual rainfall is from 200 to 300 inches (5,080 to 7,614 mm).

A working biologist, bilingual in English and Spanish, guides visitors on the trails, spotting such exotic birds as the slaty-tailed trogon and the keel-billed and chestnut-mandibled toucan (more than 314 bird species identified so far) and the home of a tent-making bat, who cuts the leaf of a wild plantain on either side of the midrib and bends it to form a tent to sleep under in daytime. Howler, white-faced capuchin, and spider monkeys are very common, as are pacas, coatis, vested anteaters, and brocket deer. Tapirs, jaguars, collared peccaries, agoutis, and three-toed sloths may be seen.

On a walk with Amos in the forest, you hear about the possibilities for sustainable production of forest plants that he hopes will convince his neighbors to harvest rather than destroy the forest, proving there is more profit in managing it than they could ever make on land cleared for crops or cattle. An understory palm once thought extinct but found here could provide seeds for export as an ornamental plant; the aerial roots of a species of philodendron can be harvested for wicker products; selective cutting of wood instead of clear-cutting can provide income while preserving rain forest habitat and biological diversity. Rara Avis and a nonprofit U.S. corporation called Rainforestry, Inc., have purchased about 3,200 acres (1,300 ha) bordering Braulio Carrillo National Park and the La Selva Protected Zone to put this thesis to the test.

The two miles of corduroy road between the two lodges are excellent for bird-watching on your own or for a relatively safe chance to have some solitary time in a tropical rain forest. People from two to seventy-six years of age have found their way to this remote spot, but access and trails can be rough for those who are not in good physical condition. There are few mosquitoes; the elevation is 2,000 feet (600 to 700 m).

Transportation: By paved road from San José to Las Horquetas, it is 48 miles (77 km) by way of Braulio Carrillo National Park, about 1½ hours; some 120 miles (193 km) via Poás Volcano, about 3 hours. The Rara Avis office can advise you of bus schedules to Las Horquetas or the cost of hiring a taxi from San José. At Río Frío, $15 and about twenty-five minutes by taxi from Las Horquetas, there is an airstrip for charter planes. For the independent traveler, scheduled trips go in Tuesday, Friday, and Sunday.

Rates: El Plástico Lodge: $45 per person per night. Waterfall Lodge: single $80 per night; double $70 per person; triple $60 per person. Prices include meals, a naturalist guide, and round-trip transportation from Las Horquetas to Rara Avis. Youth hostel members and students are entitled to special rates, with lodging at El Plástico.

Reservations: Rara Avis, Apartado 8105-1000, San José. Telephone/fax 53-0844.

Selva Verde Lodge

Dusk along the Sarapiquí behind the lodge at Selva Verde. The only sound is the rushing water; green forest that gave Selva Verde its name guards the river. Brilliant blue morpho butterflies flutter along the forest's edge above the water. Dusk becomes darkness, the magic moment is gone, and yet it lives forever.

Images of time spent at Selva Verde Lodge near Chilamate, less than three hours north of San José, crowd in. The delightful day on a river trip down the Sarapiquí was arranged at the lodge. We saw a river otter, crocodile, white-crowned parrot, kingfishers, keel-billed toucans, parakeets, blue herons, araçaris, a three-toed sloth, anhingas, egrets, flycatchers, a bananaquit, oropendolas, turtles, a scarlet-rumped tanager, trees full of vultures, and iguanas draped on limbs high above the water. We observed children playing along the river, women washing, men riding on horseback along a high bank. We passed ranches, farms, forests, and lush river vegetation.

Selva Verde has a reserve of its own along the Sarapiquí, 529 acres (214 ha), with trails that reveal the wonderland of a tropical lowland forest. You can go with Selva Verde's own bilingual guide or follow a trail map. Eight well-marked trails offer walks from easy to somewhat steep: you choose. Benches along the way provide a place to rest or a place to wait and see what the forest will reveal to you. It could be a coati, sloth, raccoon, kinkajou, brocket deer, anteater, or maybe a tiny lizard or frog. There are more than 2,000 species of plants, 700 species of butterflies, and 400 species of birds. Most commonly seen birds are tanagers, honeycreepers, oropendolas, trogons, and chachalacas. You can add what you see to a book where previous guests have already recorded species such as agoutis, tayras, river otters, kinkajous, toucans, and monkeys. A biologist natural history guide leads private tours, charging $20 for two persons for four hours. The Sarapiquí River boat trip is $20. At the tour desk, you can also arrange horseback riding, $17 per person.

Howler monkey, called *congo* in Spanish (Photo by Richard La Val)

On this side of the river are the Creek Lodge, the newer River Lodge, and the dining room. Meals are cafeteria-style, tasty and ample. A small library and reading room has bird books for reference, natural history material, and paperbacks. Both lodges have generous balconies, with hammocks and chairs from which to enjoy parrots, hummingbirds, monkeys, and other exotic species in the surrounding forest. Construction is of beautiful tropical woods; roofs are thatched. Attention to detail in the River Lodge includes convenient closet space, reading lights at each bed in the thirty-two double rooms, a small desk, lots of windows, large towels in the private baths, and even washcloths. The Creek Lodge has nine doubles upstairs over the library; shared baths. Since it is next to the highway, sounds of civilization sometimes are heard.

Guests can follow the development of botanical and butterfly gardens near the lodge. Peter Knudsen, a physicist and mathematician and a lifelong student of butterflies, is creating a flowering garden tucked among the trees on a forested hillside which attracts the butterflies and provides host plants for larvae. He is currently rearing 30 species. There are 5 species of morpho here—4 blue and 1 green-brown canopy species. Peter's collection of native plants makes it a botanical garden as well, and one section focuses on medicinal plants and endangered local species. The garden is open from dawn to dusk, free to guests at the lodge, $5 for others, with guided walks on the 2.5 miles (4 km) of easy trails. His rearing house will assure a reliable source of butterflies for the enclosed area, and some butterflies will be released to rebuild local populations.

The hub of the River Lodge is a large conference room used for talks, slide shows, or conferences. If you are traveling independently, you might be invited to join an evening presentation. I took advantage of a lecture on insects by a visiting scientist for a delightful Elderhostel group staying there and a discussion by local officials from Chilamate of issues facing a small city government. Selva Verde has a commitment to community involvement. A library for the town is being built on the property.

The gift shop also has ties to the community. Manager Betty Ann Knudsen works with local people in development and marketing of handcrafts. There is basketry made from rain-forest vines, embroidered items, belts and hat bands, primitive carvings, and jewelry made from seeds, plus lots more.

Transportation: You can take a public bus either to Puerto Viejo through Braulio Carrillo and Las Horquetas (taxi from Puerto Viejo to Selva Verde is less than $4) or a longer route toward Río Frío through Varablanca. Tell the driver to let you off at Selva Verde. The trip by taxi from San José is about $50.

Rates: Rooms in the older Creek Lodge, with shared baths, are singles $55, doubles $44 per person, including meals and taxes; in the newer River Lodge, $60 for singles, $52 per person for doubles.

Reservations: In the United States, contact Costa Rican Lodges, 3540 NW 13th Street, Gainesville, FL 32609. Telephone (800) 451-7111 or (904) 373-7118; in Florida (800) 345-7111. Fax (904) 371-3710. In Costa Rica, contact Selva Verde Lodge, Chilamate, Sarapiquí, Heredia. Telephone 20-1712, 20-2121; fax 32-3321.

Northwest

Cabinas Karen

Karen and Nils Olof Wessberg came to the Nicoya Peninsula in 1955 in search of a primitive life. On land 1 mile (1.6 km) from Montezuma, they built a palm-leaf cottage near the sea and determined to live from the land without damaging it, inspired by Fairfield Osborn's *Our Plundered Planet.*

Soon, however, they became deeply disturbed by the widespread destruction of virgin forest. Karen said they could look across the water and see the spreading patches of brown on Cabo Blanco at the tip of the peninsula, 7 miles (11 km) away. Nils began an arduous campaign to raise money to save that bit of tropical moist forest. Today Cabo Blanco Strict Nature Reserve stands in tribute to their efforts.

Though Nils died in 1975, killed on a visit to look into possibilities of conserving a part of the Osa Peninsula now known as Corcovado National Park, Karen continues conservation work—investigating and reporting the illegal entrapment of tropical birds to sell in San

José, opposing the country's electrical company when it proposed to put its lines through original forest, and protecting her own 170-acre (69-ha) reserve.

A taste of the primitive life the Wessbergs sought is still possible on that reserve. Some visitors have called it a piece of paradise. There is no electricity here: candles glow at night. Water is piped from a pure source high on the coastal mountain; the reserve stretches from shoreline to mountaintop. There is a shared open-air kitchen for the three cabins and a shared cold-water shower and outhouse. Bedding is provided. Views from the cabins are idyllic, with the blue of the Pacific shimmering through the greens of lush vegetation. The one-room wooden cabins have big shutters that open on three sides to let the jungle in. For at least one guest, that has meant a kinkajou who casually passed through one night (kinkajous are small, bright-eyed mammals related to coatis and raccoons). White-faced and howler monkeys are common, and there is a chance of seeing a paca or an agouti. Bird songs punctuate the stillness.

Trails lead to the highest point of the reserve, where there is a simple shelter for any guest who wants to spend the night under the stars, and past a small waterfall. The reserve is open only to those housed in the cabins. A panoply of colored rocks and shells fills a section of beach that stretches northeast along the shore.

Doña Karen's reserve is a thirty-minute walk from Montezuma along the shore. Guests must carry in their own gear and food.

If you get to Montezuma, do not miss the chance to visit with Doña Karen. She speaks her native Danish language as well as Swedish (her husband's language), English, and Spanish. A conservationist through and through, she is adamant that we must offer alternatives to cutting the forest. She believes, for example, that we need more studies on the nutritional content of leaves that animals eat with an eye to harvesting for human diet. She often eats leaves the monkeys consume and claims they make her feel fantastic.

Transportation: Puntarenas is the primary departure point. By car, cross the Gulf of Nicoya on the car ferry (see ferry schedule in Practical Extras) and proceed to Paquera, Cóbano, and Montezuma. By public transportation, take the launch that goes to Paquera (leaves from behind the Puntarenas downtown market). From Paquera you can hire a jeep taxi all the way to Montezuma (about $25 for the trip, with the cost shared among passengers) or take the bus to Cóbano that will be waiting at the pier in Paquera and then a taxi for the remaining few miles to Montezuma (for a total of less than $5). An open-air bus between Paquera and Montezuma costs $3 (see chap. 6). Paving proceeds bit by bit; unpaved sections can be rough but are passable without four-wheel drive.

Rates: Cost per person is $6 per night.

Reservations: No reservations, no phone. It is first come, first served. Look for the Cabinas Karen sign as you enter Montezuma. She also has two rooms at the house in town, with shared bath.

La Pacífica Ecological Center

Pacífica means peaceful or tranquil, and indeed the traveler who pulls into La Pacífica Ecological Center senses a serenity to the place. Actually it was named for the woman who designed the Costa Rican flag early in this century, but why quibble. The name fits.

The purpose of the ecological center also fits with the growing concern throughout Costa Rica that conservation and development proceed together. La Pacífica has been set up as a model for economic self-sufficiency and protection of natural resources.

Scientific researchers have been coming to "Finca La Pacífica" since the sixties. The rich diversity of habitats—tropical dry forest, river habitat, swampland, pastures—that continues to draw researchers also makes the center attractive to today's natural history tourists, who are also drawn by the modern, tastefully decorated rooms in the bungalows scattered over the spacious gardens, the restaurant, and a swimming pool that looks great on a hot Guanacaste day. Large-windowed rooms open out onto small private terraces and grounds dotted with ferns, flowers, and trees.

Guests can follow the roads and trails on their own or go with a resident, bilingual naturalist guide. Watch for informational signs along the trails. About one-third of the almost 3,300 acres (1,332 ha) is covered with forest, including tree species such as the increasingly rare *cocobolo* (rosewood), the *caoba* (mahogany), and the spiny pochote. Bird life is abundant, with 26 percent of the species found in the country seen here; 68 species are migratory. The lagoon and rivers on the property lure water birds. Forest animals include armadillos, squirrels, tamanduas (anteaters), deer, and monkeys. Studies on the howler monkey at La Pacífica go back almost twenty years.

The far-sighted Swiss agronomist who preserved the deciduous forest as part of his working ranch put the rest of the land in pasture, rice and sorghum fields, and vegetable crops. He used windbreaks that still stand to fight erosion and increase productivity; he pioneered many experimental practices in dairy farming, crop breeding, and livestock management. The new owners, also Swiss, continue to see La Pacífica as a model for the tropical Pacific lowlands. Visitors are welcome to tour the agricultural operations, including a modern dairy and an organic garden. In addition to beef and milk products, the ranch produces mangoes and cashews. Visitors can watch a reforestation project—using native species—as it develops. An hour by foot from the rooms and restaurant in a restored farmhouse with artifacts from the past century. A library at the entrance to La Pacífica focuses on the dry tropics.

The beautiful Corobicí River, popular with rafters, forms part of the boundary of the center. Staff can arrange river trips as well as guided day trips to Palo Verde, Santa Rosa, and Rincón de la Vieja national parks and Ostional Wildlife Refuge to see turtle nesting. Horseback riding is also available.

If you happen to be at La Pacífica when a group is there, you may have a chance to hear typical Guanacaste marimba music in the large, outdoor rancho used for cookouts.

All rooms have fans and private baths with hot water. Meals are à la carte in the restaurant.

La Pacífica Ecological Center is in the transition zone between tropical dry and moist forest. Annual rainfall is about 66 inches (1,674 mm). Average high temperature is around 91°F (33°C); average low, 73°F (23°C).

Transportation: The center is about 4 miles (6 km) north of Cañas on the Inter-American Highway toward Liberia, 117 miles (188 km) from San José. You can take the bus for Liberia or buses going to La Cruz or Peñas Blancas. Ask the driver to let you off at La Pacífica, or get off in Cañas and take a taxi.

Rates: Singles are $40, doubles $62. Credit cards are accepted.

Meal plans are available. The charge for a day visit is $35, which allows you use of the pool and a room plus access to trails. Guided walks with the biologist are $25 for a half day. Guided horseback tours are $3.75 an hour.

Reservations: La Pacífica Ecological Center, Apartado 8-5700, Cañas, Guanacaste. Telephone 69-0266, 69-0050; fax 69-0555.

Las Imágenes Biological Station and San Antonio Cattle Ranch
In rugged country north of Liberia between the Inter-American Highway and Rincón de la Vieja National Park is a 2,470-acre (1,000-ha) ranch with 247 acres (100 ha) of virgin forest. Las Imágenes is a working ranch that has opened a biological station for scientific study and tourism. The station is in what was the owner's modest home, a four-bedroom house with an airy, deep veranda to keep the summer sun at bay. A nearby cabin expands sleeping capacity to twenty, with shared baths. There is a delightful rancho down a path from the house that is ideal for barbecues and relaxation.

Though accommodations are on the rustic side, the setting is intriguing. The ranch offers pasture lands, *charrales* (like an overgrown field), river habitats, tropical moist forest, and mountains. The guide says he knows where some "hot" spots are: bubbling mud pots.

Horses are available for rent, or you can take off on foot. In either case, take a hat and carry water; it is thirsty country. If you have never seen the rush of water fill the cups on a Pelton wheel, here's your chance to observe how a water turbine produces electricity. The guide loves to show it. The trail takes you through lush vegetation along the river. You may find yourself reflecting on the ingenuity, hard work, and grit it takes to settle remote areas.

Butterflies are everywhere. We saw the magical morpho on the bumpy drive before we reached the station. (We had stopped to dip our hands in an irresistible stream flowing through tall forest.) More were patrolling the creek next to the station. Deer are abundant. You will see birds that look similar to some from home—various species of doves, noisy white-throated magpie jays. Parrots and parakeets remind you that you are in the tropics.

If you like, you can join ranch hands for a day on the job. We helped track lost cattle through the brush (all the while with binoculars

handy to zero in on the abundant bird life). The foreman was particularly concerned because cattle rustlers were working in the area.
Proximity to Rincón de la Vieja opens up the possibility of another
optional tour from the ranch—a visit to the national park on horseback. Or you can take off on your horse through magnificent country to visit a sister ranch owned by the same enterprise. San Antonio
Cattle Ranch does not offer accommodations for overnight visitors;
a day tour there is operated out of Hotel Las Espuelas in Liberia,
which also manages the Las Imágenes Biological Station. Near
Quebrada Grande, north of Las Imágenes, San Antonio stretches
over 5,000 acres (2,024 ha) of hills and valleys. As you ride along,
notice the influence of trade winds that blow from the east down the
slopes of the volcanoes, especially strong from December through
February. Keep your eyes and ears open—howler and white-faced
monkeys abound. Juan Valencia, a working cowman who is a good
naturalist from his years of living on the land, can show you around
at San Antonio. He knows just where to look for wildlife in the forests
along the rivers. River otters are elusive, but they do live in these
waters.

Juan will tell you that they run about a thousand head of cattle on
the ranch—Brahmans, Santa Gertrudis, Holstein, Charolais. They
are just experimenting with Herefords. It takes about 1 hectare
(roughly 2.5 acres) per animal, which doesn't mean each hectare has
one lonely cow on it. That is a rancher's way of describing how much
pasture he needs to graze a certain number of animals. They rotate
the cattle from pasture to pasture about every seven or eight days.
Cattle raising is important in the Costa Rican economy; here is a
chance to learn about it.

Transportation: Hotel Las Espuelas arranges transportation from
Liberia to the Las Imágenes Biological Station. Cost is $20.

Rates: A stay of two days and one night at Las Imágenes, including four meals, is $169; each additional day is $76, including meals.
A one-day visit with lunch is also $76. Ask about charges for optional
tours, guides, and horses. The day trip to San Antonio Cattle Ranch
from Liberia is $70, including transportation, lunch, and an after-
noon visit to Santa Rosa National Park up the road. Credit cards are
accepted.

Nature from the veranda, Selva Verde Lodge (Photo by Ree Strange Sheck)

Reservations: Hotel Las Espuelas, Apartado 1056-1007, Centro Colón, San José. Telephone 33-9955, fax 33-1787.

Los Inocentes

There's something special about waking to the dawn's early light and the bass-toned barks of the howler monkey. When you open the big windows of your south-facing room at Los Inocentes, Orosí Volcano looms big enough to touch. Teak floors, polished wood, wide L-shaped verandas, both upstairs and down—the hacienda itself is so inviting that nothing less than those intriguing barks from the forest down by the river spur one to get dressed and leave it for an early morning horseback ride.

Los Inocentes is a working ranch as well as a naturalist lodge for travelers looking to experience a bit of life and nature in Guanacaste. Perhaps that accounts for horses that are a pleasure to ride. Don't worry if you are not an expert horseman. Put yourself in the hands of Dennis Ortiz, your guide for the nature tour. He will have you riding like a pro. We found the howlers and the white-faced monkeys. Dennis patiently tracked the shyer spider monkeys three times so I could get a perfect camera angle. He tried not to laugh when a tree and I got tangled up while I was juggling cameras, lenses, and binoculars. If horses are not your thing, manager Jaime Víquez has a tractor-driven cart to take you to the forest.

The forest generally follows the *quebradas* (ravines) and the river-beds. Bird-watching is excellent in the open pastures. We heard the laughing falcon before we saw him. Both white-fronted and yellow-naped parrots are common, flying overhead in pairs or flocks. Even the elusive king vulture is among the 170 species of birds officially recorded on ranch property. Orange-fronted and orange-chinned parakeets, several species of hummingbirds, Montezuma oropendolas, and pauraques (nightjars) are among birds regularly seen. Animals to watch for include white-tailed deer, coatis, raccoons, sloths, tapirs, and peccaries. Los Inocentes is less than 1,000 feet (280 m) above sea level in premontane moist forest.

All nature tours are escorted. The guide not only knows where and what to look for in flora and fauna but he also knows the boundaries of the ranch. Bird-watchers who want a solitary trip can go to the nearby river, and the veranda offers good viewing for those who cannot tear themselves away from the charm of the house. The hacienda was built in the last century and was remodeled with an eye to maintaining the integrity of its architecture. Stone corrals also witness to the age of the property. A small swimming pool has been added, and guests can also swim in natural pools in the river.

On the south, Los Inocentes approaches Guanacaste National Park. Maybe you really do want to touch 4,879-foot (1,487-m) Orosí Volcano. You can visit one of the park's biological stations located on its slopes. A number of other day trips can be arranged: to the beach at Junquillal where you board a sailboat that takes you near Bolaños Island Wildlife Refuge and into the Santa Elena Gulf ($50), to Murciélago (a section of Santa Rosa National Park), to Las Pailas and its bubbling mud at Rincón de la Vieja National Park, to Santa Rosa. For a different kind of tour, with advance notice you can visit the two-room school located on the property where workers' children from the ranch and nearby farms attend. Local children perform traditional dances if requested beforehand. If you want to camp on the property, you must bring your own tent. A guided night tour of the forest is another possibility. At night, turn your eyes to the heavens for a bit of stargazing: there may be new constellations for you in Guanacaste's vast sky. And don't forget to ask Dennis about when it "rains fish."

Meals are something to look forward to. It is not only the milk that is fresh. The ranch makes its own cheese and brings fresh fish in from a few miles away. Fruit trees near the house include limes, mangoes, guavas, nances, and passion fruit.

The main house has eleven nicely decorated rooms and four large, shared baths—two upstairs, two down. If you like a mirror, bring one; there are none in the bedrooms. Closets are roomy.

Day visits are welcome.

Transportation: By car, go north from Liberia to just south of La Cruz and turn right toward Santa Cecilia. Los Inocentes is almost 9 miles (14 km) on paved road from the Inter-American Highway. You can also approach it from the east through Upala. Bus service is available to La Cruz, and taxis are available from La Cruz or Liberia.

Los Inocentes (Photo by Ree Strange Sheck)

When making reservations, ask about transportation; ranch personnel can sometimes pick you up in La Cruz.

Rates: The cost per person for room and meals is $50 a day. The charge for the horse and guide service is $10 a day. Talk with the staff about charges on optional tours. Cost for the day trip is $10 for lunch and $10 for a horseback tour. Credit cards are accepted.

Reservations: Los Inocentes, Apartado 1370-3000, Heredia. Telephone 39-5484, 66-9190; fax 37-8282, 39-5217.

Monteverde Cloud Forest Preserve

The flash of a resplendent quetzal above a waterfall made every bump on the road to the Monteverde cloud forest worthwhile. It was a rainy day, and the guide's search for the bird at familiar haunts had turned up nothing. Then suddenly, appearing almost a turquoise color against the rich, dark green of the forest behind, the red and emerald bird with its magnificent tail swooped across a picture postcard setting. It took my breath away.

The desire to see what many consider the most beautiful bird in tropical America brings thousands every year to this biological reserve 113 miles (182 km) northwest of San José. But the Monteverde reserve is not just quetzals: there are more than 400 species of birds, 490 species of butterflies, 100 species of mammals, 2,500 species of plants. It is the only known home of the golden toad, a two-inch brilliantly colored amphibian: males are orange; females, yellow and black with patches of scarlet. The time to see them is from the end of April to the first of June in small breeding pools formed by rain. However, they have not appeared for the past two years. Only time will tell if another species has disappeared. The preserve is home to the tapir (there is a greater chance of seeing tracks than the large form of this wary, once-common, now-endangered animal). From March to August, you are likely to hear the booming call of the three-wattled bellbird. At any time of year, the fantastic variety of epiphytes covering the trees in this cloud forest is dazzling: there are more than 300 species of orchids (blooms are most profuse in March) and 200 of ferns. Gently press the moss growing profusely on a tree trunk to get an idea of how thick it is. There are checklists on birds and mammals and an informative nature trail guide. A map of the trails is also available at the visitor center. The preserve is open from 7:30 a.m. to 4:30 p.m. year-round except October 6-7.

Monteverde Cloud Forest Preserve is not a national park, though it is now part of the Arenal Conservation Area. It is privately owned land managed by Costa Rica's Tropical Science Center, a nonprofit scientific research and education organization based in San José. Founded in 1972, the reserve encompasses some 26,116 acres (10,569

One of an estimated 2,000 species of butterflies in Costa Rica (Photo by Ree Strange Sheck)

ha) on the Continental Divide in the Tilarán Mountain Range, protecting both Atlantic and Pacific watersheds and containing eight ecological life zones.

Mean temperature at Monteverde is in the low 60s (16°-18°C). Annual rainfall is about 118 inches (3,000 mm). Bring your rain gear and rubber boots or rent boots at the preserve: trails can be muddy. Though little rain falls from December through March, mist rolls in on strong trade winds from the Atlantic and moisture forms on surfaces of the abundant forest vegetation, dripping from the canopy to the ground. For the observant, this "indirect rain" is a striking demonstration of the importance of forest conservation. Without trees and forest plants to collect and disseminate this water, the mist would vaporize in the hot dry air to the west, and rivers that flow to the lowlands would carry less water. That is why the small group of dairy-farming Quakers from the United States who settled in this area in the 1950s set aside 1,369 acres (554 ha) to protect the watershed. That parcel is now part of the reserve, leased to the Tropical Science Center for one colón a year.

To both protect habitat and ensure visitors a worthwhile experience, only 100 persons at a time are allowed on the trails. Priority is given to those coming for the preserve's guided natural history walks, led by bilingual, naturalist guides. Reservations for these walks can be made through hotels or directly with the preserve. In addition to public areas with marked trails and longer trails for backpackers, the preserve has areas where almost no use is allowed and others that are restricted to scientific investigation. Heaviest visitation is from December through May. Backpackers must make reservations for use of the shelters.

Overnight accommodations at the preserve's field station are limited to four rooms for about thirty people, with space often filled by researchers and field-course students. However, nearby hotels are available in the towns of Monteverde and Santa Elena. Parking space is very limited at the preserve. Hotels can arrange transport for you, or you might consider walking at least one way (it is 1.5 miles, 2.5 km, from the cheese plant in Monteverde to the preserve). Birds spotted along the roadside are your reward. The gift shop is worth a visit.

The abundance of plant life in the Monteverde Cloud Forest Preserve (Photo by Ree Strange Sheck)

Transportation: By car, you can reach the Monteverde Cloud Forest Preserve either by the Inter-American Highway, turning north at Sardinal or the Río Lagarto, or from Arenal, coming south through Tilarán, Quebrada Granda, and Santa Elena. On either route the last portion is unpaved and rough. An express bus goes from San José to Monteverde several days a week. The schedule changes with high and low seasons, so call 22-3854 or 61-1152 or check with the ICT office in the Plaza de la Cultura for days and times. It is a good idea to buy your ticket in advance, Calle 14, Avenidas 9/11. You do not want to stand on the trip, which takes 4 hours. There are also public buses from Puntarenas and Tilarán to Santa Elena, and taxi service from Santa Elena. See the description of the town of Monteverde in chapter 6 for other transportation possibilities.

Rates: The entrance fee is $7.50 per person for day visits, $4 for students with an identification card. Children under fifteen are admitted free. Visitors may purchase multiday passes at reduced rates. Guided walks led by bilingual guides are $12 per person. Fee for use of shelters on backpacking trips is $3 per night. Cost for room and meals in the rustic field station is $23.50 per person.

Reservations: For overnight accommodations, contact Monteverde Cloud Forest Preserve, Apartado 8-3870-1000, San José. Telephone 61-2655. Make reservations for guided natural history walks by calling the preserve or through your hotel.

South

Bosque del Cabo

If you like nighttime by candlelight, scarlet macaws flying overhead, a private outdoor shower with water heated only by the sun on the pipes, and the sound of the sea as you drop off to sleep, then Bosque del Cabo is for you.

Perched above Matapalo Beach on the tip of the Osa Peninsula, this small wilderness lodge has perhaps just the right amount of comfort and adventure. The naturalist in me thrilled at the continuous parade of tropical birds so easily seen. The explorer reveled in the horseback

Bosque del Cabo on the Osa Peninsula (Photo by Ree Strange Sheck)

ride through a tropical storm, an encounter with a snake, tracking howler monkeys on a forest trail. The romantic in me relished the private, thatched bungalows above the sea, mosquito netting draped gracefully over the beds, a shower with a forest for a backdrop. Four scarlet macaws flew over in perfect formation as I bathed my first morning there.

I confess I appreciated the modern bath with a flush toilet, the good food, the comfortable beds. I enjoyed experiencing the bungalow at night with only candles or a kerosene lantern to warm the darkness. Doors fold back to open the front of each of the four bungalows to sea and forest.

As I stood on my veranda, I counted a feeding flock of fifteen chestnut-mandibled toucans while the sounds of howler monkeys mixed with the sounds of the surf and a hummingbird whispered by my ear. The scarlet macaws are regular visitors.

Owners Philip Spier and Barbara Odio make visitors feel like welcome house guests. Attentive to needs, they also give guests the space they want. (Bosque del Cabo can house a maximum of sixteen guests.) Keeping up with one-year-old son Derek as he explores the two-level, open-air dining room could keep everyone busy. The parrot who has adopted Barbara makes sounds that Derek makes. The pet menagerie also includes two dogs, a cat, and a coati.

If you can tear yourself away from bird-watching and ocean-gazing (whales pass by at certain times of the year), you can take an hour hike to the gulf side of the peninsula to swim in gentler waters, walk on the trail down to the small river, or go on a horseback ride to the ocean side of the peninsula to visit the tide pools along a deserted beach and walk up to the waterfall. There are other horseback tours. Philip and Barbara will arrange a day trip to Corcovado that involves flying to Sirena from Puerto Jiménez.

Restaurant hours are fairly flexible to meet the needs of both bird-watchers and late sleepers. Local fruits and vegetables are incorporated in the meals that include both typical Costa Rican and North American dishes. Soft drinks and beer are available in the bar during the day. Special dietary needs can be met with advance notice. There is a generator that can provide electricity in the dining room in the evenings.

The young owners have been so busy creating Bosque del Cabo that they are just starting to compile bird and mammal lists. You can add to those lists while you are there if you wish. They say they are beginners in natural history, but if so, they are avid students, and they like to share what they are discovering.

Transportation: There are land and air possibilities. You can take the bus or fly on SANSA or Travelair to Golfito and catch a scheduled charter flight for less than $6 (10 min.) on to Puerto Jiménez. Charter flights from San José are $300 for five people. Contact Vuelos Especiales (75-0607, 41-1444) or Aeronaves de Costa Rica (32-1176, 75-0278). The taxi from Puerto Jiménez costs about $20 for the 10-mile (16-km) trip. Less-expensive transportation can be arranged on Tuesdays and Fridays (call 22-4547). If you drive, you need a four-wheel drive for the road south of Puerto Jiménez; it can be slippery and muddy, and you must cross several rivers without bridges.

Rates: Single occupancy is $75 per day, double is $55 per person, meals included. The one-day Corcovado tour is $90 each for two, $75 for four. The charge for a horse and local guide is $15 per person per day.

Reservations: No phones at Bosque del Cabo, so write or make your reservations through Costa Rican Trails in San José, telephone 22-4547, 22-7338; fax 21-3011. Philip also checks a fax in Puerto Jiménez, 78-5073. Apartado 2907-1000, San José.

Cabinas Chacón, Albergue de Montaña

At Cabinas Chacón, they do not talk about "if" you see a quetzal, they say "when." Roland Chacón, one of owner Efraín Chacón's eleven children, told me we would see one on our early morning tour, and we did. It was so easy. We drove up the mountain, and there it was sitting in the tree he expected it to be in. The red, white, and green bird so elusive in some places seemed to appear as if on cue.

The Chacón's place in San Gerardo de Dota between Cartago and San Isidro de El General in the Talamanca Mountains is famous for quetzals and for hospitality. Efraín, who has lived here for thirty-five years, started a dairy farm. Because of trout in the Savegre River that flows through his property, people started to come to fish, and some-

Cabinas Chacón in quetzal country (Photo by Ree Strange Sheck)

times they stayed late. Efraín and his wife took visitors into their home to spend the night. Eventually, they built a cabin for fishermen, and then in 1980, ecotourists began to arrive in the hope of spotting a quetzal.

Cabinas Chacón now has five modest cabins that sleep up to four, all with private bath and sitting room, and in 1990 opened a new restaurant to serve not only overnight but day visitors and local folks. Be sure to bring your appetite; food is good and plentiful. Fresh trout does make its way to the menu.

There is still a small dairy, and guests can visit the extensive apple orchards and packing plant on the property. All up and down the valley, apple trees are replacing pastures on the steep slopes.

About half of the Chacón farm is in primary forest. There is a 4 + mile (8-km) trail that takes two to three hours to hike (with fabulous views where the trail allows you at times to look out on the forest canopy) and a half-mile (1 km) one. For the real hikers, there is a trail that goes from the farm to Cerro de la Muerte. Roland suggests that people go by car to the cerro and walk back.

For those who just like gentle strolls, a walk along the country road in front affords a look at flowering trees, the rushing river that flows alongside, and a variety of birds. I watched a woodpecker gathering nuts. A good number of the more than 100 species of birds here can be seen from the cabin area. The quetzal is not the only flashy bird in the Dota Valley: trogons and emerald toucanets and iridescent hummingbirds lend color.

Animals that might be seen include porcupines, rabbits, white-faced monkeys, white-tailed deer, frogs, squirrels, and foxes. Local guides well versed in natural history can be hired for $10.

Trout fishermen and ecotourists have been joined by scientists and students in this special place. The Quetzal Education Research Complex is Southern Nazarene University's tropical campus. A research laboratory is already in operation, and classroom and lodging facilities are being built.

Cabinas Chacón is 6,890 feet (2,100 m) in elevation. Rainiest months are October and November, and there is generally little rain from December to June. You may want to bring repellent for hiking on the higher trails. The cabins are simple but comfortable. Bring a jacket for cool evenings.

Transportation: Turnoff for San Gerardo de Dota and Cabinas Chacón is at kilometer 80 on the Inter-American Highway south of San José. Buses going to San Isidro can let you off here. The Chacóns can pick you up, $20 round-trip, for the 6-mile (10-km) trip on an attention-getting road with hairpin curves.

Rates: The per-person cost is $35 including meals. Visa accepted.

Reservations: Cabinas Chacón, Apartado 482, Cartago. Telephone 71-1732.

El Salto Biological Reserve

On the ocean side, the view is of Manuel Antonio, Esterillos, and all the way north to Herradura Beach. On the land side, the magnificent Talamanca Mountains dominate: Cerro de la Muerte and other peaks with magical names like Sakira and Cerro de las Vueltas.

From a vantage point 820 feet (250 m) up, the small lodge and restaurant in El Salto Biological Reserve give one the impression of flying low over the coast. Located less than a mile (1 km) off the road between Quepos and Manuel Antonio, the reserve offers its guests proximity to one of the most visited national parks in the country and one of the most beautiful beaches as well as the facilities of a private reserve with its own forest and trails in a mountain setting.

The three trails are named for trees: *peine de mico, lengua de vaca,* and *indio desnudo,* which translated literally are monkey's comb, cow's tongue, and naked indian. It is a colorful place: greens of countless shades saturate the senses, forming a lovely background for the reds, oranges, yellows, and whites of small forest flowers. Trails are short, the longest less than a mile (1 km), and they invite walking slowly, stopping, listening, and watching. Peine de Mico leads past two waterfalls (*salto* in Spanish is sometimes used for "waterfall").

Glenn Lutz is the owner of the biological reserve. He has growing lists of flora and fauna to share with guests. On his 64 acres (26 ha), you might see howler, squirrel, or white-faced monkeys, the two-toed or three-toed sloth, tree frogs, armadillos, iguanas, boa constrictors, agoutis, and porcupines. There are birds large and small: the great tinamou, laughing falcon, golden-naped woodpecker, orange-chinned parakeet, red-lored parrot, owls, hummingbirds, and blue-gray and scarlet-rumped tanagers, to name only a few.

Talk with Hener, who also guides on these trails, and he can tell you about the sound of the sloth at night, which reminds him of someone laughing, or about the tayra that found its way to one of the terraces at the lodge, or he can help you spot the small, colorful frogs that live here.

Glenn has tours for guests to the little town of Londres and the Naranjo River for trails in another forest; to Damas Island for a boat trip through estuaries to see birds and maybe even a crocodile and to eat on a floating restaurant; to Manuel Antonio park; and to a working ranch for a horseback ride to see a cattle operation, fields of rice, and a river trail.

The small open-air restaurant with the view that won't quit serves food with a flair. It is decorated with artifacts from a ranch Glenn had in Guanacaste: branding irons, a wood stove, saddle bags, lariats. A sparkling swimming pool shares the mountaintop location, and there are covered wooden porch swings where guests can relax. Down the hill are five rooms in two buildings that can accommodate a total of fifteen. Some of the walls demonstrate an old plastering technique that has a mix of straw, giving the comfortable rooms a pleasing, earthy feeling. Baths are modern, with hot water. Rooms have windows along two sides, facing both the ocean and the Talamancas.

Transportation: The express bus to Manuel Antonio from San José passes on the road below. Glenn can pick you up there. There is also air service to Quepos.

Rates: A double room without meals is $60 and entitles guests to a tour of one of the trails. The packages are $45 per person, including lodging, breakfast, dinner, guided tour of the trails, and tax. A light lunch is available at the restaurant. The Londres-Río Naranjo tour is $10 per person, Damas Island $20, horseback tour of the farm $20 an hour. Day visits offer a half-day guided tour on the trails for $10 per person.

Reservations: El Salto Biological Reserve, Apartado 119, Quepos. Telephone 77-0130, fax 41-2938.

Genesis II—a second beginning (Photo by Ree Strange Sheck)

Genesis II

Walking through the cloud forest at Genesis II is like moving through a hanging garden in the mist. Bromeliads crowd every inch of space on the stately oaks. Mosses and mushrooms abound. I counted four orchids blooming on the same tree branch. Fallen blossoms from the canopy high above decorate the forest floor.

This cloud forest in the Talamanca Mountains, more than 7,740 feet (2,360 m) high, has an air of eternity about it. It seems to call for hushed tones, for quiet observation. Bird songs echo through the trees. It seemed appropriate that a collared redstart, known as the "friend of man," followed as we walked on the trail. Five mixed feeding flocks moved through the forest.

Birds bring many to this 100-acre (247 ha) private reserve, located about 39 miles (62 km) south of San José. The current bird list has about 100 species, and owners Steve and Paula Friedman expect it to grow to 200. The resplendent quetzal is no stranger here: from March to June, it is easily seen. The Friedmans reported seeing nine quetzals one day just from the balcony of their house.

The distinctive sounds of the three-wattled bellbird are heard here. There are collared trogons, black guans, emerald toucanets, silvery-fronted tapaculo, and hummingbirds—fiery-throated, magnificent, volcano, and purple-throated and gray-tailed mountain gems. Mammals are not as flashy but include sloths, armadillos, tayras, squirrels, and rabbits. Tracks of a tapir have been seen, probably visiting from the Río Macho Forest Reserve next door. One butterfly specialist told Steve that all of the butterflies here are in the rare category. Twelve miles (20 km) of well-maintained trails and dirt roads let guests explore the area.

An optional side trip could include a visit to Dominical, or perhaps you can get in on one of the trips scheduled to the farm of Alexander Skutch, well-known naturalist and ornithologist, near San Isidro.

Lodging at Genesis II allows a maximum of ten persons in double rooms with shared baths. Facilities are humble, but attention is first class. Paula turns out marvelous meals served family style, using many garden-fresh fruits and vegetables grown on the property. She uses many of the recipes published in her *Quetzal Cookbook*, everything from typical Costa Rican dishes to lemon chicken and lasagna.

Steve directs young people in a volunteer program helping him to re-create forest on a piece of cleared land. Activities include research on species as well as tree planting and follow-up. The program attracts people from around the world who pay to spend their vacations in this cloud forest working in conservation. Perhaps you will meet some of them while you are there. In their spare time, they teach English to adults and children in a school down the road.

And the name, Genesis II? Steve explained. He and Paula chose it to signify a "second beginning," where they would attempt to live on this land in a more proper, peaceful way.

Transportation: Buses from San José to San Isidro de El General can drop you off at the Cañon church near Kilometer 58, where the Friedmans will pick you up. Genesis II is 2.5 miles (4 km) farther. Packages include transportation.

Rates: Weekly packages include lodging, meals, guides, transportation, laundry, and taxes. Singles are $700, doubles are $890. For three days, singles are $350, doubles $400. Inquire about nonpackage rates.

Reservations: You may write to Steve and Paula Friedman, c/o Canadian Embassy, Apartado 10303-1000, San José. Telephone/fax 25-0271. This number in San José belongs to the Warringtons, who own Tres Arcos Bed and Breakfast. They will pass along the message.

Hacienda Barú

Four young coatis had dashed across the trail and scampered up a tree, quickly disappearing in a leafy world hidden from our eager eyes. We had watched a blue-black grassquit doing rapid little song-jumps, seeming to somersault in the air as it fluttered up and down from the same low branch. What sounded like a giant crashing through the forest turned out to be monkeys feeding noisily, knocking fruit and throwing branches to the ground.

This is Jack Ewing's world. He became interested in ecology about eight years ago, and today he operates Hacienda Barú just north of Dominical on the Pacific coast, a private nature reserve worth visiting. We had already gone by horseback to see pre-Columbian petroglyphs scattered in a field high above the Barú River Valley. Now we

Jack Ewing's world—Hacienda Barú (Photo by Ree Strange Sheck)

were working our way down by foot on trails that lead to lowland forest and eventually to mangrove swamps and sandy beach along the Pacific.

Jack wanted me to see a giant ceibo tree. I found out for myself that the jabillo tree has spines, and he explained that it is good for boats because the outside is resistant to salt water and the inside is usually hollow. Jack is an untiring student of the natural world. He is enthusiastic about sharing what he has learned and dedicated to conservation of it.

He said some visitors arrive expecting boas to be hanging from the trees and jaguars to appear on the trails. Boas are on his reptile list, but you are not likely to see one. And no jaguars have been spotted here, but there are pumas, jaguarundis, and ocelots. There is plenty to see. More than 231 species of birds have been counted, 30 species of mammals (not counting the various bats, mice, and marine mammals), and reptiles and amphibians that run the gamut from caimans to red-eyed tree frogs and tiny, colorful, poison dart frogs. Humpback whales pass by offshore between December and April, and olive ridley and hawksbill sea turtles lay eggs on the beach from May through November. The hacienda helps with a nursery where about 2,500 baby turtles are hatched out every year and released on the beach. Dolphins inhabit these warm waters.

About half of the 830-acre (336-ha) hacienda is forested, some in primary forest, some selectively logged a few years ago, and some regenerating forest on former pastureland. Visitors can tour the cacao plantation, taste the cocoa bean, and learn about its history and how it is processed. At the end of the tour, samples are served of how it might have been prepared by the Mayans, the Spanish conquistadors, and then the Swiss.

Most visitors come to Hacienda Barú on day visits. There are a variety of hikes with native guides: a three-hour lowland walk through mangrove, riverbank, and seashore habitat; the popular rain forest hike; and an all-day trek that goes from the beach to the petroglyphs. There are guided horseback tours to the lowlands, to the petroglyphs, and to the highlands above the river valley. Some can be combined with hikes.

Though no lodging is available yet at Hacienda Barú, there is a refuge for overnight camping (equipment supplied). This may be your chance to see nocturnal animals. The refuge has a covered area for tents in the rainy season, flush toilets, and a shower. Bird-watching from a covered observation deck is excellent: birds are easily seen in the small clearing.

Before you start out on your tours, be sure to see Diane Ewing's orchid collection, 231 species and growing, in their backyard. She is responsible for the tasty meals and for riding herd on everybody's whereabouts. No phones here, so radio communication is a way of life.

Jack came to Costa Rica in 1970 to stay for four months, and the family followed shortly after. It looks as if they are going to stay. Stop by Hacienda Barú and you will understand why.

Transportation: Bus and air service to Quepos and bus service to San Isidro de El General is a first step. Buses between Quepos and San Isidro pass by the entrance, just northwest of the Barú River. If you drive, stop by the El Ceibo gas station and information center on the road from Quepos. It is owned by the hacienda. Jack and Diane have limited editions of T-shirts with original paintings of flora and fauna done with an airbrush which are for sale at the station.

Rates: Visit to the cacao plantation is $10 per person. Charge for natural history hiking tours varies according to the number of persons. These examples are for one person, with the per-person charge going down with increased numbers: lowland walk $12.50, rain forest hike $25, all-day trek $30. The night in the jungle (including dinner, breakfast, and snacks) is $60 for one, $108 for two. These include excellent local guides. English- and French-speaking guides cost $25 extra per tour. Horseback rides cost $10 for the first hour, $5 for the second, and $3 for each additional hour.

Reservations: Hacienda Barú, Apartado 215-8000, San Isidro de El General. Telephone 71-1903; if you get a recorded message, give the tour you want, approximate time of arrival, and the number in the party. It helps to give twenty-four-hour notice. Fax 71-0441. (See chap. 6 for other lodging possibilities in the area.)

Marenco Biological Reserve

There are no roads to Marenco Biological Reserve on the Osa Peninsula. You come in either by boat from Uvita, two hours up the coast, or from Sierpe (closer), or by single-engine plane from San José, a forty-five minute flight, landing at Drake airport. From there, it is about a 25-minute boat ride south to Marenco unless the sea is too rough, in which case guests are treated to a 2-hour horseback ride.

Remote, set in a hillside clearing amidst lush premontane wet forest, the biological reserve is a center for scientific research and natural history tourism. If you are there when a researcher is visiting, you may be treated to an evening talk about what he or she is finding out. As you explore the miles of beach and forest trails on the station's 1,236 acres (500 ha), you can do some discovering of your own. In fact, you can sit on the balcony of your room and watch a veritable parade of exotic birds—parrots, toucans with their outrageous beaks, scarlet macaws, brightly colored tanagers. At certain times of the year, humpback whales pass by in the ocean below.

On forest trails you may encounter a slow-moving sloth or catch the scent of white-lipped peccaries. The resident naturalist guide will advise you to climb a nearby tree and wait until they pass if you meet a herd of the piglike peccaries. There is a subspecies of squirrel monkey, called tití in Spanish, that is endemic to southern Costa Rica and northern Panama. Watch for motion in the trees to spot them and the other three monkey species that live in Costa Rica: howler, white-faced capuchin, and spider.

You can rent one of the reserve's horses to go along the beach or forest trails, and you can walk to the cool waters of the Río Claro and take a dip beneath towering forest giants. Packages include a half-day Río Claro guided hike.

A nighttime visit to the tide pools reveals sea creatures you may never have seen before. Daytime snorkeling is great at coral gardens along Marenco's coastline, where you may see parrot fish, tangs, puffers, and angelfish. An optional boat tour to Caño Island Biological Reserve, 11 miles (17 km) west of Marenco, opens up another underwater wonderland of octopuses, lobsters, moray eels, jacks, and damselfish and triggerfish. Near the island you will probably see dolphins, and you may be startled by a manta ray. The forested island holds the secrets of both a vanished Indian culture and fabled pirate treasure troves.

A highlight for most travelers to Marenco is a day trip to nearby Corcovado National Park, entering at San Pedrillo and hiking along the beach and into the forest, where you have a chance to walk in an area of the large park that is little visited; we met only two locals during the day. Plant and bird life is outstanding, and a bilingual naturalist guide explains intricate biological relationships and points out what you are missing in front of your very eyes. You know you are treading the turf of Corcovado's animal kingdom: the jaguar, giant anteater, tapir, agouti, ocelot, kinkajou. After lunch, you board a dugout canoe for a ride on the San Pedrillo River, continuing to a pristine rain forest waterfall. A second option in Corcovado goes all the way to the magnificent waterfall at Llorona Beach. Not for the weak-kneed, the four-hour trek to Llorona is up and down hills, through the tropical forest, across small streams, sometimes along the beach. There is time for lunch and a brief swim before the four-hour hike back. It is worth every aching muscle.

Marenco itself is a buffer zone that protects the park, employs local people, and offers the traveler a chance to taste the richness. The station is considering a tropical forest and wildlife camp for young people ages fourteen to twenty, with an emphasis on tropical ecology. Write Marenco for details.

Though Sergio Miranda, of the Miranda family that owns Marenco, is quick to say that the station is not for the luxury traveler, accommodations are pleasant. Bamboo and wood bungalows contain twenty double rooms, each room with its own bath and a balcony open to a priceless view. He says the station is for those who enjoy being in a beautiful place and eating well. Meals are served family-style in a separate dining hall/meeting facility.

The generator runs from 5:30 p.m. to 9:30 p.m.; bring a flashlight to complement the candle in your room after hours. There is a radio telephone, powered by solar energy. A small reference library with some preserved local specimens of flora and fauna is worth a visit. Crafts made by local people are also available.

Busiest months at Marenco are December through April. Sergio suggests May through August or November for those who want to stay away from the "crowds" (Marenco can house forty guests). He warns that September and October are very rainy. Marenco will send you a list of recommended attire.

Transportation: Daily flights via chartered plane leave San José for Drake airport, then a boat to Marenco. Boat transportation is available from Uvita or Sierpe.

Rates: A three-night package for $575 per person includes transfer from a San José hotel to airport, airfare, boat to Marenco, rooms, meals, taxes, and guided tours to the Río Claro and Corcovado. The four-day package, $690, adds a visit to Caño Island. Inquire about packages that involve departures by boat from Uvita or Sierpe. For nonpackage travelers, the per-day charge is $75 for room and meals (plus tax); round-trip air transportation is $180 per person. Optional tours are to Río Claro at $15 per person, Corcovado for $65, and Caño Island for $75. Minimum stay is two nights. Note: Pedro Miranda, marketing and sales manager, says anyone who shows this book when making a reservation will get a 10 percent discount.

Reservations: Marenco Biological Reserve, Apartado 4025-1000, San José. Telephone 21-1594. Fax (506) 55-1340. In San José, you may go by the office at El Pueblo Commercial Center. Any taxi driver knows where El Pueblo is.

Robert and Catherine Wilson Botanical Garden

Before you even arrive at the Robert and Catherine Wilson Botanical Garden, you will be glad you came. The trip south from San José on the Inter-American Highway takes you through high mountain páramo, lowland pineapple plantations, and back up along a ridge that was the Indian route from Paso Real to Panama.

The botanical garden lies in a rural agricultural setting 3.5 miles (5.6 km) south of San Vito, near the Panamanian border. It is some 206 miles (332 km) from San José. The lofty peaks of Amistad National Park reign to the northwest, sometimes appearing above the clouds.

Founded by the Wilsons in 1962, the garden is now owned by the Organization for Tropical Studies (OTS) and is used as a field station for its graduate-level courses in tropical biology and agroecology.

Fortunately for the natural history traveler, it is not only open for day visits, from 8:00 a.m. to 5:00 p.m. every day, but also for over-nights. Space is at a premium in February and July because of courses; however, it is worth a call even then to see if you can get in.

An internationally known collection of tropical plants awaits you on the 25 acres (10 ha) of planted grounds: 80 percent of the tropical and subtropical genera of palms are grown here, the second largest collection in the world, and many can be seen on the delightful Tree Fern Hill Trail. More than 6 miles (10 km) of trails await you: Helico-nia Loop Trail; Bromeliad Walk; Orchid Walk (more than two hun-dred native and exotic species of orchids); Fern Gully (Costa Rica has 800 species of ferns); Maranta Trail; Bamboo Walk. On the Natural History Loop you will walk through Hummingbird Garden, with plants to attract this amazing creature. Costa Rica has 54 species of hummers, the garden has 12.

When you have had your fill of planted gardens, you can take off on trails that touch the adjacent 358-acre (145-ha) natural forest reserve area also belonging to OTS to see the orchids and palms and heliconias growing in their natural habitat. The slope down to the Java River is steep, but the secondary growth forest on the River Trail offers excellent bird-watching. Trails are self-guiding, and there is a brochure for the forest trail.

Since 1983 the garden has been part of the Amistad Biosphere Reserve recognized by UNESCO. The garden and forest reserve con-tain about 2,000 species of plants, 300 species of birds, 80 species of mammals, 71 species of reptiles and amphibians, and more than 3,000 kinds of moths and butterflies.

On Sundays especially, the garden is popular with area residents who come to spend the day. Admission to the park is $.30. Local out-reach and education is a prime component of a program being im-plemented by Director Luis Diego Gómez and Gail Hewson, coor-dinator of development for OTS in Costa Rica.

Overnight facilities consist of beds for thirty-four people. There are four cabins with private baths and double-occupancy rooms with bunk beds in the field station. Meals are delicious, typical Costa Rican fare, served family style. Day visitors can eat lunch at the garden with advance reservations. There is a washer and dryer for use by overnight guests. A small gift shop includes local handcrafts, some made by members of nearby Indian communities.

The Wilson Garden is located in a midelevation tropical rain forest. There is little or no rainfall from January through March, but the rest of the year there is heavy fog and, in general, afternoon rains. Annual rainfall is about 158 inches (4,000 mm). Temperatures do not vary much seasonally—in the 70s (21° to 26°C) in the daytime and the 60s (16° to 21°C) at night.

Transportation: The road is paved from San José. By car, take the Inter-American Highway through San Isidro and Buenos Aires to 9.3 miles (15 km) past the El Brujo customs checkpoint. Turn left at the sign that says San Vito 45 km. Until a bridge is completed over the Terraba River, you cross by ferry. Gasoline is available in Buenos Aires and San Vito. If you are in Golfito, you can reach the Wilson Garden via Ciudad Neily, turning north on Route 16 to Agua Buena. Taxi fare from Golfito is about $31. An express bus from San José to San Vito takes about 5 hours. Buy your tickets in advance. The taxi from San Vito to the Wilson Botanical Garden is about $6.

Rates: Per-person charge for lodging and meals is $65 for the cabins and $55 for the field station rooms. A day visit including lunch costs $12; without lunch, $4.50 for a half day and $6 for a full day.

Reservations: For overnight stays, contact Organization for Tropical Studies, Apartado 676-2050, San Pedro. Phone 40-6696, fax 40-6783. To receive a brochure about the botanical garden, contact Gail Hewson, Robert and Catherine Wilson Botanical Garden, Apartado 73, San Vito, Coto Brus. For lunch reservations for a day visit, contact the garden: telephone/fax 77-3278.

Tiskita Biological Reserve

My introduction to Tiskita Biological Reserve on the southern Pacific coast was two spectacular fiery-billed araçaris perched along the road and a group of six small squirrel monkeys cavorting through tree branches before we even reached the main lodge. Peter Aspinall, who owns Tiskita, can help you out with the name of the flashy bird if it is new to you as well as explain that you will only see this subspecies of tití monkey in southern Costa Rica.

If you enjoy birds or nature photography, you can have a field day without leaving the lodge. Planted nearby are hundreds of tropical fruit trees that draw birds like a magnet. We watched three chestnut-mandibled toucans casually eat a fruit breakfast. In the same tree were blue-crowned manakins, a lineated woodpecker, and blue-gray and scarlet-rumped tanagers. A bird book is left handy to help you identify what you spot, and there is a bird list so that you will know if anyone else has seen it before you. So far the list includes more than 275 species. Fifty-seven species of butterflies have been noted. Ask for the illustrated booklet on tide pools and the printed guide for the nature trail.

Since 1980, Peter has been growing exotic tropical fruits gathered from around the world on about 37 acres (15 ha) of his almost 400 acres (162 ha). His experimental station has the most extensive collection of tropical rare and exotic fruits in the country. Birds and guests alike can have their fill of more than a hundred varieties, tasting such delicacies as star fruit (*carambola* in Spanish), passion fruit (*maracuyá*), guava, custard apple (*anona*), jackfruit, *araza, abiu,* and dozens of others that are not yet household words. His idea is to research these fruits with an eye to nontraditional exports for Costa Rica. He reminds you that bananas and pineapples were once considered rare and exotic fruits.

Animals also come out of the primary forest that covers more than half of his land to savor the fruits. You may cross paths with all four species of monkeys found in Costa Rica, with the coati, paca, white-lipped peccary, anteater, or cats such as ocelot, jaguarundi, and margay. Trails take you through the fruit orchard, to a reforestation project of native and nonnative trees, to the beach at the bottom of the hill, and through the forest. There you find streams with clear pools where you can bathe in the company of kingfishers and humming-birds, giant trees spreading a canopy above. You can hike all the way to the hydroelectric system that, along with solar panels and a backup diesel-powered generator, provides electricity to this remote corner.

And remote it is. There is no telephone. Access is by air to a landing strip along the ocean or air to Golfito and then air or overland to Tiskita. The drive from Golfito, 37 miles (60 km), takes 2½ hours.

It is a fascinating trip through farm and ranch lands, crossing the Río Coto by ferry and fording other streams into a frontier region. A bridge now stretches across the Río Claro; I am sorry you will miss the adventure of driving through that river, especially in the rainy season. That was something to write home about. When Peter first started coming to the area, he had to come partway by boat and walk the rest of the way. He first drove to the farm in 1980.

From the hilltop where the lodge and bungalows are located, you can look out at the Pacific and across to the Osa Peninsula. A visit to Corcovado National Park is an optional tour from Tiskita. A charter flight takes you to Sirena and back, allowing three to four hours to explore.

Guests can fish or surf. Nearby is the longest breaking left wave in the country, a 1,600-yard run at Punta Pavones. An Indian reserve borders Tiskita, which, by the way, is the Guaymi name for fish eagle. A visit to the Indian settlement can be arranged; dashing hats made by the Guaymis are for sale both at Tiskita and in San José at Costa Rica Sun Tours, which arranges visits to Tiskita and is operated by Peter's brother John. Horses are available for rent.

Newest sleeping facilities at Tiskita offer rooms separated from each other by a green area—a long, covered porch connects the rooms in front. Separate bungalows nestle against the forest, a short walk from the lodge, with super baths that allow you plenty of privacy yet are open enough to let you watch the birds while you shower. All ten rooms have private baths.

Though fireflies sparkle in the evening, you will need your own flashlight for nighttime walks. In the rainy season, you will want rubber boots. Because of heavy rain, Tiskita is closed in September and October.

Transportation: Round-trip costs from San José are included in package plans.

Rates: Daily rates are $76 for singles, $60 per person for doubles, including room, meals, trail map, and taxes. Transportation can involve SANSA to Golfito (one hour) and either air charter to Tiskita (ten minutes) or jeep taxi, one way $85. Air charter direct from San José is $190 per seat one way. If you want to go from Tiskita to

Quepos or Quepos to Tiskita, charter flights are $120, minimum of two. Remember that SANSA and charters limit luggage to 26 pounds per passenger. Guided nature walks are $15, and the trip to Corcovado is $100 per person, minimum of four. Packages include transportation from and to San José, room, meals, transfers, fruit beverages, two guided walks with a naturalist guide, and taxes. For four days and three nights, rates start at $365 each for a minimum of two people, using SANSA. Fixed departures for packages are on Monday and Thursday. There are discounts for children less than fourteen years old. Tiskita donates a part of its profits to support a local clinic and school.

Reservations: Costa Rica Sun Tours, Apartado 1195-1250, Escazú. Telephone 55-3418, 55-2011; fax 55-4410. The downtown office is at Avenida 7, Calles 3/5 in San José, where you can see photos and videos of Tiskita.

Caribbean

Cabinas Chimuri

For the traveler looking for adventure, a stay at Cabinas Chimuri outside Puerto Viejo de Limón may fit the bill. Mauricio Salazar, a Bribrí Indian, and his Austrian-born wife, Colocha, have a 49-acre (20-ha) natural reserve that offers an out-of-the-ordinary experience.

Traditional Bribrí structures house guests. Built on stilts, the buildings are of tropical wood and bamboo, the roofs thatched with cane. There are three doubles and one for four persons, with shared baths a few steps away, flush toilets. You bring your own food and have use of a common kitchen or, with advance notice, a cook can be arranged. Bedding is furnished. The complex is in a clearing surrounded by forest, access via a five-minute foot trail from the road below. The Caribbean is 600 yards (500 m) from Chimuri.

The reserve offers good birding and a multitude of butterflies. An afternoon at the waterfall and inviting pools in the river is great after a morning on the trails. Mauricio will accompany you at night to watch the animals in the forest. His eyes tell you he knows the jungle; his walk, that he is one with it.

Cabinas Chimuri, in the mountains near the Caribbean coast (Photo by Ree Strange Sheck)

Right on the reserve you are likely to see sloths, porcupines, agou-tis, armadillos, tayras, coatis, anteaters, kinkajous, bats, poison dart frogs, boa contrictors, opossums, and iguanas. There are birds of prey, parrots, hummingbirds, trogons, motmots, jacamars, toucans, manakins, orioles, and tanagers. You can go on the trail by yourself or walk with Mauricio for about three hours, $10 per person. Bicy-cles and rubber boots may be rented.

If you want to explore farther than the Chimuri reserve or the nearby Caribbean coast, Mauricio offers optional tours. A one-day boat trip takes you on the Carbón River, which borders Cahuita National Park. A one-day walking or horseback tour takes you through abandoned cacao plantations to traditional Bribrí stomping grounds in the Kekoldi Indian reserve, where you will learn about various plants used by the indigenous peoples, for example, medic-inal plants and plants used for construction. Along the trails you are likely to see a sloth, a raccoon, a toucan, iguanas, perhaps a snake.

The group, limited to five people, will stop by a friend's home to eat a picnic lunch and get a glimpse of life on the Indian reserve. The return is by a different trail. Mauricio advises that it is a hard trip, intended for people in good physical condition.

If you are in really good condition, you can arrange for a three-day trip into the Talamanca Indian Reserve to experience a different type of vegetation, a wetter forest. Be prepared for rain and bring insect repellent. The trip starts on a public bus to the beginning of the hiking trail. It is on foot to Suretka, Amubri, and farther up into the reserve, to an altitude of about 3,300 feet (1,000 m). On the return, you take a boat from Coroma to Suretka. A look at the map shows that the trek is in Costa Rica's frontier region with Panama. Trails are steep, and you will be carrying your own gear. Nights are spent in a Bribrí community house; bathing is Indian-style: in a creek. This trip is also limited to six persons, and Mauricio needs one week's notice to make arrangements.

Between the two of them, Mauricio and Colocha speak English, Spanish, German, and Bribrí. Hospitality is warm. If Mauricio's mother is visiting from the reserve, she may offer you a glass of *michilanga*, a delicious beverage of cooked plantain, coconut, and cinnamon. *Chimuri*, by the way, means ripe bananas in Bribrí, and a stalk is always hanging at their house, where any hungry hand may reach and take.

Transportation: As you go into Puerto Viejo coming from Limón, watch on the right for the Cabinas Chimuri sign with a banana tree insignia on one side and a toucan on the other. From there, a short trail leads up to the cabins. For bus travel from San José, take the bus for Sixaola and ask to be let off at the sign. From Limón, take a taxi or the Limón-Puerto Viejo bus.

Rates: Cost of the double cabins is $20 per day; the quadruple, $35. The one-day tour is $25 per person. The three-day trip is $140 per person. Part of the tour fee is donated to the local Indian organization.

Reservations: Write to Mauricio Salazar, Cabinas Chimuri, Puerto Viejo de Limón, Talamanca, or call 58-3844 and leave a message. You can send a fax to 58-0854. Mauricio or Colocha will call collect to confirm your reservation.

9

Nature Tour Companies: What They Offer

Nature travel tours in Costa Rica run the gamut from two people with a guide to a microbus of travelers, from hiking, bicycling, sailing, rafting, or kayaking to the standard overland tour by horseback, car, or bus. Just as Costa Rica is small and friendly, so are the nature tours I have tried out—no Greyhound-size buses trying to maneuver narrow mountain roads, no herding people around like bodies that have to be moved. Chances are, by the time even a one-day tour is over, the guide will call you by name.

Companies included here specialize in nature travel. The listing begins with general nature travel, progressing to specializations: rafting/kayaking tours, island cruises, journeys to Tortuguero/Barra del Colorado and Coco Island. Finally, some of the companies outside of Costa Rica who organize nature tours to the country are listed. Prices, of course, are valid as of this writing but can change without notice. Listings of what each company offers are intended to give you an idea of the possibilities; they are not all-inclusive.

General Nature Travel

Two small companies that offer first-class nature travel are Geotur and Jungle Trails. Their bilingual guides are knowledgeable and personable.

Geotur is well known for its wildlife tour of Carara Biological Reserve. The one-day trip focuses on walks in the reserve, but it includes a couple of hours at Jacó Beach for lunch, swimming, or a walk along the coast. At Carara, not only do you see animals like monkeys, scarlet macaws, and crocodiles but you sometimes get a chance for a close-up look through a telescope the guide carries, depending on the animal's cooperation, of course. Part of the $69-per-person fee is returned to Carara. Geotur is building and placing wooden nests for scarlet macaws in the reserve and on neighboring property under the watchful eyes of others who are also concerned about protection of this endangered species. According to Sergio Volio, owner of Geotur, as many as 90 percent of the chicks in traditional nesting sites used by Carara's macaws are being poached to sell. He runs his own small environmental education program in nearby communities, presenting talks and natural history slide shows.

A day tour of Braulio Carrillo National Park is $69 with Geotur. Waterfalls, cloud forest, trails through lush vegetation, and encounters with wildlife are features of the tour. Outside the park, the tour continues to banana and cacao plantations on the way to Limón, and after lunch, time to swim in the Caribbean. A new one-day tour to San Gerardo de Dota is aimed at bird-watchers, with the big draw, of course, the chance to see the quetzal ($69). Binoculars are essential. Geotur offers multiday natural history tours to Guanacaste and Santa Rosa national parks (staying at the private reserve Los Inocentes) and to Cahuita National Park (with stops in Braulio Carrillo park and at CATIE in Turrialba). Telephone 34-1867, fax 53-6338. Apartado 469 Y-Griega-1011, San José.

Jungle Trails, Los Caminos de la Selva in Spanish, has an impressive array of tours and will customize expeditions throughout the country. An intriguing trip is the Let's Plant a Tropical Endangered Tree, in which people visit a native tree nursery in the Central Pacific area (where humid and dry forests meet) to learn about what each tree is good for. Each person chooses one to plant at a watershed project in cooperation with Arbofilia (Association for the Protection of Trees), a grass-roots ecological organization. After tree planting, a visit to Carara Biological Reserve shows what virgin forest is like. Part

Peace Waterfall on the road to Puerto Viejo de Sarapiqui through Varablanca (Photo by Ree Strange Sheck)

of the $75 cost buys the tree and contributes to Arbofilia. Fees for other tours also include donations to that group.

Other one-day tours with Jungle Trails ($75 each) include walking through cloud forest on Barva Volcano, Braulio Carrillo, bird-watching or customized tours to any of the nearby parks or refuges, including an early departure for Poás to see the crater before clouds roll in. A two-day trip combines either Barva and Poás or Braulio Carrillo, the Sarapiquí River area, and Poás, spending the night at Posada de Volcán Poás, $175 (minimum four persons). A three-day trip explores Rincón de la Vieja on horseback. For $270, you can visit Cartago and nearby Lankester Gardens, go to Turrialba for a visit to CATIE, and then choose either a river trip or a visit to Turrialba Volcano or Guayabo National Monument—a three-day affair. Expeditions to Chirripó and Corcovado as well as to less-visited places such as Hitoy Cerere, Caño Negro, and Barra Honda are available. Under a Trekking on Your Own program, Jungle Trails provides a hiking route with suggested campsites and information on necessary public transportation, and they will supply a guide if desired. On camping trips, all equipment except sleeping bags is furnished. Telephone for Jungle Trails is 55-3486, fax 55-2782. Apartado 2413-1000, San José. Office at Calle 38, Avenidas 5/7, near Centro Colón.

Costa Rica Expeditions, Horizontes Nature Adventures, and Costa Rica Sun Tours offer excellent nature-oriented tours of their own as well as booking a variety of tours offered by other companies.

Costa Rica Expeditions pioneered natural history travel in Costa Rica. A series of one-day trips under the heading of Tropical Forest Adventure offer travel with a professional naturalist for $65 to any of the following locations: Barva Volcano, Braulio Carrillo National Park, Carara Biological Reserve, Cerro de la Muerte, Guayabo National Monument, Poás Volcano, Tapantí Wildlife Refuge, La Virgen del Socorro. If you want to hire a naturalist guide to accompany you on a private trip, the cost is $154 a day; cost for the guide and transportation is $314 a day (covers 100 miles). A visit to Irazú Volcano and the Orosi Valley, including lunch, is $50.

This company has multiday packages that combine several destinations. For example, a 10-day trip for $1,325 (double occupancy) includes in-country travel, lodging, and most meals for either of the following: Costa Rica Experience, which combines the Monteverde Cloud Forest Preserve, Poás and Corcovado national parks, the Butterfly Farm, and white-water rafting; Costa Rica Explorer, which offers the Monteverde Cloud Forest Preserve, Carara Biological Reserve, Cahuita and Tortuguero national parks, and white-water rafting. You can write for a list of U.S. and Canadian companies who book trips for Costa Rica Expeditions, for the convenience of dealing with someone in your area. Their white-water and Tortuguero tours are mentioned under specialty tours. Telephone 57-0766, fax 57-1665. Apartado 6941-1000, San José. Office at Avenida 3, Calles Central/2.

Horizontes specializes in nature adventures and in personalized service, both for groups and individuals. Owner Tamara Budowski says the company works to provide travelers with just the right itinerary based on what they want to see or do, taking into account physical abilities, budget, and length of visit and time of year. Sometimes people take off on a trip that is too long or too tough for them. Her staff wants to make sure that does not happen to their clients.

Basically, Horizontes acts as a reservation center, booking with private reserves, hotels, naturalist guides, and nature companies that they feel will give people an excellent experience. They handle both one-day and multiday tours. Stop by their office at Calle 28, Avenidas 1/3 (just north of Pizza Hut on Paseo Colón) to see how they can help you. Telephone 22-2022, fax 55-4513. Apartado 1780-1002, San José.

Costa Rica Sun Tours operates two private nature reserves: Arenal Volcano Observatory and Tiskita Biological Reserve. Day trips to the Arenal Observatory are $95, including a guide, transportation, and time to swim in thermal waters as well as view the volcano. The tour operates every Tuesday, Thursday, and Saturday. A two-day, one-night tour, with the chance of seeing a nighttime eruption, is $150, fixed departures on Monday and Friday. You can add on a visit to Caño Negro Wildlife Refuge. If you are in your own car, there is a package without transportation. Visits to Tiskita, a remote area south of Golfito, are $365 each for a minimum of two, four days and three nights.

Where the sky meets the sea and coconut palms wave gently in the tropical breeze
(Photo by Ree Strange Sheck)

Sun Tours has a two-day, one-night trip to Monteverde Cloud Forest for $215, including a naturalist guide. To visit both Monteverde and Arenal is $320 for three nights. Or you can combine a visit to Monteverde with a day on the *Calypso* yacht in the Pacific (not Cousteau's *Calypso*, though he has been to Costa Rica); three days and two nights, $347. Ask about fixed departures for those trips. See chapter 8 for details on tours to Tiskita Biological Reserve and Arenal Volcano Observatory.

Costa Rica Sun Tours will custom design a multiday trip that takes care of the traveler from arrival at the international airport to departure. Its office on Avenida 7, Calles 3/5 (one block north of the Aurola Holiday Inn) has an Eco-Center, a reservation and information center for a number of country lodges and private reserves. You can also buy your SANSA tickets there. Drop by to see videos and photographs of possible destinations. Telephone 55-3418, fax 55-4410. Apartado 1195-1250, Escazú.

Tikal Tour Operators is a full-service travel agency that also specializes in nature travel. It has fixed departures for one-day natural history trips using professional naturalist guides, most for $65 per person. Destinations include Turrialba Volcano, Barva Volcano, Arenal Volcano, and Poás, Irazú, Cahuita, and Guayabo national parks.

Multiday trips cover the country. The Pacific Ecosafari goes to Manuel Antonio, Las Baulas, Palo Verde, and Santa Rosa national parks, Carara Biological Reserve, the private reserve at EcoAdventure Lodge, and Lake Arenal and Arenal Volcano. The Caribbean Ecosafari includes Caño Negro National Wildlife Refuge, Braulio Carrillo, Tortuguero, and Cahuita national parks, and the Bribrí Indian Reserve. Each of these tours is eight days, seven nights, $849 per person (double occupancy), leaving Sunday and Wednesday in high season. Other multiday trips center on the EcoAdventure Lodge at Coter Lake and Tango Mar on the Nicoya Peninsula.

By the way, Tikal is helpful with arranging an exit visa for visitors who overstay their legal limit. Telephone 23-2811, fax 23-1916. Apartado 6398-1000, San José. Office at Avenida 2, Calles 7/9.

Guanacaste Tours is a regional tour company that includes a variety of historical/cultural and natural history destinations. A sample of day tours with fixed departures follows: Palo Verde, Tuesday and Friday, $70; lake and volcano at Arenal, Saturday, $70; turtle tour at Ostional June through November ($45) and Playa Grande November to April ($35); Coribicí River float, Thursdays, $70; Casona at Santa Rosa, Mondays and Thursdays, $65. Pickup is in Liberia and at various beach hotels. Bilingual, biologist guides. The main office is in Las Espuelas Hotel, Liberia. Telephone 66-0306, fax 66-0307. Apartado 55-5000, Liberia, Guanacaste.

GeoVenturas is a company that specializes in "natural adventures" that can include hiking, visits to national parks, a visit to an old gold-mining area, and bicycling. A one-day cycling adventure might include Cartago, the Orosi and Reventazón valleys, and Tapantí wildlife refuge (13 miles, 21 km). Trips are on mountain bikes, and a guide/mechanic accompanies you. You can combine cycling with rafting, horseback riding, hiking, or swimming. Minimum age is 12. Telephone 82-8590, fax 82-8333. Apartado 554-2150, Moravia.

Rafting/Kayaking

Three companies that offer river tours are Aventuras Naturales, Costa Rica Expeditions, and Ríos Tropicales. All have trained, bilingual guides and good equipment. If you have never rafted or kayaked before, this is a new way to experience the natural world. There are trips for beginners, and each company offers instruction. All offer one-day trips, year-round, on the Reventazón near Turrialba (rapids and calm stetches through spectacular landscape) and the Coribicí near Cañas (float trip good for wildlife viewing, especially birds and monkeys) beginning around $65.

Aventuras Naturales has both a one-day ($85) and a two-day ($220) Pacuare River rafting trip, which is great for seeing wildlife. On the two-day, rafters hike to a nearby waterfall. A three-day trip on the General River is about $375, depending on the number of people. Sarapiquí trips are also offered. The company is run by natives of the Turrialba area, and all guides are Costa Ricans, mostly biologists. Scheduled trips are from one to three days, but staff designs custom packages. Kayaks may be rented, with lessons arranged. Telephone for Aventuras Naturales is 25-3939, fax 53-6934. Apartado 812-2050, San Pedro. Office at Avenida Central, Calles 33/35.

Costa Rica Expeditions offers a day-trip option on the Sarapiquí from July to December ($65), plus two runs for experienced rafters on the Reventazón in addition to the easy-to-moderate Reventazón run. Scheduled trips include up to three days on the Pacuare and up to five on the Chirripó (June 15 to December 15). Nine-day trips that combine a Pacuare River run with either the Chirripó or Reventazón cost $833 per person with a minimum of eight. Telephone 57-0766, fax 57-1665. Apartado 6941-1000, San José. Office at Avenida 3, Calles Central/2.

Ríos Tropicals has both raft and kayak trips. A two-day Pacuare raft trip is $220, while the one-day Sarapiquí (July to January) is $65. Their four-day Río General trip runs June to December only. There are also multiday trips to the Golfito area, to the Nicoya Peninsula near Curú Wildlife Refuge, and to Manuel Antonio, Culebra Bay, and Tortuguero. A ten-day rafting/kayaking adventure on the General, Reventazón, and Pacuare rivers is $1,050.

Trekking adventures are also offered by Ríos Tropicales, either as part of a rafting or kayaking package or separately (minimum six). Trips range from three to fifteen days and can focus on a destination such as Chirripó or involve treks in the rain forest, some of which allow for interchange with the Indian culture. Telephone 33-6455, fax 55-4354. Apartado 472-1200, Pavas. Office at Paseo Colón, Calles 22/24. U.S. representative for multiday trips with Ríos Tropicales is Baja Expeditions, (800) 843-6967.

Ríos Tropicales has a small outdoor store, Tienda de Aventura, at the same location, with equipment for camping, hiking, climbing, and some water sports. It also has a branch in Manuel Antonio.

Cruises

Companies that offer day trips by yacht through the Gulf of Nicoya to Tortuga Island include Bay Island Cruises, Calypso Tours, and Fantasia Island Cruise. Passengers are wined and dined during the daylong outing, with time for swimming, snorkeling, or just relaxing. All charge $70 from San José.

Bay Island Cruises. Telephone 39-4951, fax 39-4404. Apartado 145-1007, San José.

Fantasia Island Cruise. Telephone 55-0791, fax 23-1013. Apartado 123, Puntarenas.

Calypso Tours. The originator of the island cruise to Tortuga Island, Calypso Tours also offers several packages that combine the island cruise with something else: a visit to Monteverde (three days,

Tortuga Island beach (Photo by Ree Strange Sheck)

two nights, $347 per person, double occupancy); a raft trip on the Corobicí (two days, $175 for double occupancy). A three-day tour to Tango Mar on the Nicoya Peninsula is $342. These prices are based on double occupancy. Telephone 33-3617, fax 33-0401. Apartado 6941-1000, San José.

An offshoot of Calypso Tours is Seaventures, which has an afternoon sailing from Puntarenas to Jacó Beach, $49, and a three-day tour to Cabo Blanco Nature Reserve, $445 (minimum four). The company also does a ten-day charter trip to Coco Island, with a cost of $800 per day for the yacht. Telephone 55-3022, fax 33-0401. Apartado 6941-1000, San José.

Costa Sol Tropical Cruises does a one-day trip to a private beach near Tambor for $70, with scheduled trips on Thursday, Saturday, and Sunday. Telephone 20-0722, fax 20-2095. United States and Canada (800) 245-8420.

Cruceros de Sur offers multiday sailing trips on the *Temptress*, a cruise ship with a capacity of 64 passengers, air-conditioned, private baths. Staff includes bilingual naturalists and diving and photography instructors (ship has its own photo lab). The *Temptress* southern cruise (November-May) goes to Palo Verde, Manuel Antonio, and Corcovado parks, Chira Island, Caño Island Biological Reserve, and Drake Bay. The northern cruise goes to Cuajiniquil, Culebra Bay in Guanacastre, Guiones Beach, Santa Rosa park, and Murciélago Island. Cost for the seven days on either cruise is $1,495. The company also offers trips to Coco Island, with first available space in 1993, 10 days for $2,195 per person. Telephone 32-6672, fax 31-6533. Apartado 5452-1000, San José.

Canal Trips—Tortuguero/Barra del Colorado

Four of the companies that offer package trips along the canals in the Caribbean lowlands are Adventure Tours, Costa Rica Expeditions, Cotur, and Ilan-Ilan. The companies have fixed departure dates. This is definitely a trip where the journey is as important as the destination. The April 1991 earthquake that struck hard on the Caribbean coast made access by canal from Limón difficult. Departures for larger boats are sometimes now from Hamburgo, and some companies are using the Sarapiquí/San Juan rivers. Once the problem section of the canal has been dredged, itineraries may change.

Adventure Tours is affiliated with the Río Colorado Lodge in Barra del Colorado, where overnight guests are lodged. With more peaceful conditions along the northern border with Nicaragua, Adventure Tours has reopened the route Río Colorado Lodge pioneered, a two-day, one-night tour on the Río Sarapiquí to the San Juan River (on the frontier) and then on the Colorado River, which flows through Barra del Colorado National Park. Includes lodging at Río Colorado Lodge and a visit to Tortuguero National Park. Optional nighttime turtle tour mid-July through November, $25. The river trip is aboard the twenty-four passenger *Colorado Queen*, departing from Puerto Viejo de Sarapiquí. The leg of the journey by bus goes through Varablanca and returns through Ciudad Quesada and Zarcero. Cost is $195. Telephone 32-4063, fax 31-5987. Apartado 5094-1000, San José. Office in Hotel Coribicí. In the United States, reservations and information at (800) 243-9777.

Costa Rica Expeditions offers a three-day, two-night tour to Tortuguero that combines visits to Braulio Carrillo National Park and banana and cacao plantations with the canal trip and a return by air. Cost for double occupancy begins at $299 per person. The first night is spent in Limón. A one-day, one-night tour starts at $199, adding $67 for a second day. Telephone 57-0766, fax 57-1665. Apartado 6941-1000, San José. Office at Avenida 3, Calles Central/2.

Cotur has a three-day, two-night tour to Tortuguero for $198 double occupancy, with accommodations at the Jungle Lodge and the canal trip on the *Miss America* going and coming. Air transportation is arranged for an additional charge. Departures Tuesday, Friday, and Sunday. Telephone 33-0133, fax 33-0778. Apartado 1818-1002, San José. Office at Paseo Colón/Avenida 1, Calle 36.

Ilan-Ilan has a three-day, two-night visit to Tortuguero, cruising on the canals in the *Colorado Prince* or *Tortuguero Prince*. On the way, there is a stop in Braulio Carrillo park. Lodging is at the Hotel Ilan-Ilan. Cost is $180 per person. Price includes three guided jungle walks. Optional turtle observation tour July-September. Telephone 55-2031, fax 55-1946. Apartado 91-1150, San José. Office is on Paseo Colón just west of the Children's Hospital.

Some U.S. Companies with Nature Tours to Costa Rica

Many tour companies offer trips to Costa Rica. Here are a few of those that specialize in nature travel.

Costa Rica Connection has a national parks tour that begins at $1,199 from Los Angeles, $1,089 from Miami, with visits to Tortuguero and Manuel Antonio parks—nine days, eight nights. It can be extended to Santa Rosa and Corcovado parks. A donation to foundations who support national parks and private reserves is made for each parks tour sold. Specialty tours include birding, orchids, beaches, kayaking/rafting, and language and culture. The San José Special, which includes airfare and six nights at the Amstel Hotel, begins at $589 from Miami and $699 from Los Angeles. Send for their brochure to see the exciting array of programs. Here are a few: a twelve-day tropical birding tour, eight-day Costa Rica National Orchid Show and Tour, twelve-day Coco Island Diving Adventure, eleven-day family tour, a Spanish language program that runs from two to four weeks. Telephone (805) 543-8823, fax (805) 543-3626. 958 Higuera Street, San Luis Obispo, CA 93401. In U.S., (800) 345-7422.

Geo Expeditions has a ten-day natural history tour that focuses on Poás National Park, Monteverde Cloud Forest Preserve, and the Osa Peninsula, with visits to Corcovado National Park and Caño Island, accompanied by first-class naturalist guides. Contact for costs and departure dates. Telephone (800) 351-5041, (209) 532-0152; fax (209) 532-1979. Box 3656, Sonora, CA 95370.

Geostar Travel's eight- to seventeen-day tours focus on general natural history, botany, horticulture, and birds. Trips are escorted by professional biologists, and costs range from $1,275 to $3,065, excluding international airfare. Geostar plans individual trips as well as for organizations such as Nature Conservancy. Part of the cost of the Costa Rican Natural History tour goes to support a conservation project near Tortuguero, including visits to Poás, Manuel Antonio, and Tortuguero parks, the cloud forest at Monteverde, and Tamarindo beach. There is an orchid tour, a horticultural and natural history tour, and a biking and rafting tour. Telephone: (800) 624-6633, (707) 579-2420; fax (707) 579-2704. 1240 Century Court, Santa Rosa, CA 95403.

Wildland Adventures offers tours as well as an individual trip planner that allows you to build your own program. You can choose from prearranged tours such as the wildlands camping and hiking safari, a family odyssey planned for parents and kids, nature-oriented honeymoon adventures, and one called Tropical Trails Less Traveled specially designed for the independent traveler. The bilingual trip leaders are biologists and active conservationists. Telephone (800) 345-4453, (206) 365-0686; fax (206) 363-6615. 3516 NE 155, Seattle, WA 98155.

Halintours has ten itineraries for independent travelers available anytime, escorted tours with fixed departures (each one includes an opportunity to mix with local people, whether in a volunteer project, a local fiesta, or a picnic), and special programs (Spanish language and a working-learning vacation focusing on ecology, with Halintours making a donation to the Children's Alliance for Protection of the Environment for each paying participant). The independent tours, excluding international airfare, meals in San José or at beach resorts, begin as low as $340 for seven days. Telephone (512) 450-0955, fax (512) 450-0958. Box 49705, Austin, TX 78765.

Osprey Tours specializes in travel to Costa Rica and other parts of Central America, on both an individual and group basis. Natural history tours with a bent toward birding are offered, along with general natural history, botany, archaeology, and geology. Escorted tour includes Palo Verde and Tortuguero parks, Lomas Barbudal and Carara biological reserves, and the Gulf of Nicoya. Company specializes in planning tours to accommodate travelers whether they want to camp out or stay in luxury hotels, to travel by bus and horseback or charter a plane. Two offices. Box 030211, Fort Lauderdale, FL 33303-0211. Telephone (305) 767-4823, fax (305) 767-4824. Also Box 832, West Tisbury, Martha's Vineyard, MA 02575. Telephone (508) 645-9049, fax (508) 645-3244.

Preferred Adventures does customized individual travel as well as tours for special interest groups: birders, horticulturists, and natural history travelers. Prices range from ten days for $1,325 to fifteen days for $2,695, excluding international airfare. Telephone (612) 222-8131, fax (612) 222-4221. One West Water Street, Suite 300, St. Paul, MN 55107.

Americas Tours and Travel emphasizes Costa Rica as a nature destination, doing itineraries for individuals that fit their wishes. The company encourages travel to the private reserves and to less-visited parks and reserves as well as the more popular ones. Telephone (206) 623-8850, (800) 553-2513; fax (206) 467-0454. 1402 Third Avenue No. 1019, Seattle, WA 98101-2110.

Practical Extras

International Airline Information

In San José

Airline	Address	Reservations	Airport
American	Across from Hotel Corobicí, Calle 42	22-5655	41-1168
Continental	Avenida 2, Calles 19/21	33-0266	41-8156
LACSA	Calle 1, Avenida 5	31-0033	41-6244
Mexicana	Calle 1, Avenidas 2/4	22-1711	41-9377
SAHSA	Avenida 5, Calles 1/3	21-5561	41-1064
TACA	Calle 1, Avenida 3	22-1790	41-5090

Reservation Numbers—United States and Canada

American	(800) 433-7300, United States and Canada
Continental	(800) 525-0280, United States
LACSA	(800) 225-2272, United States and Canada
Mexicana	(800) 531-7921, United States
	(800) 531-7923, Canada
SAHSA	(800) 327-1225, United States
	(416) 675-2007, Canada
TACA	(800) 535-8780, United States and Canada

Costa Rican National Tourist Bureau

San José
Plaza de la Cultura
Calle 5, Avenidas Central/2
Telephone   22-1090
                     23-1733, extension 277
                     42-1820 (airport office)

U.S. Offices
1101 Brickell Avenue
BIV Tower, Suite 801
Miami, FL 33131
Telephone   (305) 358-2150
                     (800) 327-7033

Private Information Service

INFOTUR: Computerized Information Service
San José
Calle 3, Avenidas 8/10
Telephone 23-4481 or 23-0407, fax 23-4476
Branch offices in Liberia, Puntarenas, Limón, Paso Canoas,
   Peñas Blancas
Access via computer:
1. (506) 57-2000 or (506) 53-2000
2. Press H (capital) and enter
3. Press Ninfrac-211201000 and enter
4. Communicate via menus, using first two letters of option. In internal level, use number codes.
5. For net users, the code is 0712211201000

Embassies in San José

U.S. Embassy
Road to Pavas in front of
  Centro Comercial
(any taxi driver can take you)
Telephone   20-3939

Canadian Embassy
Edificio Cromo, sixth floor
Avenida Central, Calle 3
Telephone   55-3522

Transportation Tidbits

Ferries

Puntarenas Ferry (Puntarenas-Playa Naranjo on Nicoya Peninsula)
Leaves Puntarenas 7:00 a.m. and 4:00 p.m. daily; adds 11:00 a.m.
  departure on Thursday and weekends
Leaves Playa Naranjo 9:00 a.m. and 6:00 p.m. daily; adds 1:00 p.m.
  departure Thursday and weekends

Tempisque Ferry (across mouth of Tempisque River)
Leaves continuously between 7:00 a.m. and 6:00 p.m.

Paquera Launch (Puntarenas to Paquera on Nicoya Peninsula)
Leaves Puntarenas from behind the market at 6:00 a.m. and 3:00 p.m.
  daily
Leaves Paquera 8:00 a.m. and 5:00 p.m.

Domestic Airline Scheduled Service
SANSA
San José office at Calle 24, Paseó Colón/Avenida 1, telephone
  33-0397, 33-3258
San José to and from Barra del Colorado: Tuesday, Thursday, Saturday
San José to and from Coto 47: daily except Sunday
San José to and from Palmar Sur and Golfito: Monday, Thursday,
  Friday

Travelair
San José office at Tobias Bolaños Airport in Pavas, telephone
  32-7883, 20-3054, fax 20-0413.
Daily flights to Barra del Colorado, Golfito, Quepos, Tamarindo.

San José to and from Golfito: daily except Sunday
San José to and from Nosara: Monday, Wednesday, Friday
San José to and from Quepos: daily except Sunday
San José to and from Tamarindo and Sámara: Monday, Wednesday,
Friday

Intercity Buses

These are the addresses of bus stops in San José for the cities indicated, phone numbers, and length of trip. Sometimes there is a terminal; sometimes there is only a sign on the street indicating the bus
stop. Check with the ICT Information Office or INFOTUR for departure times, and make sure the bus stop has not moved.

Alajuela: Avenida 2, Calles 12/14 (leaves every 15 minutes), 22-5325,
20 minutes
Cahuita: Avenida 11, Calles Central/1 (twice daily—this is the bus
for Sixaola), 58-1572, 4 hours
Cañas: Calle 16, Avenidas 3/5 (tickets in advance), 22-3006, 3 hours
Cartago: Avenida Central, Calles 13/15 (every 10 minutes), 33-5350,
45 minutes
Ciudad Quesada (San Carlos: Calle 16, Avenidas 1/3 (every hour),
55-4318, 3 hours
Fortuna: Calle 16, Avenidas 1/3 (daily express), 32-5660, 4½ hours
Golfito: Avenida 18, Calles 2/4 (express bus twice a day; buy ticket
in advance), 21-4214, 8 hours
Heredia: Calle 1, Avenidas 7/9 (every 10 minutes), 33-8392, 25
minutes
Jacó Beach: Calle 16, Avenidas 1/3, 32-1829, 2½ hours
Junquillal: Calle 20, Avenida 3 (daily express), 21-7202, 5 hours
La Cruz or Peñas Blancas: Calle 16, Avenidas 3/5, 38-2725, 6 hours
Liberia: Calle 14, Avenidas 1/3 (several express buses daily, buy
ticket in advance), 22-1650, 4 hours
Limón: Avenida 3, Calles 19/21 (every hour), 23-7811, 2½ hours
Monteverde: Calle 14, Avenidas 9/11, 22-3854, 4 hours
Nicoya: Calle 14, Avenidas 3/5 (tickets in advance), 22-2750, 6 hours

Playa del Coco: Calle 14, Avenidas 1/3, 22-1650, 5 hours

Puerto Viejo de Sarapiquí: Calle 12, Avenidas 7/9, 4 hours

Puerto Viejo de Limón: Avenida 11, Calles Central/1 (bus for Sixaola), 58-1572, 4½ hours (get off at El Cruce)

Puntarenas: Calle 12, Avenidas 7/9 (express leaves every 40 minutes), 22-0064, 2 hours

Quepos and Manuel Antonio: Calle 16, Avenida 1/3 (express bus leaves from lot behind Hotel Musoc; buy ticket in advance inside adjacent market), 23-5567, 3½ hours

Sámara: Calle 14, Avenidas 3/5 (daily express), 22-2750, 6 hours

Santa Cruz: Calle 20, Avenidas 1/3 (tickets in advance), 21-7202, 5 hours

San Isidro de El General: Calle 16, Avenidas 1/3 (express every hour, buy tickets in advance), 22-2422, 3 hours

San Vito: Avenida 5, Calle 16 (tickets in advance), 22-2750, 5 hours

Tamarindo: Calle 20, Avenidas 3/5, 21-7202, 6 hours

Turrialba: Calle 13, Avenidas 6/8 (express every hour), 56-0073, 2 hours

Zarcero: Calle 16, Avenidas 1/3 (express every hour), 55-4318, 1½ hours

Metric Conversion Tables

To change	to	Multiply by
Hectares	Acres	2.4710
Meters	Feet	3.2808
Kilometers	Miles	.6214
Millimeters	Inches	.0394
Square kilometers	Square miles	.3861
Liters	Gallons (U.S.)	.2642
Kilograms	Pounds	2.2050

Temperature

Celsius to Fahrenheit: multiply by 9/5 and add 32.

Fahrenheit to Celsius: subtract 32 and multiply by 5/9.

Here are some reference points to save some of the math:

Celsius	Fahrenheit
0	32
10	50
20	68
30	86
35	95
40	104

Fauna: English and Spanish Names

English	Spanish
Howler monkey	Mono congo
Spider monkey	Mono colorado, mono araña
Squirrel monkey	Mono tití, mono ardilla
White-faced capuchin monkey	Mono cara blanca
Agouti	Guatusa
Coati	Pizote
Paca	Tepezcuintle
Kinkajou	Martilla
Cougar, mountain lion	Puma, león
Jaguar	Jaguar, tigre
Jaguarundi	León breñero
Margay	Caucel, tigrillo
Ocelot	Manigordo
Armadillo	Cusuco
Tapir	Danta
Sloth	Perezoso, perica
White-lipped peccary	Cariblanco
Collared peccary	Saíno
White-tailed deer	Venado cola blanca
Brocket deer	Cabra de monte
Squirrel	Ardilla, chisa
Lesser anteater, tamandua	Oso hormiguero
Silky anteater	Serafín
Bat	Murciélago
Gopher	Taltusa
Opossum	Zorro
Skunk	Zorro hediondo
Raccoon	Mapachín
River otter	Nutria, perro de agua

English	Spanish
Tayra	Tolomuco
Frog	Rana
Toad	Sapo
Turtle	Tortuga
Caiman	Caimán
Crocodile	Cocodrilo
Snake	Serpiente, culebra
Bird	Pájaro, ave
Parrot	Loro
Scarlet macaw	Lapa
Butterfly	Mariposa

Recommended Reading

A Naturalist in Costa Rica, Alexander F. Skutch. Gainesville: University of Florida Press, 1971.

The Costa Ricans, Richard Biesanz, Karen Zubris Biesanz, and Mavis Hiltunen Biesanz. Englewood Cliffs, N.J.: Prentice-Hall, 1982.

Costa Rica National Parks, Mario A. Boza. Madrid: Incafo (for Fundación Neotrópica de Costa Rica), 1988.

Costa Rican Natural History, edited by Daniel H. Janzen. Chicago: University of Chicago Press, 1983.

The Butterflies of Costa Rica and Their Natural History, Philip J. De-Vries. Princeton: Princeton University Press, 1987.

The Rivers of Costa Rica: A Canoeing, Kayaking, and Rafting Guide, Michael W. Mayfield and Rafael E. Gallo. Birmingham, Ala.: Menasha Ridge Press, 1988.

Journey through a Tropical Jungle, Adrian Forsyth. Toronto: Greey de Pencier Books, 1988.

A Guide to the Birds of Costa Rica, F. Gary Stiles and Alexander F. Skutch. Ithaca: Cornell University Press, 1989.

The New Key to Costa Rica, Beatrice Blake. San José: Publications in English, 1991.

Index

Other Books from John Muir Publications

Adventure Vacations: From Trekking in New Guinea to Swimming in Siberia, Bangs 256 pp. $17.95

Asia Through the Back Door, 3rd ed., Steves and Gottberg 326 pp. $15.95

Belize: A Natural Destination, Mahler, Wotkyns, Schafer 304 pp. $16.95

Buddhist America: Centers, Retreats, Practices, Morreale 400 pp. $12.95

Bus Touring: Charter Vacations, U.S.A., Warren with Bloch 168 pp. $9.95

California Public Gardens: A Visitor's Guide, Sigg 304 pp. $16.95

Catholic America: Self-Renewal Centers and Retreats, Christian-Meyer 325 pp. $13.95

Costa Rica: A Natural Destination, Sheck 280 pp. $15.95 (**2nd ed.** available 3/92 $16.95)

Elderhostels: The Students' Choice, 2nd ed., Hyman 312 pp. $15.95

Environmental Vacations: Volunteer Projects to Save the Planet, Ocko 240 pp. $15.95 (**2nd ed.** available 2/92 $16.95)

Europe 101: History & Art for the Traveler, 4th ed., Steves and Openshaw 372 pp. $15.95

Europe Through the Back Door, 9th ed., Steves 432 pp. $16.95 (**10th ed.** available 1/92 $16.95)

Floating Vacations: River, Lake, and Ocean Adventures, White 256 pp. $17.95

Great Cities of Eastern Europe, Rapoport 240 pp. $16.95

Gypsying After 40: A Guide to Adventure and Self-Discovery, Harris 264 pp. $14.95

The Heart of Jerusalem, Nellhaus 336 pp. $12.95

Indian America: A Traveler's Companion, Eagle/Walking Turtle 448 pp. $17.95

Mona Winks: Self-Guided Tours of Europe's Top Museums, Steves and Openshaw 456 pp. $14.95

Opera! The Guide to Western Europe's Great Houses, Zietz 296 pp. $18.95

Paintbrushes and Pistols: How the Taos Artists Sold the West, Taggett and Schwarz 280 pp. $17.95

The People's Guide to Mexico, 8th ed., Franz 608 pp. $17.95

The People's Guide to RV Camping in Mexico, Franz with Rogers 320 pp. $13.95

Ranch Vacations: The Complete Guide to Guest and Resort, Fly-Fishing, and Cross-Country Skiing Ranches, 2nd ed., Kilgore 396 pp. $18.95

The Shopper's Guide to Art and Crafts in the Hawaiian Islands, Schuchter 272 pp. $13.95

The Shopper's Guide to Mexico, Rogers and Rosa 224 pp. $9.95

Ski Tech's Guide to Equipment, Skiwear, and Accessories, ed. Tanler 144 pp. $11.95

Ski Tech's Guide to Maintenance and Repair, ed. Tanler 160 pp. $11.95

A Traveler's Guide to Asian Culture, Chambers 224 pp. $13.95

Traveler's Guide to Healing Centers and Retreats in North America, Rudee and Blease 240 pp. $11.95

Understanding Europeans, Miller 272 pp. $14.95

Undiscovered Islands of the Caribbean, 2nd ed., Willes 232 pp. $14.95

Undiscovered Islands of the Mediterranean, Moyer and Willes 232 pp. $14.95

Undiscovered Islands of the U.S. and Canadian West Coast, Moyer and Willes 208 pp. $12.95

A Viewer's Guide to Art: A Glossary of Gods, People, and Creatures, Shaw and Warren 144 pp. $10.95

2 to 22 Days Series
Each title offers 22 flexible daily itineraries that can be used to get the most out of vacations of any length. Included are not only "must see" attractions but also little-known villages and hidden "jewels" as well as valuable general information.

22 Days Around the World, 1992 ed., Rapoport and Willes 256 pp. $12.95
2 to 22 Days Around the Great Lakes, 1992 ed., Schuchter 192 pp. $9.95
22 Days in Alaska, Lanier 128 pp. $7.95
2 to 22 Days in the American Southwest, 1992 ed., Harris 176 pp. $9.95
2 to 22 Days in Asia, 1992 ed., Rapoport and Willes 176 pp. $9.95
2 to 22 Days in Australia, 1992 ed., Gottberg 192 pp. $9.95
22 Days in California, 2nd ed., Rapoport 176 pp. $9.95
22 Days in China, Duke and Victor 144 pp. $7.95
2 to 22 Days in Europe, 1992 ed., Steves 276 pp. $12.95
2 to 22 Days in Florida, 1992 ed., Harris 192 pp. $9.95
2 to 22 Days in France, 1992 ed., Steves 192 pp. $9.95
2 to 22 Days in Germany, Austria, & Switzerland, 1992 ed., Steves 224 pp. $9.95
2 to 22 Days in Great Britain, 1992 ed., Steves 192 pp. $9.95
2 to 22 Days in Hawaii, 1992 ed., Schuchter 176 pp. $9.95
22 Days in India, Mathur 136 pp. $7.95
22 Days in Japan, Old 136 pp. $7.95
22 Days in Mexico, 2nd ed., Rogers and Rosa 128 pp. $7.95
2 to 22 Days in New England, 1992 ed., Wright 192 pp. $9.95
2 to 22 Days in New Zealand, 1991 ed., Schuchter 176 pp. $9.95
2 to 22 Days in Norway, Sweden, & Denmark, 1992 ed., Steves 192 pp. $9.95
2 to 22 Days in the Pacific Northwest, 1992 ed., Harris 192 pp. $9.95
2 to 22 Days in the Rockies, 1992 ed., Rapoport 176 pp. $9.95
2 to 22 Days in Spain & Portugal, 1992 ed., Steves 192 pp. $9.95
22 Days in Texas, Harris 176 pp. $9.95

22 Days in Thailand, Richardson 176 pp. $9.95
22 Days in the West Indies, Morreale and Morreale 136 pp. $7.95

Parenting Series
Being a Father: Family, Work, and Self, *Mothering* Magazine 176 pp. $12.95
Preconception: A Woman's Guide to Preparing for Pregnancy and Parenthood, Aikey-Keller 232 pp. $14.95
Schooling at Home: Parents, Kids, and Learning, *Mothering* Magazine 264 pp. $14.95
Teens: A Fresh Look, *Mothering* Magazine 240 pp. $14.95

"Kidding Around" Travel Guides for Young Readers
Written for kids eight years of age and older.

Kidding Around Atlanta, Pedersen 64 pp. $9.95
Kidding Around Boston, Byers 64 pp. $9.95
Kidding Around Chicago, Davis 64 pp. $9.95
Kidding Around the Hawaiian Islands, Lovett 64 pp. $9.95
Kidding Around London, Lovett 64 pp. $9.95
Kidding Around Los Angeles, Cash 64 pp. $9.95
Kidding Around the National Parks of the Southwest, Lovett 108 pp. $12.95
Kidding Around New York City, Lovett 64 pp. $9.95
Kidding Around Paris, Clay 64 pp. $9.95
Kidding Around Philadelphia, Clay 64 pp. $9.95
Kidding Around San Diego, Luhrs 64 pp. $9.95
Kidding Around San Francisco, Zibart 64 pp. $9.95
Kidding Around Santa Fe, York 64 pp. $9.95
Kidding Around Seattle, Steves 64 pp. $9.95
Kidding Around Spain, Biggs 108 pp. $12.95
Kidding Around Washington, D.C., Pedersen 64 pp. $9.95

Environmental Books for Young Readers

Written for kids eight years and older.

The Indian Way: Learning to Communicate with Mother Earth, McLain 114 pp. $9.95

The Kids' Environment Book: What's Awry and Why, Pedersen 192 pp. $13.95

Rads, Ergs, and Cheeseburgers: The Kids' Guide to Energy and the Environment, Yanda 108 pp. $12.95

"Extremely Weird" Series for Young Readers

Written for kids eight years of age and older.

Extremely Weird Bats, Lovett 48 pp. $9.95

Extremely Weird Frogs, Lovett 48 pp. $9.95

Extremely Weird Primates, Lovett 48 pp. $9.95

Extremely Weird Reptiles, Lovett 48 pp. $9.95

Extremely Weird Spiders, Lovett 48 pp. $9.95

Quill Hedgehog Adventures Series

Written for kids eight years of age and older. Our new series of green fiction for kids follows the adventures of Quill Hedgehog and his Animalfolk friends.

Quill's Adventures in the Great Beyond. Waddington-Feather 96 pp. $5.95

Quill's Adventures in Wasteland, Waddington-Feather 132 pp. $5.95

Quill's Adventures in Grozzieland, Waddington-Feather 132 pp. $5.95

Other Young Readers Titles

Kids Explore America's Hispanic Heritage, edited by Cozzens 112 pp. $7.95 (avail. 2/92)

Automotive Repair Manuals

How to Keep Your VW Alive, 14th ed., 440 pp. $21.95

How to Keep Your Subaru Alive 480 pp. $21.95

How to Keep Your Toyota Pickup Alive 392 pp. $21.95

How to Keep Your Datsun/Nissan Alive 544 pp. $21.95

Other Automotive Books

The Greaseless Guide to Car Care Confidence: Take the Terror Out of Talking to Your Mechanic, Jackson 224 pp. $14.95

Off-Road Emergency Repair & Survival, Ristow 160 pp. $9.95

Ordering Information

If you cannot find our books in your local bookstore, you can order directly from us. Please check the "Available" date above. If you send us money for a book not yet available, we will hold your money until we can ship you the book. Your books will be sent to you via UPS (for U.S. destinations). UPS will not deliver to a P.O. Box; please give us a street address. Include $3.25 for the first item ordered and $.50 for each additional item to cover shipping and handling costs. For airmail within the U.S., enclose $4.00. All foreign orders will be shipped surface rate; please enclose $3.00 for the first item and $1.00 for each additional item. Please inquire about foreign airmail rates.

Method of Payment

Your order may be paid by check, money order, or credit card. We cannot be responsible for cash sent through the mail. All payments must be made in U.S. dollars drawn on a U.S. bank. Canadian postal money orders in U.S. dollars are acceptable. For VISA, MasterCard, or American Express orders, include your card number, expiration date, and your signature, or call (800) 888-7504. Books ordered on American Express cards can be shipped only to the billing address of the cardholder. Sorry, no C.O.D.'s. Residents of sunny New Mexico, add 5.875% tax to the total.

Address all orders and inquiries to:
John Muir Publications
P.O. Box 613
Santa Fe, NM 87504
(505) 982-4078
(800) 888-7504